Autobiography of a Saint

St Thérèse of Lisieux was a Carmelite nun who died in 1897 at the age of twenty-four. This, her autobiography, is among the greatest books of spirituality ever written.

It is a complete and authorised version translated from photostats of the original manuscripts with seven thousand alterations and twenty-five per cent. new material. In a faithful, beautiful and vigorous style, Ronald Knox has given us in his translation the true flavour of Thérèse's writings and enabled the many millions of people who are her admirers to meet her as a real person.

THÉRÈSE OF LISIEUX

Autobiography of a Saint

The complete and authorised text of
L'Histoire d'une Âme
newly translated by Ronald Knox

With a Foreword by Vernon Johnson

Fount

An Imprint of HarperCollins*Publishers*

First published 1958
First issued in Fontana Books 1960
Seventh impression September 1973
Reprinted in Fountain Books January 1977

This edition reprinted in 1991 by
Fount Paperbacks, an imprint of
HarperCollins Religious,
part of HarperCollins Publishers,
77–85 Fulham Palace Road
Hammersmith, London W6 8JB

Printed and bound in Great Britain by
HarperCollins Manufacturing, Glasgow

NIHIL OBSTAT:
JOANNES M. T. BARTON, S.T.D., L.S.S.
CENSOR DEPUTATUS
IMPRIMATUR:
✠ E. MORROGH BERNARD, VIC. GEN.
WESTMONASTERII, DIE 27A JANUARII, 1958

FOREWORD

No MODERN saint has exerted such an influence on the men and women of our time as Saint Thérèse of Lisieux. The publication therefore of the original manuscript of her Autobiography, just as it came from her pen, will be of the greatest interest to everyone. It is here being given for the first time to the English public through an admirable translation made by Monsignor Ronald Knox—in actual fact the last important work that he undertook.

Till now we have been familiar with the Autobiography as edited by Mother Agnes. Mother Agnes was specially commissioned to do this by the Saint herself, and the edition thus edited was the one sanctioned for publication by the Holy See, to whom both versions were submitted during the Process of Canonisation.

That some editing was absolutely necessary at that time is made clear in the excellent Introduction of Fr François which follows this Foreword. The first part of the manuscript is full of personal family details which at that early stage would have been tedious to the public and would have obscured the message of the Saint. That Mother Agnes interpreted her commission very liberally is undoubtedly true, but as Fr François points out the portrait of the Saint and her doctrine remain in each text substantially the same.

Saint Thérèse is now a canonised saint, her teaching has been proposed by four Popes to the faithful for their imitation. It is of vital importance that the manuscript should be available exactly as she wrote it—that is what the English public now have before them. In this translation, the critics will find the complete answer to all their questions, while the faithful, eager to know all that is to be known about Saint Thérèse, will find a wealth of detail, fresh, vivid and spontaneous, which will tell them a great deal more about the Saint, though she remains substantially the same as we have always known her. One delightful trait runs throughout, namely a delicious vein of humour making her most vividly human, and who could better interpret the humour of Saint Thérèse than Monsignor Knox?

The Carmel of Lisieux wishes that this should become the authorised edition. It has been brilliantly translated in a style powerful, clear, forceful and free, abounding in light and shade, emancipated entirely from the limitation and convention of the period in which the manuscript was actually written and which has often proved a hindrance to English readers. This book may well herald a revival of interest in the message of this remarkable Saint in wide circles where hitherto she has never been really understood.

VERNON JOHNSON

CONTENTS

BOOK ONE

MANUSCRIPT DEDICATED TO
THE REVEREND MOTHER AGNES OF JESUS

CONTENTS

BOOK TWO

LETTER TO SISTER MARIE OF
THE SACRED HEART

BOOK THREE

MANUSCRIPT DEDICATED TO MOTHER MARIE
DE GONZAGUE

LIST OF PLATES

NOTE

The present translation was made by Monsignor
Ronald Knox from the facsimile edition. The
division into chapters was made by him. The
Biblical quotations are taken from his translation
of the Bible.

INTRODUCTION

THE AUTOBIOGRAPHY of St. Thérèse of the Child Jesus, up to now known under the title of *The Story of a Soul*, is not a continuous text but a collection of three MSS of unequal length written at different times, addressed to different people and differing from one another in character.

The first, entitled by Thérèse "The Story of a Little White Flower" and dedicated to the Reverend Mother Agnes of Jesus (her sister Pauline), was written between the beginning of January, 1895, and the 20th January, 1896.

The second is a letter to Sister Marie of the Sacred Heart (her eldest sister Marie), written at her request in three days between the 13th and 16th September, 1896.

The third, a note-book written for the Reverend Mother Marie de Gonzague, was begun on 3rd June and finished early in July, 1897.

Mother Agnes has herself described how, as she sat with her sisters on a winter evening in the one room of the Carmel where there was a fire, the writing of the first manuscript was decided.

"One evening in the beginning of the year 1895, two and a half years before the death of Sister Thérèse, I was with my two sisters Marie and Thérèse. Sister Thérèse of the Child Jesus told me several happenings of her childhood and Sister Marie of the Sacred Heart (my eldest sister Marie) said to me: 'O Mother, what a pity that all this should not be written down for us. If you were to ask Sister Thérèse of the Child Jesus to write down her childhood memories, how much pleasure this would give us!' . . . I turned to Sister Thérèse of the Child Jesus, who laughed as though we were teasing her, and said: 'I order you to write down your memories of your childhood.'"[1]

The account given by Sister Marie of the Sacred Heart agrees with this statement but adds some details showing how hesitant Mother Agnes was in giving so unusual an order.

[1] Affidavit by the Reverend Mother Agnes of Jesus. *Actes officiels du Procès déposés dans les Archives de l'Evêché de Bayeux*, Vol. I.

Indeed, "nothing of the sort had ever been done since the foundation of the Carmel of Lisieux," Mother Agnes stated at the Canonisation Process.[2]

When Thérèse realised that the order had been given in all seriousness she had a moment of alarm. She was afraid of distraction; besides "what could I write that you don't already know?" she asked her sisters.[3] Obedience, however, forced her to comply. But the circumstances in which the writing was done could hardly have been more difficult— never any consecutive hours in which to write; except on feast days nothing but the short moments of leisure, such as those after Compline; the rest of the day was taken up with "earning one's living."[4]

So it was generally in the evenings that Thérèse wrote, sitting on her little bench with an old writing-case on her knees (she had found it thrown away in the loft). The light was poor, for though her cousin Marie Guérin had got her a small paraffin lamp, it was so old that it no longer worked properly and the wick had to be pushed up with a pin.[5]

The work was finished, as requested, in time for Mother Agnes's feast day. At evening meditation the night before (20th January, 1896), as she passed before the Prioress on her way to her stall, Thérèse knelt before her and offered her the manuscript. She heard nothing more about it.

Mother Agnes, regarding it as no more than a "family souvenir," kept it "for afterwards."[6] She did not open it until two months later. By then Mother Marie de Gonzague had been elected Prioress and Mother Agnes, who was once again a simple community nun, had more free time. She then read the manuscript and showed it to her sisters. She only informed the Prioress of its existence on the 2nd June, 1897.

On Sunday, 13th September, 1896, Sister Marie of the Sacred Heart (eldest sister and godmother of Thérèse) wrote to her goddaughter reminding her of a conversation in which

[2] *Ibid.*   [3] *Ibid.*

[4] "Thérèse never wasted her time. When she was advised not to overtire herself she replied that her vow of poverty obliged her to work." *Bayeux*, Vol. I.

[5] *Lettres de Sainte Thérèse de l'Enfant Jésus,* Carmel of Lisieux, 1948. p. 48.

[6] Affidavit by Sister Geneviève of St. Teresa. *Bayeux*, Vol. I.

Thérèse had told her of her spiritual discoveries; now she asked her to write them down[7] and added (by way of stressing the urgency of the task): "Reverend Mother gives you permission to reply by return of post."

Thérèse replied in ten closely written pages. Her many corrections show that she wrote in great haste and in a state of extreme fatigue.

The origin of the third part of the Saint's "souvenirs" was described by Mother Agnes in the following terms at the Informative Process.

"It seemed to me that these accounts were incomplete. Sister Thérèse of the Child Jesus had concentrated on her childhood and early youth as I had asked her to do, her life as a nun was hardly sketched in. . . . I thought it a great pity that she had not described the development of her life in the Carmel in the same way, but just then I ceased to be Reverend Mother and Mother Marie de Gonzague held this office. I was afraid she would not attach the same interest as I did to these writings and I dared not say anything to her about it. But then, seeing that Sister Thérèse was so ill, I determined to try the impossible. About midnight on the evening of the 2nd June, 1897, four months before the death of Sister Thérèse, I went to see Mother Prioress. 'Mother,' I said, 'I can't go to sleep without having told you a secret: when I was Prioress Sister Thérèse, in order to please me and by obedience, wrote down some recollections of her childhood. I re-read them the other day. They are charming, but you will not get much out of them to help you compose her "Circular"[8] after her death, because they contain very little about her life as a religious. If you were to order her to do so, she could write something more valuable, and I don't doubt that you would have something incomparably better than I have.' God blessed my action and the next morning Reverend Mother ordered Sister Thérèse of the Child Jesus to go on with her account."[9]

[7] In the Canonisation Proceedings Sister Marie of the Sacred Heart stated: "I had asked Sister Thérèse of the Child Jesus to write down for me what I described as 'her little way of trust and love.'" *Bayeux*, Vol. I.

[8] It was usual for an obituary circular to be sent to the convents of the Order after the death of a Sister.

[9] *Bayeux*, Vol. I.

Most of this manuscript was written during the month of June, 1897. Thérèse spent long afternoons under the chestnut trees where her invalid chair had been wheeled. But she had no uninterrupted quiet. There was the coming and going of zealous infirmary sisters, the novices who wanted to tell her their difficulties, the lay sisters who were happy to exchange a word or two with her.

Thérèse stopped writing in the first days of July, 1897.[10] She had to finish in pencil, so great was her weakness. Eventually the pencil fell from her hand as she wrote the last word, " love." It is the final word of all three manuscripts.[11]

The extraordinarily wide circulation of *The Story of a Soul*, which has become part of the patrimony of the Church, may tend to make the reader forget that its original character was that of an intimate family document. Witnesses at the Canonisation Process stressed this point, especially in regard to the first manuscript. " She wrote only under obedience, trying however to relate some specific facts to each member of her family, in order to give pleasure to all. . . . Her manuscript was, in fact, a family album intended only for her sisters."[12]

By a privilege rare in the annals of sainthood Thérèse found two of her sisters in the cloister and was soon joined by her third sister Céline, who had been her playfellow, and by her cousin Marie Guérin. No doubt, their earlier intimacy was sacrificed, but on the other hand the bonds of the spirit strengthened those of kinship. In the first manuscript the Saint is writing to one who is " doubly her mother," in the second to one who is " doubly her sister." This explains the tone of certain passages, their intimate allusions and the description of some trivial childhood incidents. All these were meant to form part of the " family album," they were not intended for the scrutiny of the Universal Church.

10 MS. C. Fol. 6.
11 *Note on the Physical appearance of the MSS:* MS. A (dedicated to Mother Agnes) was written on the very bad paper of two school copy-books; MS. B (letter to Sister Marie of the Sacred Heart) was written on squared writing-paper; MS. C (dedicated to Mother Marie de Gonzague) was written in a copy-book of good qaulity bound in black oil-cloth.
12 Affidavit by Sister Geneviève of St. Teresa at the Diocesan Process, *Bayeux*, Vol. I.

When the text was finished it still had to pass the family censorship. The Proceedings record that this first manuscript was sent to Thérèse's uncle, M. Guérin, and Mother Agnes certainly suggested to Thérèse the addition of a line here or there as she considered the reactions of this or that member of the family.[13]

As for the third manuscript, it was written for Mother Marie de Gonzague to whom Thérèse was not related by blood; but as the Prioress of a small convent she knew nearly as much about Thérèse's life as did her sisters. The writing is less spontaneous but it is no less intimate.

The circumstances in which the work was written are extremely important to its understanding. Thérèse, we must remember, was writing in a convent where the smallest acts were governed by the rule of obedience. She was not, therefore, acting on her own initiative or following an impulse to produce a literary work. She was, nevertheless, conscious of technical weaknesses in her writing. She often complained that her style was "not very pleasing" and thought that she had expressed herself badly.

Her style was in fact conversational, though she occasionally recalled the lessons she had once had in the "art of expressing oneself." The result is a curious mixture; the tone of some passages is frank, direct, colourful or naïve, while that of others is less happy.

Thérèse's last words concerning her writings have been preserved for us by Mother Agnes and they help us to understand how it came about that Sister Thérèse gradually became accustomed to the idea of her autobiography being one day published and, at the end of her life, made certain dispositions to this effect.[14]

[13] For instance, the note on Folio 29, MS. A: "The only visit which I liked was that of my Uncle and Aunt," together with the additions at the bottom of the page, was, according to the experts, written after the rest of the MS. It was added by Thérèse herself in order to give pleasure to the uncle and aunt by recalling their devotion to her during a childhood illness.

[14] The last words of St. Thérèse were recorded by Mother Agnes. (1) Five green copy-books were made out by Mother Agnes from earlier notes for the Beatification Process and sent to Mgr. de Teil in 1909. (2) One yellow copy-book, also by Mother Agnes, describing the last conversations of St. Thérèse was written during the nineteen-twenties. (3) A small typescript which is, in fact, a copy

The question naturally arises: did she have any idea of eventual publication at the time when she was actually writing the first two manuscripts?

So far as the first of them is concerned, everyone is agreed that she did not.[15] Of the second, Mother Agnes definitely stated at the Diocesan Process that these pages " were written exclusively for her sister Marie, who asked for them"; later, however, at the Apostolic Process, she seemed less positive: " nor did she think (of publication), I believe . . ."

But what of the note-book written for Mother Marie de Gonzague? A week before Mother Agnes approached the Prioress, Thérèse had been consulted about her " obituary circular": material for the circular was all that was as yet in question. She replied:

Thursday, 27th May, Ascension
" I would like a circular because I have always thought that I must do something to earn the Office of the Dead which every Carmelite will say for me. I really don't understand why some of the nuns do not want obituary circulars. It is so pleasant to know each other, to know a little about those with whom we shall live in eternity."

When, a week later, on the 3rd June, Mother Marie de Gonzague ordered her to go on with her autobiography, it was at first still only intended to provide material for the obituary. But once permission to write it had been granted, the question of a wider circulation arose. In her Affidavit at the Apostolic Process Sister Geneviève of St. Teresa spoke of a " book"; in " the composition of the (last) section, which was undertaken at the request of Mother Marie de Gonzague, when the Servant of God was already very ill, she foresaw, I think, not that her notes would be published as they were, but that they would be used, with amendments, for a book which would be published in order to make known the path by which she had gone to the good God and which would encourage others to follow the same way."[16]

of the yellow copy-book with certain corrections, dates from *circa* 1924.

[15] *Bayeux*, Vol. I.   [16] *Bayeux*, Vol. II.

Once the manuscript was finished bolder views arose and in the intimate circle of her sisters it was considered that the work might go to Rome. To the suggestion that what she had written " might very well go to the Holy Father," Thérèse smilingly replied by a *jeu de mots*: " *Et nunc et semper.*"[17]

She made it clear that she had complete confidence in Mother Agnes:

Saturday, 10th July
" I have not had time to write what I have wished to write. It isn't complete. But listen to me, Mother: anything you want to cut or add to the note-book of my life, it is as though I were myself cutting or adding. Remember this later and have no scruples on this subject."[18]

On another occasion she is quoted as saying: " My thought is there, you will only need to tidy it up."[19]

She was clearly aware by now of the importance of her writings and of the influence they were to have after her death. She gives the credit to God:

Sunday, 11th July
" Everyone will see very that it all comes from the good God and whatever fame I may have will be a gratuitous gift which will not belong to me; this will be quite clear to all . . ."[20]

What was at stake was so important that, with her prudence and foresight, she felt obliged to give this warning:

Sunday, 1st August
" After my death you must not speak about my manuscript till it has been published; only to our Reverend Mother should it be mentioned. Otherwise the Devil will set traps for you so that he may spoil God's work . . . such an important work . . ."[21]

---

[17] Yellow copy-book.   [18] Green copy-book.
[19] Deposition by Mother Agnes of Jesus, *Bayeux*, Vol. I.
[20] Yellow copy-book.   [21] *Ibid.*

Before she died Thérèse solemnly ratified all she had written:

Saturday, 25th September
" Oh, Mother, it is very easy to write beautiful things about suffering but to write is nothing—nothing at all. One must be in it to know . . . I feel very certain now that all I have said and written is true . . . It is true that I wanted to suffer a great deal for God and it is true that I still desire to do so."[22]

Strengthened by the authority which Thérèse had given her, Mother Agnes began seriously to consider the possibility of publishing the autobiography in place of the usual obituary circular.

Mother Marie de Gonzague, who may not have known of this plan until after the death of the Saint, was consulted, for her permission was necessary. She agreed, but the condition she imposed clearly shows the sickly jealousy which spoilt her very real qualities; the first two manuscripts were to be altered in such a way as to make it seem that all three were addressed to her personally.

Besides the permission of the Prioress, that of the Bishop had also to be obtained before going to press. As a first step, a few weeks after Thérèse's death, Mother Marie de Gonzague wrote to the Reverend Godefroid Madelaine, the Prior of the Abbey of Mondaye, a friend of the community who had known Thérèse. She sent him a copy of the manuscripts, though whether this was a copy of the original text or of a text already edited by Mother Agnes is not known.

In his reply, Dom Madelaine said: " For you, everything in the manuscript is precious, but for the public, there are details so intimate, so far above the ordinary level, that I think it would be preferable not to print them." He also mentioned faults of style, some passages which might be shortened, and some repetitions; he said that he would mark with a blue pencil what he thought had better be cut.

After writing this letter, it might be supposed that Dom Madelaine handled the blue pencil vigorously, but at the

[22] Yellow copy-book.

Canonisation Process he stated that he had only made very small corrections.

On the 7th March, 1898, Dom Madelaine went to see the Bishop, manuscript in hand. The Bishop warned him at first to beware of the imagination of women. However, he consented to give the necessary *Imprimatur*,[28] but declined to write the introductory note for which he had also been asked. Dom Madelaine supplied the deficiency and also contributed the title, *The Story of a Soul,* as well as dividing the work into chapters.[24]

In his editing of the work he had been assisted by another priest, Dom Norbert, who, like Dom Madelaine, had encouraged the Prioress to allow Mother Agnes to make her own corrections: "Do not deprive Mother Agnes of Jesus (who is, I understand, a sister of Sister Thérèse) of the pleasure of putting some last touches to her sister's work, which she does so well. Only a woman's hand, and that of a Carmelite, can do such delicate work."

It would certainly have been impossible to publish Thérèse's manuscript word for word at the time; nobody who has looked at the facsimiles can doubt this. In a period when so much importance was attached to perfect correctness of style and scrupulous respect for literary conventions, to publish the rough notes of a young and unknown nun would have meant making oneself ridiculous as well as betraying the author.

The content also seemed to need some editing. The "too intimate details" and those "too far above the ordinary level," passages concerning third persons and trivial incidents, all these, it seemed, had better be left out, at any rate for the time being. Sometimes too an added detail might enrich the text without doing it any harm. And the sequence could occasionally by changed for the sake of clarity. In brief, the three operations suggested by Thérèse herself—adding, cutting and arranging—were carried out. But it must be admitted that the scale on which this work was done was very generous.

Mother Agnes in fact rewrote Thérèse's autobiography.

[28] Permission necessary for the publication of a work by a religious.
[24] Apart from this division the three MSS. were published as a consecutive text, MS. B following MS. C.

It is enough to compare the manuscripts with the printed text of *The Story of a Soul* to be convinced of this. There is no doubt that the content remains substantially the same, so does the basis of the doctrine, but the form differs to the extent that the temperament of Mother Agnes differed from that of Thérèse. These changes have certainly not prevented souls from really meeting Thérèse or understanding her doctrine. But it would be useless to claim that the way in which the text was re-handled conforms to the standards of literary scholarship accepted to-day.

To note every alteration would be an endless and a useless task. We have listed more than seven thousand variations, from the smallest to the most important. The exact figure must depend on the standard adopted for this kind of work, but the number roughly shows the scale.

The corrections which were considered necessary before going to press might well have been made on the printer's copy and have left the original manuscripts intact. Unfortunately these were also retouched and some passages erased and over-written in such a way that it is to-day impossible to know in every case whether the correction was made by Thérèse or by one of her editors.

It is certain that Thérèse made many corrections herself. In those days every Carmelite kept an eraser in her writing-case and used it generously and with precision. Of the changes made by other hands there were those, to start with, on which the Prioress insisted in order that all three manuscripts should seem to be addressed to her. In deference to her wishes, Mother Agnes made them not only in the published text but on Thérèse's manuscripts as well, and in going through them for this purpose she cut other details which might have displeased Mother Marie de Gonzague. The original names were later restored by the nuns, but other corrections continued to be made at different times after the publication of the book. The effect of all these erasures and rewritings on the thin paper of the cheap copy-book can well be imagined.

In 1910, when the cause of Thérèse's beatification was introduced, the original text was reconstituted by the nuns in order to be submitted to Rome, though the published text continued to be the one edited by Mother Agnes. In prepar-

ing the facsimile edition[25] the impossible had been done at
the wish of the Lisieux Carmelites themselves to decipher
the original manuscripts, for even where the rubbing out
and rewriting had been done by the Saint, it was interesting
to know what she had written first. By comparing the auto-
graph pages and their photographs, by examining them micro-
scopically and with the help of ultra-violet and ultra-red rays
the maximum has been achieved.

The Story of a Soul was first published on the 30th September, 1898; two thousand copies were printed and there was
much timid speculation as to whether such a number could
ever be disposed of. Printed by a provincial firm, distributed
by a convent of enclosed nuns, would its destiny be any
different from that of other pious " lives " which accumulate
on the shelves of Convent Repositories?

Apart from the technical difficulties of distribution, it is
hard for us to-day to imagine how bold even the version
edited for contemporary taste seemed to the readers of those
days. Even some of the houses of the Order reacted unfav-
ourably. Three Carmelite convents did not like it at all,
Mother Agnes stated at the Apostolic Process.[26]

Even more courage was needed to face the Lisieux community, book in hand. When the text was read aloud in the
refectory, the listeners included the " Sister who had a talent
for displeasing me in everything," the " Sister who never
stopped rattling her rosary or I don't know what else," the
one who, as she washed the handkerchiefs, always splashed
Thérèse. How would these Sisters and others accept the
description of their mishaps and harmless foibles? How
would Mother Marie de Gonzague feel when her severity
towards Thérèse was recalled before the whole community?

Mother Agnes was not withheld by considerations of
prudence, she carried out the mission entrusted to her by the
Saint; for this she deserves our gratitude. Her courage made
it possible for *The Story of a Soul* to become widely known
in religious circles.

It was as if a spark had set off a vast conflagration. By 1911 the Carmel was receiving fifty letters a day, by 1914 the number had risen to five hundred. In the first twelve years after publication forty-seven thousand copies of the book were sold; a hundred and sixty-four thousand were sold between 1910 and 1915. To-day the sales can only be counted in millions.

During the Canonisation Process the original text and the published version were compared. Eventually, as the fame of the Saint grew, so did the demand that the original texts should be made public.

In August 1947 the Bishop of Bayeux and Lisieux gave permission for their publication and the Definitor General of the Order, the Very Reverend Marie-Eugène of the Child Jesus, wrote to Mother Agnes: " The Church has spoken. The sainthood and the doctrinal mission of St. Thérèse of the Child Jesus are universally recognised. From now on she belongs to the Church and to history. To avoid and to refute partial or mistaken interpretations of her doctrine and in order that her doctrine and her soul should be still more deeply understood, the documents which you have so generously given us are insufficient. Only the original texts can allow us to discover the movement of her thought, its living rhythm, and disclose all the light contained in her definitions, which are usually so firm and so precise."

Shaken by this official advice, Mother Agnes seriously considered the publication of the original text. But Mother Agnes was old; she had been given contrary advice as well; she was torn between a wish to put an end to all the arguments by publishing the texts and a fear—for which allowance must be made—of upsetting some of the devotees of the Saint.

She had been appointed Prioress for life. By courtesy to her, the Holy See pronounced the Decree *Dilata* suspending the publication for her lifetime. Relieved by this decision, Mother Agnes instructed Sister Geneviève of the Holy Face (her sister Céline and the only surviving member of the family) to take charge of the publication of the facsimiles after her death: " After my death I order you to do it in my name."

Mother Agnes died on the 28th July, 1951, and a year later steps were taken in Rome to get permission for the publication of the Manuscripts. On 19th September, 1952, the decree suspending it was lifted.

It was in 1953 that the Carmel of Lisieux asked me to undertake the work of producing the facsimile edition which alone could satisfy the most exacting minds and close the discussion.

FR. FRANCOISE DE SAINTE MARIE, O.C.D.

BOOK ONE

Manuscript Dedicated to
the Reverend Mother Agnes of Jesus

Chapter 1

THERESE'S FAMILY

DEAREST MOTHER, it is to you, who are my mother twice over*, that I am going to tell the history of my soul. When you first asked me to do it, I was frightened: it looked as if it meant wasting my spiritual energies on introspection. But, since then, our Lord has made it clear to me that all he wanted of me was plain obedience. And in any case, what I shall be doing is only what will be my task in eternity— telling over and over again the story of God's mercies to me.[1]

Before taking up my pen, I knelt down before our Lady's statue; the one which has so often assured us that the Queen of Heaven looks on our family with special favour. My prayer was that she would guide my hand, and never let my pen write a single line which wasn't as she wanted it to be. After that, I opened the gospels at random, and the words my eyes fell on were these: "Then he went up on to the mountain side, and called to him those whom it pleased him to call; so these came to him."[2] There it all was, the history of my life, of my whole vocation; above all, of the special claims Jesus makes on my soul. He doesn't call the people who are worthy of it; no, just the people it pleases him to call; as St. Paul says, God shews pity on those he pities, shews mercy where he is merciful; the effect comes from God's mercy, not from man's will or man's alacrity."[3]

I had always wondered why it was that God has his preferences, instead of giving each soul an equal degree of grace. Why does he shower such extraordinary favours on the Saints

who at one time have been his enemies, people like St. Paul
and St. Augustine, compelling them (you might say) to accept
the graces he sends them? Why do you find, in reading the
lives of the Saints, that there are some of them our Lord sees
fit to hold in his arms, all the way from the cradle to the
grave? Never an obstacle in their path, as they make their
way up to him; grace still heading them off, so that they
never manage to soil the robe of baptismal innocence! And
again, I used to wonder about the poor savages and people
like that, who die, such numbers of them, without ever so
much as hearing the name of God mentioned. But Jesus has
been gracious enough to teach me a lesson about this mystery,
simply by holding up to my eyes the book of nature. I
realised, then, that all the flowers he has made are beautiful;
the rose in its glory, the lily in its whiteness, don't rob the
tiny violet of its sweet smell, or the daisy of its charming
simplicity. I saw that if all these lesser blooms wanted to be
roses instead, nature would lose the gaiety of her springtide
dress—there would be no little flowers to make a pattern over
the countryside. And so it is with the world of souls, which
is his garden. He wanted to have great Saints, to be his
lilies and roses, but he has made lesser Saints as well; and
these lesser ones must be content to rank as daisies and
violets, lying at his feet and giving pleasure to his eye like
that. Perfection consists simply in doing his will, and being
just what he wants us to be.

This, too, was made clear to me—that our Lord's love
makes itself seen quite as much in the simplest of souls as in
the most highly gifted, as long as there is no resistance offered
to his grace. After all, the whole point of love is making
yourself small; and if we were all like the great Doctors
who have shed lustre on the Church by their brilliant teaching, there wouldn't be much condescension on God's part,
would there, about coming into hearts like these? But no, he
has created little children, who have no idea what's going on
and can only express themselves by helpless crying: he has
made the poor savages, with nothing better than the natural
law to live by; and he is content to forget his dignity and
come into their hearts too—these are the wild flowers that
delight him by their simplicity. It is by such condescension
that God shews his infinite greatness. The sun's light, that

plays on the cedar-trees, plays on each tiny flower as if it were the only one in existence; and in the same way our Lord takes a special interest in each soul, as if there were no other like it. Everything conspires for the good of each individual soul, just as the march of the seasons is designed to make the most insignificant daisy unfold its petals on the day appointed for it.

Dear Mother, you must be wondering by now what all this is leading up to; not a word yet to suggest that I am telling the story of my life! But, you see, you told me to write down, without reserve, all the thoughts which came into my mind, and it isn't exactly an account of my life that I mean to write; these are the thoughts which occur to me about the graces which God in his mercy has seen fit to grant me. I am now at a moment of my life when I can afford to look back at the past. The fire of sufferings, outward and inward, has brought me to maturity; I am like a flower that can lift its head, refreshed, after the storm has passed by. I can read my own experience in the words of the twenty-second psalm: " The Lord is my shepherd; how can I lack anything? He gives me a resting-place where there is green pasture, leads me out to the cool water's brink, refreshed and content. As in honour pledged, by sure paths he leads me: dark be the valley about my path, hurt I fear none while thou, Lord, art with me." To me, the Lord has always been " pitying and gracious, patient and rich in mercy."[1]

What happiness, Mother, to " put the Lord's mercies on record " with you at my side! It's for you only that I mean to write down the story of the little flower Jesus has picked, so I can talk to you quite freely, without any qualms about my style, or about wandering away from the point so often. A mother's instinct can always understand, even when her child can only talk baby-language; and you, Mother, who had the shaping of my heart and gave it to Jesus, surely you will be able to understand, and to guess what I mean.

If a wild flower could talk, I imagine it would tell us quite candidly about all God has done for it; there would be no point in hushing up his gifts to it, out of mock humility, and pretending that it was ugly, that it had no smell, that the sun had robbed it of its bloom, or the wind broken its stem,

[1] Psalm 102, 8.

knowing that all that wasn't true. Anyhow, this isn't going to be the autobiography of a flower like that. On the contrary, I'm delighted to be able to put them on record, the favours our Lord has shown me, all quite undeserved. I fully realise that there was nothing about me which could have claimed his divine attention; anything which is good in me is the effect of his mercy—that and nothing else.

It was he that chose the soil I was to grow in—holy ground, all steeped (you might say) in the scent of purity. He saw to it that eight lilies of dazzling whiteness should grow up there before me. Even so, his little flower must be lovingly protected from the pestilential airs of worldliness; he would transplant it, when its petals were only just beginning to open, to Mount Carmel—a place perfumed already by the scent of two lilies that had blessed her spring-tide with their gentle companionship. It is seven years now since that flower took root in the garden where the Lover of Souls had planted it; and now there are *three* lilies to lift their heads close by; a fourth is unfolding, still under the watchful care of Jesus, not far away. And what of our parents, the blessed stock from which we all sprang? They have been reunited, for all eternity, in their heavenly country, and found there, waiting for them, those other four lilies that never unfolded to earthly eyes. May Jesus be merciful to us, who are still exiles here, and not leave us long on this alien shore; soon, soon may the lily-plant be complete in heaven!

So far, Mother, I've just been giving a brief summary of the blessings God has granted me; now I must talk about my childhood in detail. Anybody else would find it a dull story, but you, with your mother's heart, will find something there that appeals to you. Besides, the memories I'm going to conjure up are your memories as well as mine; my childhood was passed in your near neighbourhood, and I had the happiness to claim the same parents—parents you couldn't have matched anywhere; the same loving care surrounded both of us. May they have a blessing to spare for the youngest of their children, and help her to set on record the story of the Divine mercies.

Chapter II

HER INFANCY

I'M DIVIDING up the course of my life before I entered Carmel into three distinct periods; the first of these is short, but rich in memories. It begins with the dawn of reason in me; it ends with the day when our dear Mother left us for a better home in heaven. God, in his goodness, allowed my mind to develop early, and impressed the memories of childhood on it so firmly that all the events I'm going to tell you about feel as if they'd happened yesterday. I suppose our Lord had a loving design in that; he wanted me to realise what a wonderful mother he'd given me, although he was so soon to reward her with a heavenly crown.

God has seen fit to surround me with love at every moment of my life: all my earliest impressions are of smiles and of endearments. And if he planted love all about me, he planted it in my childish heart too, gave me a loving and sensitive nature. How fond I was of Papa and Mamma! I shewed my affection for them in any number of ways, like the demonstrative child I was: and some of these were rather unusual. Witness the following extract from one of Mamma's letters:

" Baby is such a queer little creature as you never saw: she comes up and puts her arms round me and wishes I were dead. 'Oh, poor little Mother,' she says, 'I do wish you'd die.' Then, when you scold her, she explains: 'Oh, but it's only because I want you to go to heaven: you told me yourself one can't go to heaven without dying.' She wants to kill off her father too, when she gets really affectionate."

I was very fond, too, of my dear godmother.[1] I used to pay great attention, without shewing it, to everything people were doing or saying, and I really think I still judge things to-day

[1] That is, her sister Marie.

29

as I did then. When Marie was teaching Céline to do things, I listened very carefully, so as to be able to follow suit.

This is what Mamma said about me on June 25th, when I was scarcely eighteen months old:

" Your father has just put up a swing, and Céline couldn't be happier. But you ought to see Baby swinging: it's so amusing, the grown-up way she sits there, and you can be quite sure that she will hang on to the rope. But soon she starts yelling because it isn't going fast enough, and then she has to be strapped down with another rope in front—even so, it makes me nervous to see her perched up there. I had such a queer adventure with Baby the other day. I usually go out to Mass at half past five, but at first, of course, I didn't like to leave her alone. Then, finding that she never woke up, I decided to go all the same. My plan is to put her down on my own bed, with the cradle so close beside it that she can't fall out. Only one day I forgot to bring the cradle up, and when I came back there was no Baby to be seen in my bed! But just then I heard a groan, and when I looked round, there was Baby sitting on a chair opposite the end of my bed, with her little head on the bolster—asleep, but sleeping badly because she was uncomfortable. How she managed to reach the chair in a sitting position, when she'd been lying down on the bed, I couldn't imagine; I just thanked God no harm had come of it. It was really providential: she might so easily have fallen off on to the ground, if she hadn't been protected by her guardian angel and the holy souls in Purgatory—I say a prayer for her to them every day. That's my account of the matter; you must account for it as you think fit."

At the end of her letter Mamma added:

" Here's Baby coming to stroke my face with her tiny hand and give me a hug. The poor little thing stays with me all the time, and hates being parted from me. She's very fond of going into the garden, but if I'm not there she won't stay in it; she cries till she's brought back to me."

Here's a passage from another letter of hers:

"Little Thérèse asked me the other day whether she would get into heaven. I said Yes, if she was good; and her answer was: 'But if I was naughty, I suppose I'd go to hell. D'you know what I'd do then? You'd be in heaven, so I'd take refuge with you, and how would God manage to catch me then? Because you'd be holding me ever so tight in your arms.' And there was a look in her eyes which told me that she really did think that: if she was in her mother's arms God wouldn't be able to do anything to her. Marie is very fond of her little sister and finds her charming; no wonder, because the poor little thing is desperately afraid of annoying her. Yesterday I wanted to give her a rose, because she always likes that, but she implored me not to cut it—Marie had said they weren't to be cut; she got quite red in the face over it. When I cut two all the same, she wouldn't shew her face inside the house: it was no good telling her the roses belonged to me. she said: 'No, no, it's Marie's.' She's certainly a very temperamental child; any misadventure she has must be made public property immediately. Yesterday, by accident, she pulled down a bit of the wall-paper, and the effect was piteous; her father must be told at once, at once! He didn't come in till four hours later, when everybody had forgotten about it; but Thérèse made straight for Marie. 'Quick, tell Papa about my tearing the paper.' There she stands, like a criminal awaiting sentence, but always with the idea in her little head that she will be forgiven more readily if she owns up."

When Marie came back from school at the Visitation, there was one treat I specially coveted—being allowed into her room while she was giving Céline her lessons. That meant being very good and doing exactly what she, Marie, told me; on her side, she used to shower presents on me, not very expensive presents, which delighted me all the same. I was very proud of both my big sisters, but it was Pauline who was the model of my childish ambitions. Sometimes, after I'd begun to talk, Mamma would ask me: "What are you thinking about?" and the answer was invariably: "Pauline." Or

I would trace lines, with my tiny hand, on the window-pane, and announce: "I'm writing Pauline." I often heard people say that she was certain to become a nun, and without knowing much about it I used to tell myself: "I'll be a nun too." One of my earliest memories, and I never changed my mind! So you see, Mother, it was through you that our Lord saw fit to betroth me to himself. We weren't seeing much of one another at the time, but already you were my ideal; I wanted to be like you, and it was your example that led me, ever since I was two years old, to set my heart on a Heavenly Bridegroom. Such a wealth of happy memories I should like you to share with me! But no, I'm only concerned with the growth of one particular flower in the garden; I must go on filling in the outlines of that. If I tried to tell you in detail what Pauline meant to me, my story would never get finished.

Dear little Léonie—she, too, claimed a lot of my affection. She was so fond of me; and when the rest of the family went out for a walk in the evening, it was she who looked after me. I can still hear the soft lullabies with which she used to put me to sleep. She was determined to keep me happy at all costs, and, for my part, I should have hated to cause her the least uneasiness. I remember so well the day of her first Communion, and above all the moment when she took me in her arms to carry me with her into the presbytery; I thought it wonderful being carried by a big sister in a dress as white as my own. I was put to bed early that night, because I was too young to sit up for late dinner; but I can still see Papa coming up at dessert-time, to bring his dear little princess some bits of iced cake. Next day or a few days after that, we went with Mamma to see the girl who'd made her first Communion with Léonie; and I think it must have been then that this kindest of mothers took us off behind a wall to give us some wine after dinner. She didn't want to hurt the feelings of our hostess, Madame Dagorau, who wasn't at all well off, and at the same time she didn't want us to go short of anything. A mother's heart is so considerate: her love shews itself, again and again, by such thoughtful, such unexpected attentions.

Chapter III

THERESE AND CELINE

I'VE STILL got to talk about dear Céline, who shared the nursery with me; but I've so many memories of her that I don't know how to choose between them. What I'll do is to give some extracts from the letters Mamma wrote to you at school. It would take too long if I gave them in full. This is what she wrote on the 10th of July, 1873, the year of my birth:

"On Thursday Nurse brought little Thérèse.* She did nothing but laugh, Céline was a great favourite with her and they roared with laughter together, apparently she wants to play games already. That will come before long; she holds herself up on her little legs as stiff as a post, and we're expecting her to walk soon. I think she'll be a good girl; she seems very intelligent and has a face as chubby as a cherub's."*

But it wasn't till I left my foster-mother that I began to shew how fond I was of dear little Céline. We understood one another perfectly; the only difference was that I was much more lively, and had a less simple nature than she had. Although I was three and a half years younger, I always felt as if we were the same age. Here is a passage from one of Mamma's letters, which will give you some idea of the nice child Céline was, the naughty child I was:

"My little Céline's propensities are good in every way; to be good is the leading idea in her nature; she has an innocent mind and a horror of evil. It's difficult to see how the other little imp is going to turn out; she's so young and so thoughtless. She's cleverer than Céline, but she hasn't got her sweet temper; so obstinate that you can't do anything with her—once she's said No, nothing will make her budge. You could lock her up all day in the cellar, and she'd sleep the night there rather than say Yes. And yet at heart she's as good as gold, so loving and so open. You should see her running after me to tell me when she's been naughty. 'Mamma, I gave Céline a shove once, and I've slapped her once, but I'm not going to do it again'—it's always like that. On Thursday afternoon we went for a walk by the station, and she insisted on going into the waiting-room to look for Pauline. There she was running in front of me, so happy that it did you good to see her; but when she realised that we'd got to go home without taking the train to look for Pauline, she cried all the way home.'

That last part of the letter reminds me of the happiness I used to feel when you came back from school;* in a moment, Mother, I was in your arms and Céline in Marie's, and I would kiss you again and again, and lean over your shoulder to admire your long plaits. Then you would give me a stick of chocolate you'd been keeping for me for three months; you can imagine how I treated it as a kind of relic. I remember, too, the journey to Le Mans, the first time I ever went by train; it was so wonderful to be on our travels, just Mamma and I, all by ourselves. But somehow I started crying, I don't know why; and when we got to my aunt's at Le Mans poor Mother had to introduce her to a horrible little fright, all red in the face from crying on the journey. The only memory I have of Aunt's convent parlour is of the moment when she handed me a little white sugar-mouse, and a cardboard basket full of sweets. There were two pretty rings lying on the top of them, made of sugar, just the size of my finger; so I shouted "Hurrah! There'll be one for Céline too." But unfortunately when we left I carried the basket by its handle (my other hand being in Mamma's), and a few yards farther on, when I looked down at the basket, I found nearly all my sweets were scattered about in the street, like the stones in Hop-o'-my-thumb. A closer inspection shewed that one of my two precious rings had gone the way of the sweets—there was nothing left to give to Céline! This led to an outburst of grief; we must go back, go back! When Mamma didn't seem to take any notice, it was too much altogether; the tears stopped, and the yelling began—how could she be so indifferent to my misery? That made it all so much worse!

I must go back to the letters Mamma wrote to you about
Céline and me; it's the best way of describing to you the kind
of child I was. Here is one that shews up my defects rather
luridly:

"At the moment, Céline is playing bricks to amuse
Baby. Every now and then they start arguing, but Céline
gives way; another pearl (she thinks) for her crown. Baby,
when things aren't going well for her, gets pitiably worked
up, so that I have to talk her round; she seems to think
that all is lost, and sometimes the feeling is too much for
her, and she chokes with indignation. She's such a very
excitable child;* and yet she's quite good and very intelligent; she remembers everything she's told."

You can see for yourself, Mother, that I wasn't exactly a
model child. It couldn't even be said of me that I was "well-
behaved enough when I was asleep," because I gave more
trouble at night than by day. First I would give all my bed-
clothes leave of absence, and then, still asleep, knock up
against the wood of my bedstead; the pain woke me up, and
then it was: "Mamma, I've bumped myself!" Poor Mamma
had to get up and verify, from the bruises on my forehead,
the fact of the bumping; she would put the clothes on and go
back to bed, to be told a moment later that I'd bumped myself again. There was nothing for it but to tie me down in
bed; so every night, Céline used to come and tie me up in
any number of knots, little fidget that I was, to prevent me
waking Mamma. After that, I was at least well-behaved in
my sleep.

There was another fault I had, a waking fault this time,
which Mamma doesn't mention in her letters—a great self-
esteem. I'll only give you two instances of that, because I
mustn't make my story too long. "Thérèse, my pet," Mamma
said to me one day, "I'll give you a halfpenny to kiss the
ground." A halfpenny was a fortune in those days, and it
wasn't a great loss of dignity because I wasn't much height
from the ground; but no, my pride was up in arms at the idea
of kissing the ground. I held myself up very straight and
said to Mamma: "I think not, dear Mother; I'd rather go
without the halfpenny." Another time, when we were going

to Madame Monnier's house at Grogny, Mamma told Marie
to dress me in my light-blue frock with the lace edging, but
not to leave my arms bare for fear of sunburn. I let her dress
me without protest, as children do at that age; but inwardly
I was reflecting all the time that I should have looked much
prettier with my arms bare.

With a nature like mine, I might have turned out thoroughly wicked, and perhaps lost my soul, if I had been
brought up by indifferent parents, or if Louise* had spoilt me
as she spoilt Céline. But I'd promised myself to our Lord, and
he was looking after me; he saw to it that the faults in my
character were checked in good time, and actually helped me
to grow up to the full height of my possibilities. Self-esteem
I had, but I also had a love of goodness; and as soon as I began
to think seriously (as I did when I was still quite young), it
was enough to tell me once for all: "That's not a very good
thing to do," and I'd no wish to hear it said again. I'm glad
to know, from reading Mamma's letters, that as I grew older
I was more of a comfort to her. I had good examples all
around me, and it was natural that I should imitate them. This
is what she wrote in 1876:

"Even Thérèse sometimes wants to take part in their
pious practices.* She is a delicious child, thin as a ghost,*
very lively, but with a sensitive nature. She and Céline are
fast friends, and need no company but their own to keep
themselves amused. Every day, immediately after dinner,
Céline gets hold of her little bantam-cock, and then goes
off to catch Thérèse's hen—a thing I can never do, but she's
so smart that she can catch it with one spring. Then they
both come in and sit down one on each side of the fire, and
keep happy like that for hours. It was little Rose[1] who'd
made me a present of both birds, and I'd given the cock to
Céline. The other day Céline had got into my bed, and
Thérèse was upstairs in Céline's. She'd asked Louise to
come and take her downstairs to be dressed, but when
Louise went to look for her she found the bed empty—
Thérèse had heard Céline calling and come down to be
with her. 'What!' said Louise. 'Don't you want to come
down and be dressed after all?' And the answer was: 'Oh,
[1] Rose Tarthé, the foster-mother of Thérèse.

I'm sorry, Louise, but we're like the two bantams, we're inseparable.' And as they said it they hugged one another ever so tight. Then, in the evening, Louise, Céline and Léonie went off to the Catholic social evening,* not taking Thérèse, who quite realised that she was too young to go. ' Well,' she said, ' couldn't I be put to sleep in Céline's bed?' It appeared that she couldn't; so she said nothing, and was left alone with her bed-side lamp; in a quarter of an hour she was fast asleep."

Under another date Mamma writes:

" Céline and Thérèse are quite inseparable; you've never seen two children so fond of one another. When Marie comes to look for Céline, because it's time for her lessons, poor Thérèse is in a flood of tears. Oh dear, what will become of her, left without a friend in the world? Marie's heart is melted, and she takes Thérèse along too; there she sits for two or three hours on end, poor mite, with some beads to thread or a bit of sewing to do: never daring to move, but heaving a great sigh now and again. When the thread comes out of her needle, she tries to thread it again, but it's never a success—but of course she mustn't disturb Marie. Watch her; before long you will see two big tears trickling down her cheeks. Marie comes to the rescue at once, and the poor little angel smiles through her tears after all."

To be sure, yes : I can remember how I couldn't bear to be separated from Céline; I would leave my own dessert unfinished, so as to go off with her the moment she rose from the table. I would turn round in my high chair asking to get down, and we would run off to play together. Sometimes it was with the préfet's* daughter; we liked that because of the park, and the lovely toys she shewed us. But I really went there to please Céline: I preferred staying in our own little garden, where we scraped the walls and carried off the shiny bits of stone we found there, to sell them to Papa; he bought them from us with the utmost seriousness.

Chapter IV

CHILDHOOD AT ALENCON

I WAS TOO young to go to Church on Sundays, and Mamma stayed behind to look after me. I behaved beautifully and went about on tiptoe all the time Mass was going on; but when I saw the gate opening, it was the signal for an outburst of delirious joy. I rushed at my small sister, who was looking beautiful in her Sunday best, shouting: "Quick, quick, Céline, the *pain bénit*!*" Sometimes she hadn't brought any, because she'd got to Church late; here was a state of things! I couldn't go without; it counted in my own mind as my attendance at Mass. There was only one thing for it: "If you haven't brought any blessed bread, you'll jolly well have to bless some." No sooner said than done; she'd opened the cupboard, secured the bread and cut a mouthful of it, over which she said a Hail Mary. Then she gave it me, and after making the sign of the Cross with it, I ate it with great devotion; somehow for me it had exactly the taste of the real *pain bénit*.

Often enough we engaged in discussions about religion. Here's an instance, taken from Mamma's letters:

"Céline and Thérèse, the little dears, are angels of goodness—really angelic characters. Marie is so delighted with Thérèse, and so proud of her: you wouldn't believe how much credit she takes for it. And it's quite true her answers are very quick for a child of her age; she doesn't let Céline, who is twice as old, forget it. Céline asked the other day how God could be there in a tiny Host like that; and Baby said: 'There's nothing surprising about it at all; God is Almighty.' 'Almighty, what does that mean?' 'It means he can do anything he wants to.'"

A day came when Léonie, thinking she was too old now to play with dolls, came along to us with a basket full of dresses and pretty little bits of stuff for making others, with her own doll lying on the top. " Here you are, darlings," she said, " choose which of these you'd like; they're all for you." Céline put her hand in and brought out a little ball of silken braid which had taken her fancy. I thought for a moment, and then said, as I held out my hand: " I choose the whole lot!" Then, without further ceremony, I took over the basket. Everybody said I was quite within my rights, and Céline never dreamt of making any protest. (As a matter of fact she was never hard up for toys; her godfather was always giving her presents, and Louise could always manage to get her anything she wanted.)

Only a childish trait, perhaps, but in a sense it's been the key to my whole life. Later on, when the idea of religious perfection came within my horizon, I realised at once that there was no reaching sanctity unless you were prepared to suffer a great deal, to be always on the look-out for something higher still, and to forget yourself. There were plenty of degrees in spiritual advancement, and every soul was free to answer our Lord's invitation by doing a little for him, or by doing a lot for him; in fact, he gave it a *choice* between various kinds of self-sacrifice he wanted it to offer. And then, as in babyhood, I found myself crying out: " My God, I choose the whole lot. No point in becoming a Saint by halves. I'm not afraid of suffering for your sake; the only thing I'm afraid of is clinging to my own will. Take it, I want the whole lot, everything whatsoever that is your will for me."

But I must call a halt; I'm not talking yet about what I was like in my youth, I'm only talking about a little imp of four years old. I can remember a dream I had, which must have come to me about that time; it impressed itself deeply on my imagination. I dreamt one night that I went out for a walk alone in the garden, and when I got to the bottom of the steps that led up to it, I stopped, overcome with fright. In front of me, quite close to the arbour one has to go through, there was a barrel of lime; and on it I saw two horrible little demons, dancing about with a surprising quickness of movement—surprising because they wore flat-irons on their feet. All of a sudden their flashing eyes fell on me, and thereupon, apparently much more frightened of me than I was of them, they jumped down off the barrel and took refuge in the linen-room, just in front of them. Their nervousness encouraged me to go and see what they were up to, so I went up to the linen-room window; there they were, the poor little demons, running about over the tables in a frantic effort to get out of sight. Sometimes they would come up to the window, looking anxiously to see if I was still there; and finding that I went on watching them, they began to run to and fro as if in desperation. There was nothing very extraordinary, to be sure, about this dream of mine; but I suppose God allowed me to remember it for a special purpose. He wanted me to see that the soul, when in a state of grace, has nothing to fear from the spirits of evil; they are cowards, so cowardly that they run away at a glance from a child.

Here's another passage I find in Mamma's letters (poor dear Mother, she foresaw that her exile on earth wasn't going to last much longer): *

"I'm not worried about the two tiny ones; they're so well-behaved, both of them. With natures of such rare quality, they're sure to turn out well; you and Marie will have no difficulty in managing their education. Céline is never guilty of the slightest wilful fault, and Baby will do well too; she wouldn't tell a lie for all the money in the world, and there's more originality about her than I've ever seen in any of you. She was at the grocer's the other day with Céline and Louise; she was talking hard to Céline about her rule of life.* 'What *does* she mean?' asked the good lady behind the counter. 'She talks about nothing but her rule of life when they're playing out there in the garden. Madame Gaucheron spends her time leaning out of the window to try and discover what it's all about, this rule-of-life business!' Poor mite, she's a joy to all of us; she'll grow up into a good woman. You can see the germs of it already; she's always talking about Almighty God, and she wouldn't miss her prayers for anything. I wish you could be there when she's reciting nursery tales; I've never seen anything so attractive—she finds out exactly the right expression and the right tone of voice all by herself. The best of all is when she repeats: 'Tell me, dear little Golden-hair, Whether you look to find God there.' When she gets to 'Up into heaven, so deep and blue,' she looks up with a quite angelic expression on her face; it's so lovely that we're never tired of making her do it, that expression of hers is so completely ravishing."

What a happy childhood it was, Mother! I'd already begun to taste the joys of life, and at the same time virtue was, for me, something attractive—I suppose I was really very much like what I am now, with a great instinct, already, of self-control. These sunny days of childhood, how quickly they pass! And yet, how those delightful memories have stamped themselves on my soul! I remember the thrill of going out for a walk with Papa to the pavilion in the park;* the smallest details of them have left their impress on my mind, especially the Sunday walks, when Mamma always went with us. I can still recall the deep poetic feelings which sprang up in my heart at the sight of standing crops all dotted with corn-flowers and such wild growths. Already I had a feeling for distances, and wide views, and huge trees[1] with their branches sweeping the ground; they made much the same impression on me as the beauties of nature still do.

We often met poor people on these long walks of ours, and always little Thérèse, to her great delight, was their almoner; except when Papa thought the distance was too long for his dear little princess, and took her home in front of the others, which she didn't like at all. Céline would try to console me by filling the small basket she carried with daisies, and giving them to me when she got home; but alas, Grandmama, dear good soul, sometimes thought there were too many of them for one small girl, and carried off a whole lot of them for our Lady's statue. I minded that, but I was careful not to say anything about it. I always made a point of not complaining when things were taken away from me and when I was blamed for something I hadn't done, I held my tongue instead of making excuses. I don't take any credit for that; it was instinctive generosity in me. Unfortunately, this generosity was soon to vanish.

[1] Pine trees.

Chapter V

THE MOVE TO LISIEUX

THERE'S NO denying it, the world was treating me very well; flowers at my feet everywhere, and a happy disposition which helped to make life pleasant for me. But now my soul had got to start on a new period of its existence; I was to pass through the searching fires of trial, and be apprenticed early to suffering, so as to be offered to our Lord the sooner. The spring flowers begin to put out their buds down under the snow, before they can be unfolded by the sun's rays. I've compared myself to a little wild flower; no wonder that I should have to undergo the test of winter-time.

All the details of dear Mother's illness are still a poignant memory to me; her last days on earth I remember especially well. Céline and I were a couple of tiny exiles; Madame Leriche came round every morning, and we spent the day with her. One day we hadn't had time to say our prayers before we left home, and Céline whispered to me on the way: "Ought we to tell her we haven't said our prayers?" I said Yes, and she explained things, very shyly, to Madame Leriche, who replied: "Never mind, you'll say them now," and went off, leaving us together in one of the big rooms. Céline looked at me, and we both agreed: "Mamma would never have done that. She always made sure we got our prayers said." All the time we were playing with other children, the thought of our dear Mother was haunting us. I remember how Céline, when she was given a lovely apricot, leant over to me and whispered: "We won't eat it: I'll give it to Mamma." But indeed our poor Mother was too ill, now, to enjoy the fruits of earth; she was to find her refreshment in the sight of God's glory in heaven; she was to partake of that mysterious "fruit of the vine" which our Lord, at the Last Supper, promised to share with us in his Father's kingdom.[1] The touching ceremonies of Extreme

[1] Luke 22, 18.

Unction impressed themselves deeply on my imagination: I can still see the place where I knelt beside Céline—all five of us were there, in order of age, and poor dear Father knelt there too, sobbing.

He took me in his arms on the day of Mamma's death, or perhaps it was the day after, and said: "Come and give your poor Mother a last kiss." I put my lips to dear Mother's forehead without saying a word; I don't think I was crying much; my feelings were too deep to be shared with anybody. In silence I looked and listened; nobody was bothering about me, so I was conscious of many sights that would otherwise have been spared me. Once I found myself in view of the coffin lid, and stood a long time looking at it; I'd never seen one before, but I understood what it all meant. Mamma was so small, and yet I had to lift my head well up before I could see the whole length of it; I hated the size of it. Fifteen years later, I found myself standing before another coffin, that of Mother Geneviève; it was the same size as Mamma's, and it took me straight back to my childhood. All my memories came back to me in a flood; baby Thérèse and I were one and the same person. Only, now that I'd grown up, the coffin looked quite small; I lifted up my head, not to look at the coffin, but to gaze towards a heaven which now seemed so joyful, with all my trials over, the winter of my soul for ever past.

So the day came when the Church gave our dear Mother's mortal remains the blessing of heaven; it was God's will to give me on that same day, of my own free choice, a new mother on earth. We were all together, the five of us, each looking miserably at the rest; Louise was there too, and the sight of Céline and myself made her say: "Poor mites, you have no mother now." Céline threw herself into the arms of Marie. "All right," she said, "then you've got to be Mamma." It was a habit with me always to imitate Céline, but it was to you, dear Mother, that I turned instead, and as if a veil had already been torn away from the future,[1] threw myself into *your* arms, shouting: "My Mamma's going to be Pauline."

All this (as I said just above) was an epoch; I was to enter, now, on the second period of my life; it was also the

[1]Pauline was, of course, the Mother Agnes for whom this part of the memoir was written.

most painful—especially after this new mother of my choice had entered Carmel. It lasted from the time when I was four up to my fourteenth year; it was only then that I really became a child again, though it was just the moment when I was beginning to take life seriously. It must be confessed, Mother, that after Mamma's death my character, which had been so happy in its disposition till then, underwent a complete change. I, who had been so lively, so communicative, was now a shy and quiet little girl, and over-sensitive. Merely to be looked at made me burst into tears; I was only happy when nobody was paying any attention to me; I hated having strange people about, and could only recover my good spirits when I was alone with the family. And indeed, all this time I was surrounded by love and thoughtfulness on every side; Papa's compassionate nature made him a mother as well as a father to me, and hadn't I two mothers as well in you and Marie, the best, the most unselfish mothers that ever were? It is as if God had seen that the little flower I wrote of needed some rays of sunshine, if it was to take root here at all. Rain and wind all the time would have been too much for it; warmth and dew and the spring breeze must play their part as well. Such blessings our Lord wanted me to have, even when I was undergoing the test of winter.

I can't remember that I minded leaving Alençon; children enjoy a change, and I welcomed our arrival at Lisieux. I remember the journey, and how we reached our aunt's house when it was already evening. Jeanne and Marie were waiting for us at the door; it was nice to have such pretty cousins, and I grew very fond of them, as I did of my aunt and still more of my uncle, though he frightened me; I was never really at my ease there, as I was at Les Buissonnets: it was at Les Buissonnets that I really found life enjoyable. Every day you came in, and asked me whether I'd made my morning offering; then you'd dress me, talking to me about God all the time, and then I knelt beside you and said my prayers. Later on came the reading lesson; the first word I ever learned to read was "Heaven." It was my dear godmother who taught me to write; you did all the rest. I wasn't very good at learning things, but I had an excellent memory. Catechism and Bible History were what I liked best; I enjoyed *them*; but there were plenty of tears shed over grammar—do you re-

member the trouble about masculine and feminine? As soon
as class was over I went up to the sunny room at the top of
the house, carrying my badge and my marks* to Papa. How
proud I was when I was able to announce: "I got five marks
and none taken off—Pauline said it of her own accord!" The
point being that when I had to ask you whether I'd got five
full marks and wait for you to say Yes, I always felt it was
one degree less creditable. You gave me special good marks,
too, and when I'd collected enough of these I was given a
reward and a holiday, a whole day of freedom. I remember I
used to find these days went much more slowly than the
others, and you were glad to hear that, because it meant that
I wasn't really fond of doing nothing.

Every afternoon I used to go for a walk with Papa, and we
made our visit to the Blessed Sacrament together. We used
to go round all the churches in turn, and that's how I had
my first experience of going into the chapel at Carmel. There,
Papa shewed me the grille that shuts off the choir, and told
me that there were nuns beyond it; the suspicion never
crossed my mind that nine years later I should be one of
them. Before we finished our walk, Papa always bought me
some tiny present; when it was over, I finished my arrears of
work, and spent the rest of my time romping about in the
garden, close to him—I never had the knack of playing with
dolls. I was very fond of making curious concoctions of my
own, from seeds and bits of bark which I found lying about,
and offering them to Papa in a doll's cup. Poor dear, he had
to stop working, and give me a smile, and make a pretence
of drinking. Before he gave me back the cup he would ask,
in an aside, whether he was to empty it out; sometimes he
was allowed to, but more often I took my precious *tisane*
away, to do duty several times over. I enjoyed gardening, too,
in the little plot Papa had given me; it contained a recess, in
which I used to put up little toy altars. When one of these
was finished, I ran off to fetch Papa and dragged him to the
spot, making him keep his eyes shut till he was told to open
them. Obediently he would follow me to my little garden,
and when I shouted: "Open your eyes, Papa!" he would
humour me by going into ecstasies of admiration at what
seemed to me a masterpiece. I could go on for ever recalling
details like that, so characteristic of him, that crowd into

the mind. But I could never acknowledge all the kindness he shewed to his dear little princess: speech, and even thought, can't always do justice to the gratitude the heart feels.

He went out fishing sometimes, this Prince Charming of mine, and it was a great day when he took me with him; I did so love the countryside, with all the birds and the flowers. I even tried fishing too, with a small rod of my own; but I preferred sitting there on the grass, with the flowers for my company. My thoughts went deep at such times, and although I knew nothing about meditating, my soul did sink into a state of genuine prayer. Noises came to me from a distance, the sighing of the wind, and faint echoes, even, of music from soldiers on the march,* inducing a mood of agreeable melancholy. Earth seemed a place of exile, and I could dream of heaven. How quickly the afternoon was over and we had to go back to Les Buissonnets! But first I'd got to finish the food I'd brought with me in my basket; those jam sandwiches you cut for me, the bright contrast of their colours all faded, now, into a dull pink—no, this world was a depressing place, and there was to be no unclouded happiness this side of heaven.

Talking of clouds, I remember one of these days in the country when the blue sky grew suddenly overcast, and we heard the rumblings of a storm; the dark clouds were furrowed by flashes of lightning, and I saw a thunderbolt fall not far off. I wasn't the least bit frightened; on the contrary, I was delighted; God seemed so near me. Papa didn't altogether share my delight; he wasn't afraid of the storm, but already the grass at my feet and the tall daisies above me seemed as if they were spangled with jewels, and it looked as if these jewels were going to make his little daughter rather wet. So, as we had several fields to cross before we got back to the road, he arranged his fishing tackle as best he could, and carried me on his back.

When I went for walks with Papa, he was fond of sending me to give money to the poor people we met. One day, we saw a man dragging himself painfully along on crutches, but when I went up to him with my penny he turned out not to be as poor as all that; he smiled sadly and wouldn't take it. I can't describe my emotions; here was this man I should have liked to comfort and console, and instead of that I'd injured his feelings. I dare say the poor cripple guessed what was passing through my mind, because he turned back to smile at me. How would it be to give him the cake Papa had just bought for me? No, I hadn't the courage; but I did wish I could offer him something, something it would be impossible to refuse; I felt so terribly sorry for him. Then I remembered having been told that on your first Communion day you could get any prayer granted. That was a comforting thought; I was only six years old then, but when I made my first Communion I would remember my poor man. That promise I kept, five years later, and I hope the prayer was answered; a prayer God himself had inspired; a prayer for one of his suffering members.

Chapter VI

EARLY RELIGIOUS IMPRESSIONS

I HAD LEARNED already to love God, love him deeply; and I constantly made him the gift of my heart, using the short formula which Mamma had taught me. But I must tell you about a fault by which I offended him one evening in May (of all months!); it's worth recalling, because it's good for my humility,* though I trust by now I've repented of it perfectly. I was too young to go to May devotions, so I stayed at home with Victoire,[1] and, with her, celebrated May devotions of my own on a small scale, with tiny candlesticks and flower-pots and a couple of wax matches which lit up the scene splendidly. Now and again she brought me, as a surprise present, two butt-ends of wax tapers, but that didn't often happen. Well, one evening we were all ready to start on the prayers, and I said: "Do you mind starting the *Memorare,* Victoire? I'm just going to light up." She made as if to start, but didn't say a word, only looked at me and laughed. There were my precious matches burning themselves out all too quickly; and when I'd asked her again to start the prayer and nothing happened, I told her out loud that she was a naughty girl, and stamped my foot—I, who was so gentle as a rule—as hard as I could. Poor Victoire no longer found it a laughing matter; there was nothing but astonishment in her eyes as she produced the pieces of taper she'd brought for me. The tears of anger gave place to tears of genuine contrition; I was quite resolved that I "wasn't going to do it again."

I had another set-to with Victoire, but this time there was no access of repentance; I kept perfectly cool the whole time. I wanted to get hold of an ink-pot which was on the kitchen mantelpiece, and as I was too small to reach it I asked Victoire, quite politely, to get it down for me. Would she do it? No; she told me to get up on a chair. Well, I went and got the chair without saying anything more about it; but it

[1] Victoire was the Martins' maid.

did seem to me it wasn't very nice of her, and by way of making that clear, I fished about in my childish vocabulary for the most offensive word I knew. When she was annoyed with me, she often called me a " little brat," which I found very wounding. So, before I got down off the chair, I turned round with a dignified air and said: " Victoire, you're a brat." Then I ran for cover, leaving her to digest this deep insult. Things moved quickly after that; it wasn't long before I heard her shouting out: " Miss Marie, here's Thérèse been calling me a brat!" Then Marie came and told me to apologise, so I did, but without really being sorry. If Victoire wouldn't even stretch out her great long arm to oblige me, what else would you call her?

All the same, we were very fond of one another. Hadn't she rescued me from a position of grave peril which I had brought on myself? She was ironing with a pail of water beside her, and I sat watching her, balancing, as usual, on a chair. All of a sudden the chair slipped, and instead of falling on to the ground I fell into the pail, where I remained with my feet touching my head, fitting in as neatly as a chicken in its egg! Poor Victoire could only stand there gaping at a situation which had never come her way before; much as I wished to get out of the pail, I couldn't manage it because my prison-cell made all movement impossible. Well, she did rescue me, with a little difficulty, from the terrible danger I've been describing—though she wasn't so lucky with my clothes, which had to be changed completely; I was soaked like a piece of bread in the soup. Another time I fell into the fire-place, but fortunately the fire wasn't lit, so Victoire had only to pick me up and shake the cinders off me. It was on Wednesday evenings, when you and Marie were away at choir practice, that these thrilling adventures used to occur.

It was on a Wednesday, too, that M. Ducellier* paid a pastoral call, and, being told by Victoire that there was nobody in except little Thérèse, came right through into the kitchen to see me, and had a look at my lessons. You may imagine how proud I felt about entertaining my confessor— I'd made my first confession only a short time before. My first confession—that is one of my most delightful memories. You'd prepared me for it so well, dear Mother, explaining to

me that I was really going to tell God about my sins, not just
a man. That sank in, and I made my confession full of the
spirit of faith; I even asked you: "If it's God I'm going to
talk to in his person, ought I to tell M. Ducellier that I love
him with my whole heart?" I knew exactly what to do and
say, so I went and knelt down in the confessional; unfortunately when he opened the grille M. Ducellier couldn't see
anybody there, because I was so small that my head didn't
reach the arm-rest! So he told me to stand up, and I stood
up and took a good look at him, then I made my confession
as if I had been quite a big girl. How devoutly I received
his blessing! You'd told me that the tears of the Child Jesus
were going to wash my soul clean. I remember his advice, the
first advice I ever received in the confessional; it was chiefly
about devotion to our Blessed Lady, so I promised myself that
I'd love her better than ever. I came out so pleased with life,
so light-hearted! Never before had my soul known such
happiness.

From then onwards, I went to confession as each big feast
day came round, and, for me, it seemed to make the holiday a
real holiday. Those big feasts are full of memories for me,
because I was so fond of them; you, dear Mother, were so good
at explaining the mysteries that lay at the heart of them,
they seemed like days spent in heaven. Above all, I liked the
Corpus Christi procession, a chance for me to strew God's
path with flowers; and not just dropping them but throwing
them as high as I could, with the thrill, sometimes, of seeing
my rose-petals touch the monstrance itself. Big feasts, of
course, only came now and then, but every week brought one
feast to which I had a real devotion—Sunday. There was
nothing like Sunday, God's own holiday, the day of rest.
I stayed longer in bed to begin with than usual; it was
Pauline who spoilt me by bringing me my chocolate in
bed, and then dressed me up like a princess; it was Marie
who came in to curl my hair, and I wasn't always very nice
to her when she pulled it tight. But it was a very happy
little girl who went downstairs to put her hand in Papa's
and be greeted with a specially loving kiss in honour of the
day; and then we all went off to High Mass.

All the way to Church, and even when we'd got into
Church, Papa let the little princess hold his hand; my place

was next to him, and when we had to go down into the body
of the Church for the sermon, two chairs must be found side
by side. That wasn't difficult to arrange; people seemed so
impressed by the sight of this fine old man and his tiny
daughter that they moved up to give us places. And there
was my uncle, sitting in the church-wardens' pew, beaming
with pleasure—he used to say I was like a ray of sunshine to
him. Personally, I wasn't much worried by people looking at
us, because I was always listening very attentively to the
sermon, without understanding a great deal of it. The first
sermon I did understand, and very moving I found it, was
one which M. Ducellier preached about the Passion; all the
other sermons came easier after that. When the preacher
referred to St. Teresa, Papa would lean over to me and
whisper: "Listen carefully, princess; this is about your
patron Saint." I listened, sure enough, but my eyes weren't
on the preacher so much as on Papa; there was so much
written in that handsome face of his! His eyes, sometimes,
would be full of tears which he tried vainly to keep back—it
was as if he didn't belong to earth any more, and his soul
could only find its own level in eternal truths. Not that his
span of life was nearly over; long years must pass before
heaven dawned on those welcoming eyes, and God wiped
away the tears from them, in reward of his faithful service.

But I must go back to our Sundays. The day passed too
quickly, as happy days will, not without a hint of melancholy.
Up to the time of Compline, I remember, my happiness was
unalloyed; it was during Compline that I said to myself:
" The day of rest will soon be coming to an end." To-morrow
I should have to pick up life again, do my work and learn
my lessons—it gave me the sense of being an exile, longing
for the eternal rest of heaven, those endless sabbaths in our
true home. Even the walks we took before going back to Les
Buissonnets had a feeling of sadness about them, because it
was then that the family broke up. To please my uncle, Papa
would leave Marie or Pauline behind to spend Sunday evening with him. I must say that I enjoyed it when I was left
behind too; it was so much better than going there alone,
when too much attention was paid to me. What I really
liked was sitting and listening to all my uncle said; what I
didn't like was being asked questions, and the terrifying thing

was when he took me on one knee and sang "Bluebeard" in a voice that unnerved me.

I was quite glad at the sight of Papa when he came round to fetch us. On the way home I would look up at the stars that shone so quietly, and the sight took me out of myself. In particular, there was a string of golden beads which seemed, to my great delight, to be in the form of the letter T. I used to shew it to Papa and tell him that my name was written in heaven; then, determined that I wasn't going to waste any more time looking at an ugly thing like the earth, I would ask him to steer me along, and walk with my head well in the air, not looking where I was going—I could gaze for ever at that starry vault!

Chapter VII

THERESE AND HER FATHER

EVENINGS IN winter, especially Sunday evenings in winter—
how am I to do justice to them? When the game of draughts
was over, and Papa took Céline and me one on either knee,
what songs he sang to us in that fine voice of his, moving my
soul to deep thoughts! Or else, by way of lullaby, he would
recite poetry to us, poetry that bore the stamp of eternal
truth. After that we went up to say our prayers together, but
for the little princess there was nobody there except her
prince—you had only to watch him to see what Saints are
like when they pray. And the climax was when all of us, in
order of age, went to get a kiss from Papa; naturally I was
the last, and he would take me up by the elbows as I shouted
out: "Good night, Papa, good night, sleep well," my invari-
able formula. Then I was carried up to Céline's bed in the
arms of my young mother, and I would ask: "Have I been
good to-day, Pauline? Will there be little angels hovering
round me?" The answer had to be Yes, or it would have
meant a night spent in tears.

So, when Pauline and Marie had kissed me and gone downstairs, poor little Thérèse was left all alone in the darkness;
try as she would to picture the angels hovering round her,
fears assailed her before long; the darkness was so terrifying
when you couldn't, from your bed, see the calm shining of the
stars. I look upon it as a real grace, dear Mother, that you
helped me to get accustomed to fears of this kind. Sometimes
you would send me, all by myself, to fetch something at night
from a room at the other end of the house. But for this good
training, I might have grown up into a nervous woman; as it
is, it takes a lot to frighten me. I often wonder how you
managed to look after me so lovingly, so considerately, yet
always without spoiling me. I'm certain no fault of mine
was passed over, and I fancy no reproach of yours was ever
undeserved. You never went back on a decision you'd once

53

made; that was so clear to me that I couldn't and wouldn't have put one foot before the other against your orders. Even Papa had to fall in with your wishes; I couldn't go for a walk without leave from Pauline. "Come along, Thérèse," Papa would say, and the only answer was: "Pauline doesn't want me to"; so he had to go and get your leave, and even then I knew well enough when you said Yes without really wanting me to—then there would be tears, and all consolation would be useless, until Pauline had said Yes really meaning it, and kissed me.

When I was ill—and that used to happen every winter—I was so wonderfully looked after; I can't tell you what it was like; you were a real mother to me. You would put me in your own bed (which was the greatest treat imaginable) and then give me anything I wanted. I remember one day you looked under the bolster and brought out a sweet little pocket-knife which was your very own. "Pauline," I cried out, delighted beyond words by such a present, "how you must love me! Are you really prepared to do without a lovely knife like that, and a little star on it too, all in mother-of-pearl? Look here, Pauline, supposing I was dying, would you, to save my life, give me your watch?" And you said: "Save your life? Why, I'd give it up at once if it was even going to make you get well quicker." I can't explain to you how surprised I felt, and how grateful. Occasionally in the summer I felt sick, and you were no less attentive. The great thing was to keep me amused, and you would give me a ride in a wheel-barrow all round the garden; then you'd tell me to get out and load up with a small daisy-plant, which had to be wheeled along to my garden very carefully, and dug in there with a good deal of ceremony.

If I had confidences to impart, they must be imparted to Pauline; if I had doubts, Pauline must resolve them. I remember being bothered about why God doesn't give the same degree of glory to all the elect when they get to heaven; surely that must make some of them unhappy? Whereupon you sent me to fetch Papa's big drinking-mug, which you put down side by side with my tiny thimble; then you poured water into both, and asked me which was fuller? I had to say that each was as full as the other; neither could hold any more. And then, dear Mother, you explained to me that in heaven God gives each soul the amount of glory it can accommodate and no more; so there's no reason why the lowest should envy the highest. So it wasn't only my body you looked after; you managed to attend to the needs of my soul, because you had the knack of bringing the most mysterious truths down to my level.

Every year I had the thrill of a prize-giving ceremony. Here as everywhere, strict justice was maintained; I was never given a prize I hadn't honestly earned. There I stood all by myself before an august family assembly, and there was the King of France and Navarre, as I called him, pronouncing sentence on me. How my heart beat when I went up to get my prizes and my crown! It felt like the Day of Judgment. When the distribution was over I got out of my white dress, and was hastily got up as one of the characters in the great pageant which followed.

They were great days, those occasions of family rejoicing. When you saw Papa so radiantly happy, you couldn't guess the trials that were in store for him. And yet in a way we were prepared for it beforehand, by a strange apparition which God saw fit to send me. Papa had been away several days, and wasn't expected back for two days more. It must have been about two or three in the afternoon; the sun was shining brightly, and nature was in its holiday best. I was standing, all alone, at an attic window which gave on to the main garden, looking out in that direction and full of my own untroubled thoughts. Suddenly I saw, in front of the laundry just opposite, a man dressed exactly like Papa, of his own height and walking just as he did, only much more bent as he walked. His face I couldn't see, because his head was muffled in an apron of some indeterminate colour; he wore the kind of hat Papa usually wore. I saw him move steadily onwards, past my own little garden; and all at once I was overcome by the sense of something uncanny about him. Then it occurred to me that Papa must have come home early, and was going about in disguise to give me a start, so I shouted, in a voice shrill with alarm: "Father, Father!" There was no sign that the mysterious visitor had heard me; he went steadily on without even turning round, and I watched him making for the little clump of trees which cut the main walk in two; I waited to see him come out on the farther side of those spreading branches. But no, the warning apparition had vanished.

All this happened in a moment, but it impressed itself so clearly on my mind that even now, after fifteen years, the memory of it is as fresh as if the sight were still before my eyes. Marie was next door with you, Mother, in a room which communicated with the one I was in, and when she heard me call to Papa she felt—so she told me afterwards—a thrill of terror, as if something extraordinary must be happening. But she wasn't going to betray her feelings; she ran in to find me and asked what on earth I meant by shouting out to Papa, when he was at Alençon. Then I told her what I'd seen.

Well, she tried to calm me down; it must have been Victoire trying to give me a fright, with her head muffled up in an apron. But when we asked Victoire, she insisted that she'd never left the kitchen: and besides I was quite positive that I'd seen this man, a man who had all the outward appearance of Papa. We went down, all three of us, behind the screen of trees, and found no trace of anyone having passed that way, so you both told me not to think about it any more. Not think about it! It was no use saying that; constantly I recalled, in imagination, the mysterious scene I had witnessed; constantly I tried to lift the veil which hid its meaning from me. That it had a meaning, which one day would be made clear to me, was my profound conviction. But it was not till fourteen years later that God tore the veil aside.

Once, when Sister Marie of the Sacred Heart[1] and I had leave to talk, we found as usual two subjects of conversation—the world to come, and our memories of childhood. I reminded her of this apparition which came to me when I was six or seven years old, and as we recalled the details of that strange scene, we realised, both of us at the same moment, its significance. It really was Papa I saw, all bent with age; it really was Papa—that venerable face, those grey hairs, bearing the marks of that strange affliction which prepared him for heaven.[2] Wasn't the adorable face of Jesus

[1] Thérèse's sister Marie.
[2] At the end of his life M. Martin had a stroke and went out of his mind; in the early stages of this infirmity he often insisted, it appears, on keeping his face muffled up.

veiled during his Passion? And this faithful servant of his was to go about with his face veiled when suffering came to him so that it might shine the brighter in the presence of his Master. At rest, now, amid heavenly glories past our knowing, our dear Father himself has won us the grace to understand the vision granted to his youngest daughter, too young, surely, to be the prey of an illusion. At rest, now, he has won for us the great comfort of knowing that God was preparing us, ten years beforehand, for the ordeal we were to undergo. So a father might give his children a glimpse of the honours that lie in wait for them; might take pleasure in the thought of the great riches they were one day to share.

But why did God grant it to me, this light on coming events? I was far too young to understand what it meant, and if I had understood what it meant, the grief of it would have killed me; why, then, was I chosen? We shall understand, in heaven, the Wisdom which decreed such things, and spend an eternity in admiring it. God is so good to us, the trials he sends us are the ones we are strong enough to bear. As I say, at the time, the mere thought of the suffering which lay ahead of us would have been too much for me. The very idea that Papa might die some day was enough to make me tremble all over. Once when he was at the top of a ladder, and I was just underneath, he shouted: "Stand clear, Tiny; if I fell off now I should squash you flat." All my instincts rebelled; instead of moving away, I clung to the ladder—if he did fall, I could spare myself the pain of witnessing his death by dying when he died.

I simply can't explain how fond I was of Papa; everything about him filled me with admiration. Sometimes he used to tell me his ideas about things in general, just as if I'd been a big girl; and I used to say, in my innocence, that if he put all that to the important Government people they'd be certain to take him and make a king of him, and then France would be happier than she'd ever been. But at heart, although I felt it was rather selfish of me, I was quite content that things should remain as they were, and that I should be the only person who really understood him through and through. Because if he'd been made King of "France and Navarre," he'd certainly have been unhappy—all kings were; and besides, he was my own prince and I wanted to keep him to myself.

I was seven or eight years old when Papa took us to Trouville, and I shall never forget the impression made on me by my first sight of the sea. I couldn't take my eyes off it, its vastness, the ceaseless roaring of the waves, spoke to me of the greatness and the power of God. It was there, I remember, while we were walking on the beach, and I was scampering about near Papa, that a lady and a gentleman came up to ask if that pretty little girl was his daughter. I noticed that Papa, as he said Yes, made a sign to shew that he didn't want them to pay me compliments. It was the first time I'd heard myself called pretty, and I enjoyed it, because I didn't think I was pretty at all. You'd been so careful, dear Mother, to keep me away from anything of that sort, anything which could spoil my natural innocence or wake an echo of vanity in my heart. I never took any notice of what other people said, except you and Papa, and neither of you had ever paid me any compliments, so I wasn't much interested in the lady's comments, or the admiring looks she gave me.

That evening, about the time when the sun looks as if it were sinking into an endless waste of waves, and leaving a long track of light in between, Pauline and I were sitting on a rock by ourselves watching it. I was reminded of that touching story called "The Golden Track";[1] and for a long time I sat there thinking about this track of light and of its heavenly counterpart—the grace which pierces the darkness and guides the little white-sailed ship on its course. Sitting there beside Pauline, I made a resolve that I would always think of our Lord as watching me, and travel straight on in his line of vision till I came safe to the shore of my heavenly country.

[1] This came in a collection of stories made by Louise Swanton Belloc, Hilaire Belloc's grandmother.

Chapter VIII

SCHOOL DAYS

So IT WENT on, this life of peace and happiness, and the love which surrounded me at Les Buissonnets did, after a fashion, help me to grow up. But I was old enough now to enter on the battle of life, to make closer acquaintance with the world and its tragedies. I was eight and a half when Léonie finished her schooling, and I took her place at the Abbey. I've often heard it said that one's school-days are the best and the happiest days of one's life; but I can't say I found them so. I've never been so melancholy as I was during those five years, and if I hadn't had dear Céline there with me, I couldn't have spent a month there without losing my health. I was like some little flower that has always been accustomed to put out its frail roots in a soil specially prepared for it; such a flower does not take kindly to a garden which it shares with a variety of others, many of them hardier than itself, and draw, from a common soil, the vitality it needs.

You'd been so successful over my education, dear Mother, that when I got to school I found myself ahead of other girls of the same age, and I was put in a class where all the rest were my seniors. One of these, a girl of thirteen or fourteen, who wasn't particularly bright, but had a knack of impressing her school-fellows and even her mistresses, didn't like to see a small creature like me nearly always head of the class, and petted by the nuns. These school-girl jealousies are pardonable enough, but she did pay me out, in all sorts of ways, for such successes as I won. Shy and sensitive as I was, I had no means of protecting myself, and I cried over it a lot, but without telling a soul. I didn't even tell *you* what I was going through. I hadn't the strength of soul to rise superior to vexations of this kind, and my sensitive feelings suffered terribly.

Fortunately it only lasted till evening: every evening I went home, where I could expand and blossom out; when I'd jumped on to Papa's knee and told him all about my marks, and he'd kissed me, all my misery was forgotten. How splendid to be able to announce the success of the first paper I did, one about Bible History, in which I should have got full marks if I'd known the name of Moses's father! I'd come out top, and brought a silver badge home with me. Papa rewarded me with a shiny threepenny bit,* and I put it away in a box which was to be the home of many other contributions, all of the same value; they came nearly every Thursday. To this box I regularly went, when certain feast-days came round, and I wanted to make a private donation to the Society for the Propogation of the Faith, or something like that. Pauline, delighted with the success of her old pupil, presented me with a lovely hoop, to keep me keen on my lessons. I needed these family attentions, poor mite; without them, school life would have been altogether too much for me.

Every Thursday afternoon was a holiday, but it wasn't like the holidays Pauline used to give me, which I spent in the sunny room upstairs with Papa. I had to play games, and not just with Céline—I always liked that when we were alone together—but with my Guérin cousins and the Maudelonde girls. I looked on it as a penance; I didn't know how to play the games other children played, and I can't have been a very amusing companion, in spite of my unsuccessful efforts to do just as they did. I was dreadfully bored, especially when I had to spend a whole afternoon dancing quadrilles. The only thing I enjoyed was going off to the Park, the Star Park as it was called, where we were allowed to pick the flowers; that gave me a chance to shine, because I could pick them fast and knew where to find the prettiest ones, to everybody's envy.

Once I did really enjoy myself; it was when I was alone with my cousin Marie—no Céline Maudelonde pressing her to join in the ordinary games—and she allowed me to choose what I'd like to play at. My game was a completely new invention; we two, Marie and Thérèse, had become hermits, with no possessions except a rude hut, a small cornfield, and a few vegetables we grew. Our rule was one of uninterrupted contemplation; when either of us was engaged in active work, the other carried on with the prayers. There was no quarrelling, there was complete silence, and our behaviour as religious left nothing to be desired. When my aunt came to find us and sent us out for a walk, we kept up our game as we went along the street, saying the rosary together as hermits should, but only on our fingers, so as not to attract the attention of the general public. (The junior hermit wasn't always so careful; I can remember making an enormous sign of the cross over a bun which had been given me for my lunch, which caused some amusement among the profane.)

Marie and I were twin souls; we always had the same instincts, and there was one occasion when the thing went too far. Coming back from school one evening, I said: " Marie, you've got to steer me along; I'm going to shut my eyes," and of course the answer was: " I'm going to shut mine too." All right, go! There was no arguing about it; it was each for herself—we were on the pavement, so there was no danger from the traffic. For several minutes we made a good passage, enjoying the experience of walking without looking where you are going; but there was a shop-front with goods displayed in boxes outside, and we two idiots fell over those boxes both at the same moment, or rather knocked them over. The shopkeeper who came out to pick the things up wasn't at all pleased; we had to pick ourselves up as best we could, no longer artificially blind, but walking as fast as we could with eyes wide open, while Jeanne Guérin, who shared the shopkeeper's annoyance, scolded us as we deserved. She determined to punish us by keeping us apart, and from then on Marie and Céline went together while I walked with Jeanne. This put an end to our fatal unanimity, and it wasn't a bad thing for the two elder ones either, because they weren't twin souls at all, they used to argue all the way home. Now it was perfect peace all round.

I've said nothing so far about my personal relations with Céline at this time; if I tried to give a full account of them, I should never stop. Since we got to Lisieux, we had exchanged rôles; it was she, now, who was the mischievous little imp, whereas I was a very gentle little girl, and much too fond of crying. But we grew more and more fond of one another—I don't mean that we didn't have an argument now and again, but it never amounted to anything serious; fundamentally we were always in agreement. Dear little Céline, I can answer for it that she never did anything to hurt my feelings; she was a ray of sunshine to me, a continual

source of happiness and comfort. I wish I could describe
how bravely she stood up for me when people taunted me at
school. And I got tired, sometimes, of the way she looked
after my health.

What I didn't get tired of was watching her at play. She
would collect all our dolls and hold a class for them, in the
best school-mistress manner, always careful that her own
should behave well, while mine were put in the corner for
being naughty. She used to tell me about the things she'd
learnt in her lessons, which interested me deeply, and I regarded her as a fountainhead of information. They used to
call me " Céline's little daughter," and when she was angry
with me her most effective way of shewing disapproval was
to say : " You're not my little daughter any longer; that's all
done with, and I'm never, never going to forget it ! " But I'd
only got to turn to and cry like a penitent Magdalen, implor-
ing her to be my mother again, and before long she'd be
kissing me and promising to forget all about it. To make me
cheer up, she'd take one of her dolls and tell it to give Auntie
a nice hug; I remember one occasion when the doll, in its
anxiety to do this, managed to get its fingers up my nose, and
hung there till Auntie dislodged it, to the surprise and the
great amusement of Céline, who hadn't in the least intended
it.

It would have made you laugh to see us buying our New
Year presents together at the bazaar, each taking great care
to hide her proceedings from the other. We each had about a
shilling* to spend and five or six presents to buy, so there was
a lot of competition to see who would buy the nicest things.
What bargains we made, and how impatiently we waited for
New Year's Day, when the all-important presentations would
take place ! It was a great thing, that morning, to wake up
first and be the first to say "Happy New Year"; then the
presents were exchanged, and we went into ecstasies over our
shilling's-worth of treasures. I really think these small tokens
gave us more pleasure than the splendid presents we got from
our uncle. Meanwhile, the fun had only just started; we got
dressed in no time, and both of us were on tenter-hooks
waiting to hang round Papa's neck. The moment he came out
of his room, the whole house rang with our cries of delight,
and poor Father looked as if he was happy to see us

enjoying ourselves. The maternal presents we got from Marie and Pauline weren't very expensive perhaps, but what pleasure we got out of them! We weren't old enough yet, Céline and I, to be *blasées*; one's soul, at that age, has all the freshness and the expansiveness of a flower drinking in the morning dew. Two stalks swaying in the same breeze—what brought joy or grief to either brought joy or grief to both.

Certainly we shared our joys; that fact came home to me on the great day when dear Céline made her first Communion. This was before I went to school, when I was only seven; but I still remember—it is one of my most cherished memories—the preparation which you, Mother, gave to Céline. Every evening you would put her on your knee and talk to her about this great step she was taking, and I used to listen, because I wanted badly to prepare for my own first Communion; how I minded it when you told me (as often happened) to go away because I was too young! How could four years be too long a preparation for receiving God himself? I heard you, one evening, say that with one's first Communion one should start living a new life, so I decided not to wait: I'd start my new life when Céline started hers.

I'd never realised how fond I was of her till that three days' retreat when, for the first time in my life, I was separated from her, and couldn't be put to sleep in her bed. I forgot, on the first day, that she wouldn't be coming home, and saved up a bunch of cherries Papa had bought for me; and I was miserable when she didn't come back to share them with me. Papa had to console me by promising that he'd take me to see her at the Abbey next day, with a new bunch of cherries to give her. The actual day of her first Communion couldn't have made more impression on me if it had been my own. I woke up, all alone in the double bed, bursting with happiness: "It's come! To-day's the day!" was the refrain I went on repeating to myself, and I really felt as if I, not Céline, had been the person concerned. Great graces, I think, were bestowed on me that day; it was certainly one of the happiest in my life.

Chapter IX

THERESE'S ILLNESS

I'VE HAD to go back a bit on my story, in recalling these delightful, these comforting memories. Now I have to describe a very different experience, a heart-breaking experience; the ordeal I went through, so young, when our Lord took you away from me—you, Pauline, whom I loved like a mother. I'd told Pauline once that I'd like to be an anchoress; couldn't we both go off into some desert a long way away? And her answer was that my ambition was hers too; only *she would have to wait* until I was old enough to go with her. Of course, she hadn't meant that seriously, but it had been taken quite seriously by the small creature she was talking to. Imagine, then, my transports of grief when I overheard my beloved Pauline, in conversation with Marie, talk about going off, quite soon, to Carmel. I didn't exactly know what Carmel was, but I realised that Pauline was leaving me; Pauline was going into a convent without waiting for me; I was going to lose my Mother all over again! I can't tell you what misery I went through at that moment; this was life, I told myself, life, that hadn't hitherto semed so bad. Life, when you saw it as it really was, just meant continual suffering, continual separation. I cried bitterly over it, having no idea as yet of the joy that comes from sacrifice; I was a feeble creature, so feeble that I feel it's a triumph of grace I should have got through such an exacting ordeal at all. It wouldn't have been so bad if the news of Pauline's going off had been broken to me gently; it was the suddenness of the announcement that drove the wound so deep.

Well, dear Mother, I shan't forget your gentleness in trying to console me. And you went on to describe the life at Carmel, which seemed to me absolutely splendid. Thinking it over, I came to the conclusion that this must be the desert in which God meant me, too, to take refuge. So strong was my feeling about this that it left no shadow of doubt in my mind;

it wasn't just the dream of an impressionable child, it was certain with all the certainty of a divine vocation. I didn't want to go into Carmel for Pauline's sake, but for our Lord's sake and for no other reason. Words won't do justice to all that was in my mind, but now I was completely at rest. Next day, I told Pauline my secret, and she interpreted these longings of mine as an indication of the divine will; she would take me, quite soon, to see Mother Prioress at Carmel, and I was to explain to her what God had put into my mind.

A Sunday was fixed for this important visit. I felt very awkward when I was told that Marie Guérin was to stay behind with me; she was still of an age at which one is allowed to see the Carmelites instead of talking to them through a veil. This would never do; I wanted to stay behind alone. I had an idea about this; I told Marie that it was a great privilege to see Mother Prioress; and we'd got to be on our very best behaviour. Now the right thing to do with a Mother Prioress was to make her the confidante of all your secrets. So the only thing was for each of us to go out for a bit and leave the other alone with her. Marie took my word for it; not having any secrets, she wasn't particularly keen on confiding them to anybody, but we each stayed behind in turn, and I told Mother Marie de Gonzague my great news. She quite agreed that I had a vocation, but she explained that they couldn't take postulants of nine years old; I should have to wait till I was sixteen. I'd been hoping to enter Carmel at once, and make my first Communion there the day Pauline was clothed; but I had to resign myself to the situation. It was on this visit that I received my second compliment—Sister Thérèse of St. Augustine came to see me and kept on saying how pretty I was. Well, I hadn't been meaning to join Carmel so as to have bouquets thrown at me; and when the parlour was over I told Almighty God, not once but many times, that it was for his sake and his sake only I wanted to be a Carmelite.

I tried to see as much of my dear Pauline as I could, during those last few weeks when she was still in the world. Every day Céline and I bought her a cake and some sweets, because we thought such things would be passing out of her life before long; we stuck to her all the time, never giving her a moment's peace. At last the day came, that second day of October which was the source of so many tears, so many blessings; the day when our Lord picked the first flower in this garden of his, you, who were to be a mother to the rest of us when, before long, we came to join you. I can still see the place where Pauline gave me her last kiss. After that, my aunt took us all to Mass, while Papa climbed Mount Carmel to offer his first sacrifice. The whole family was in tears, so that we were greeted with looks of astonishment as we came into Church; but that was all one to me, my tears still flowed. If the whole earth had crumbled about me, I don't think I should have noticed it. I looked up at the clear sky, and wondered how the sun could shine so brightly when my own heart was plunged in sorrow.

Dear Mother, do you suspect me of exaggerating what I felt? I quite see, of course, that my grief ought not to have been so deep as it was, considering that I hoped to join you in Carmel later on. But my soul, then, hadn't nearly reached the stage of ripeness; there were fiery trials to be gone through before that welcome moment came.

The second of October was the day on which we were due back at school; and back I had to go, with a heavy heart. In the afternoon my aunt came for us and took us to Carmel, where I saw my beloved Pauline through the grille. It's terrible to think what I've gone through in this parlour of ours at Carmel. I'm writing the history of my soul, and who has a right to hear the whole story, if not my Mother? I must admit to her that what I went through before she entered the convent was nothing to what I went through later. Every Thursday we went up to Carmel in a body; and I, who was used to getting hold of Pauline for a heart-to-heart talk, was now reduced to two or three minutes at the end of our stay in the parlour; I spent them in crying, and went away torn with emotion. I didn't realise that it was just kindness to my aunt when you talked to Jeanne and Marie for preference, leaving your own little ones out in the cold. I couldn't understand it, and deep in my heart I felt: "Pauline is lost to me."

Stimulated by all this unhappiness, my intellectual perceptions developed with surprising rapidity; developed to such a point that in a very short time I fell ill. It was, beyond doubt, the devil's work, this illness which overtook me; your

entry into Carmel had enraged him, and he was determined
to get his own back for all the loss of influence in which our
family was to involve him. He didn't reckon with the power
of our Blessed Lady, waiting there so calmly in heaven, ready
to still the storm before this tiny flower could be overwhelmed by it. It was towards the end of that year that I
was attacked by continual headaches, which weren't very
painful—I went on with my school work, and nobody was
worried about me. That went on up to the Easter of 1883, at
which time my father took Marie and Léonie to Paris, leaving Céline and me in the charge of our aunt. My uncle took
me with him one evening, and talked to me about Mamma
and about old days with a kindliness which went to my heart
and made me cry. He made out that I was too sensitive; what
I wanted was plenty of distraction; he and my aunt agreed
between them that I must be given a good time during the
Easter holidays. We were due to go off to the Catholic social
evening, but my aunt thought I was too tired, and put me to
bed. It was while I was undressing that I had a strange fit of
trembling, which my aunt put down to the cold; but though
she piled bed-clothes on me and plied me with hot-water
bottles it did no good; I shivered and shook nearly all night
long.

My uncle, coming back from the social evening with
Céline and my cousins, couldn't make it out at all, and thought
it must be something quite serious, but he didn't say so for
fear of distressing my aunt; next day he called in Dr. Notta,
who agreed with him that I was suffering from a very serious
complaint—he'd never heard of anybody being attacked by it
so young. Everybody was thoroughly alarmed, and I had to
stay on with my aunt, who looked after me with all the
anxiety of a mother. When Papa and my elder sisters got
back from Paris, Aimée, the maid-servant, met them with
such a long face that Marie thought I must be dead. But no,
this illness, like that of Lazarus, was not fatal. It was meant
for God's honour. And God was honoured, both in the
wonderful resignation of my father (who was convinced
that his little daughter would either die or go mad) and in that
of Marie. Poor Marie, what she went through, what unselfish
care she lavished on me! I can never be grateful enough;
her instinct told her the right things to do for me. After all,

a mother's instincts are better than the skill of any doctor; she can guess what treatment her child's illness needs.

She had to come and settle down at my uncle's; there was no chance, then, of moving me to Les Buissonnets. Meanwhile, it was nearly time for Pauline's clothing. Nobody dared to mention it in my presence because they thought I should be so disappointed at having to miss it; I talked about it freely, declaring that I should be well enough to go and see dear Pauline. And I was right; Almighty God wanted me to have this bit of consolation—or rather, it was a kind of wedding-day treat for you, after all the anxiety you'd had about your ailing daughter. I've always noticed that our Lord doesn't give his children trials to undergo on the actual day of their betrothal to him; that must be a cloudless day, a foretaste of heaven; that's been true five times in my experience. I did get the chance of hugging this dear mother of mine, of climbing on her knee and covering her with kisses; I did get the chance of seeing her, looking so lovely, in her wedding-dress. A day of real happiness, among all those dark days of trial; but it was over all too soon. Before long I had to get into the carriage and drive away, away from Pauline and from dear Carmel. They made me go to bed when we got back to Les Buissonnets, very unwillingly, because I thought I was all right now, and shouldn't need to be treated as an invalid any longer. Unfortunately, though, I was only at the beginning of my ordeal. Next morning I was as bad as ever, and my illness took such a grave turn that there was no human probability I should recover.

I wish I could describe this strange illness of mine. I'm fully persuaded, now, that it was the work of the devil; but for a long time after I got well I was convinced that I had made myself ill on purpose, and that became a real torment to me. I mentioned this to Marie, who did her best, in the goodness of her heart, to reassure me. I mentioned it in confession, and there again my confessor tried to calm my doubts; it wouldn't have been possible, he said, to make myself as ill as all that merely by shamming ill. I suppose Almighty God meant to purify and above all to humble me, so he allowed this secret torment of mine to go on right up to the time when I entered Carmel. When I got to Carmel, our spiritual father removed all my scruples just like *that*; I've never felt the slightest uneasiness about it since.

It's not surprising, really, that I should have had these doubts. How could I be certain that I hadn't been in perfectly good physical health, and playing the invalid? Because my words and actions didn't in the least correspond to my thoughts: I was delirious nearly all the time and talking utter nonsense, and yet I'm quite certain that I never, for a moment, lost the use of my reason. Often I seemed to be in a dead faint, without making the slightest movement: anybody could do anything they liked with me—you could have killed me unresisting; and yet all the time I heard everything that was being said round me, and I remember it all still. Once, for quite a long time, I couldn't open my eyes, and yet when I was left alone I opened them for a moment. It seems to me that the devil had been given power over the outward part of me, but couldn't reach my soul; he couldn't reach my reason either, except by making me terrified of certain things—certain medicines, for example, of a quite ordinary kind which they wanted me to take, but I wouldn't.

But if Almighty God allowed the devil to come very close, he also sent me angels in visible form. Marie was always at my bedside, looking after me and comforting me with a mother's tenderness; not once did she shew the least sign that she was tired of it, although I gave her endless trouble, and wouldn't let her out of my sight. Still, of course, she had to go off and join Papa at his meals, but I was calling out for her all the time she was away; Victoire, who was left in charge, had to go and fetch her now and again, because I was calling for "Mama." When she went out, it was either to hear Mass or to see Pauline, and I never remonstrated then. And then Uncle and Aunt were so kind to me; Aunt came to see me every day, and spoilt me by loading me with presents. There were friends of the family, too, who came to see me, but I implored Marie to tell them that I was not up to receiving callers. I couldn't bear " seeing people sitting round my bed like a great string of onions, watching me as if I were a strange beast." Uncle and Aunt were the only visitors I wanted. I can't tell you how much this illness increased my affection for them. " Not many people have relations like that "—those words were often on poor Father's lips, and he was right. He was to learn from experience, later on, that he hadn't misjudged them; where he is now, he can win the divine aid, the divine blessing; what can I do, still in exile? I have only the comfort of being able to pray for them, these dear relations of ours, who have been and are so good to me.

Léonie, too, was full of kindness, doing all she could to keep me in good spirits: only I'm afraid sometimes I must have wounded her, by making it clear that nobody could be quite what Marie was to me. And dear Céline, there was nothing she ·wouldn't do for her Thérèse. When she was home from school on Sundays, instead of going out for a walk, to shut herself up for hours with a sister who to all appearances was a lunatic, when she could easily have kept clear of me—oh, that was love! Dear, dear sisters, the burden I've been to you! Who ever gave so much trouble, or received so much love? Well, there's always heaven, and I shall hope to get my own back there. Our Lord is so rich; I can dig, dig deep in his treasure-house, and repay, a hundred times over, what I owe you.

Chapter X

HER RECOVERY
SOME STRAY MEMORIES

WHAT CHEERED me up most of all during my illness was a letter from Pauline, which I read again and again till I knew it by heart. There was one time too, dear Mother, when you sent me a little hour-glass, and one of my dolls dressed up as a Carmelite; I can't tell you how pleased I was. My uncle didn't like it; he thought it would be better to make me forget about Carmel than to remind me of it like that; my own feeling was that the hope of being a Carmelite one day was the only thing that was keeping me alive. What I really enjoyed was doing bits of work for Pauline, cutting things out of cardboard for her. I also spent a good deal of time in making wreaths of daisy and forget-me-not for our Lady's statue, because it was May month—May month, when nature was decked out in its best, and there was life and happiness everywhere, and here was I, one poor little flower, doomed to fade away and disappear, it seemed, for want of sunshine! But no, the sunshine was there, close at hand; it came to me from that wonder-working statue of the Madonna which had twice[1] given Mother the Message she needed. Towards this statue I would turn continually, like a flower that turns its head towards the sun.

One day, I saw Papa come into Marie's room, where I was lying; how sad he looked, as he handed her some gold coins he wanted her to send off to Paris, for Masses in honour of our Lady of Victories, for his little daughter's recovery! I was so touched by this evidence of his faith and his love for me, that I longed to be able to tell him : "It's all right, I'm cured." But I'd so often cheated him with false hopes already —no amount of willing on my part would produce a miracle, and a miracle was wanted if I was to get better. It came, and it came from our Lady of Victories. While the novena of Masses was still being said, Marie went out into the garden,

[1] Once only, according to a note supplied by Mother Agnes.

one Sunday morning, leaving me in charge of Léonie, who
was reading near the window. After a few minutes I began to
call for Marie, in a voice hardly above a whisper: " Mama!
Mama!" Léonie didn't pay any attention; she was used to
hearing me call out like that. It went on and on; my cries
became louder; and in the end Marie came back. I was quite
conscious of her entering the room, but I couldn't recognise
with any certainty who it was, so I went on calling for
" Mama " louder than ever. It was very painful to me, to
have this unnatural conflict going on in my mind; and it
must have been still more painful for Marie. When she
found she couldn't convince me that she was really there, she
knelt down beside my bed, with Léonie and Céline, turned
towards our Lady's statue and prayed for me like a mother
praying for her child's life. And her prayer, Marie's prayer,
was granted.

There was no help, it seemed, for poor Thérèse on earth;
so I, too, had turned towards the statue, and all my heart went
out into a prayer that my Mother in Heaven would have pity
on me. All at once, she let me see her in her beauty, a beauty
that surpassed all my experience—her face wore such a look
of kindness and of pity as I can't describe; but what pierced
me to the heart was her smile, " that entrancing smile of the
Blessed Virgin's."[1] With that, all my distress came to an
end; two big tears started up from my eyes, and ran softly
down my cheeks; but they were tears of joy, unadulterated
joy. And I said to myself: " To think that the Blessed Virgin
should have smiled down at me! Oh, I'm so happy! But I
mustn't tell anybody about it; my happiness would disappear if I did." I had no difficulty, then, in lowering my
eyes, and I could see Marie looking at me tenderly—pro-
foundly moved and yet not quite certain about the grace our
Lady had granted me. Or rather, granted her; it was to her
pathetic prayers that I owed this privilege of a smile from

[1] This sentence begins in the original " tout à coup la Sainte Vierge
me parut belle, si belle " etc. The implication seems to be that the
statue took on, at this moment, an appearance of supernatural
beauty. But the Saint's punctuation is always irregular; and if we
read " tout à coup la Sainte Vierge me parut, belle, si belle " etc.,
the reference will no longer be to the statue, but to an apparition
quite distinct from it. The concluding words of the sentence are
written in inverted commas, as if they were a quotation.

the Queen of Heaven herself. The moment she saw my eyes
fixed on the statue, she thought: "Thérèse has recovered!"
And she was right; the faded flower had come to life again,
and the ray of sunlight which had restored freshness to it
wasn't going to leave its work unfinished. It wouldn't happen
all at once; gently, by easy stages, the flower learned to raise
its head again, and grew so strong that it could unfold itself,
five years later, on the rich mountain soil of Carmel.

As I say, Marie had guessed that, in some mysterious way,
the Blessed Virgin had been gracious to me. And when we
were alone together, she wanted to know what it was that
I'd seen; how was I to resist such loving, eager inquiries as
hers? Somehow, my secret had been discovered without my
saying anything about it; to Marie, then, I told the whole
story. My instinct had been all too true; from that moment,
my happiness disappeared, and I regretted bitterly what I'd
done. For four years the memory of that wonderful grace I'd
received was a real torment to me, and when I found happiness again, it was only at the feet of our Lady of Victories.
It was given back to me, then, in full measure; but I must tell
you about that later on, about that second grace which our
Lady had in store for me. For the moment, dear Mother, let
me be content to tell you how it was that my joy turned into
sadness.

I told the story to Marie as simply and openly as I could;
and when she asked leave to pass it on to the nuns at Carmel,
somehow I couldn't say No. When I next went to Carmel,
there was my dear Pauline wearing our Lady's habit; and I was
so overwhelmed with joy at the sight, the occasion was so
precious to both of us, that I forgot all the things I wanted to
say—my heart was too full for words. But meanwhile, dear
Mother Marie Gonzague was there, all kindness and attentive-
ness; and then some of the other nuns came in, and I found
myself being questioned about the grace that had been given
me. Was the Blessed Virgin carrying the Child Jesus in her
arms? Was there a great blaze of light? And so on. These
questions worried me and made me feel unhappy; I could
only go on saying: "The Blessed Virgin looked very beautiful indeed, and I saw her smile down at me." After all, it was
only her face, really, that had caught my attention; and here
were these Carmelites getting the whole thing wrong! The

whole subject of my illness became painful to me; had I, perhaps, been telling lies? I feel sure that if I had kept my secret, I could have kept my peace of mind; as it was, our Lady allowed this trial to befall me, for my soul's good; without it, I might have given way to vanity, instead of accepting humiliation as my lot, and never looking upon myself without feelings of deep disgust. But what suffering it brought me! I shall never be able to describe it—not in this world.

Talking of that visit to the Carmelites reminds me of my first visit, soon after Pauline entered—I forgot to describe it earlier on, but there's one detail which I mustn't leave out. It was the morning of the day when I was to go and see her in the parlour, and I was lying in bed, alone with my thoughts— I always found myself sunk deepest in prayer when I lay in bed like that; unlike the Bride in the Canticles, I never found that my loving search for my heavenly Father went unrewarded.[1] Well, that morning I was wondering what my name would be in religion; Carmel had its Teresa of Jesus already, and yet it wouldn't do to give up the name of Thérèse, such a lovely name. And all at once I remembered my devotion to the Sacred Infancy, and thought how wonderful it would be to be called Thérèse of the Child Jesus. I didn't say anything about this day-dream of mine; but sure enough, when dear Mother Marie Gonzague asked the sisters what I ought to be called, this dream-name of mine was the one they thought of. How pleased I was! It looked like a special favour from the Child Jesus, this happy piece of thought-transference.

There are other little details dating from my childhood, before you entered religion, that I have forgotten to put down. I've said nothing about my fondness for pictures and for reading. But it is to you, dear Mother, and to the lovely pictures you used to shew me when I'd deserved a treat, that I owe one of the greatest joys in my life, and one of the most powerful impressions that awoke in me the love of holiness. The hours passed unnoticed as I sat gazing at them; one of them was called " A little flower at the door of the

[1] Canticles III, 1.

Tabernacle,"[1] and it had so much to tell me that I got quite absorbed in it. Someone had written Pauline's name just under the flower; why couldn't the name of Thérèse be there too? So it was that I offered myself, under the figure of a little flower, to Jesus. And reading, too, I was fond of that, although I never cared much for playing games; I could have spent a life-time in reading. It was lucky for me that I had people like you, angels in human form, to choose for me the kind of books that would be good mental and spiritual food, instead of just keeping me interested. Perhaps lucky, too, that my time for reading was limited; what a wrench it was to break off my reading just in the middle of a passage that specially appealed to me! This love of reading lasted with me right up to the time when I entered Carmel; I couldn't possibly reckon up the number of books that passed through my hands, but God's Providence saw to it that I never read a single one that could be harmful to me.

There were, of course, romantic tales which made me forget, at the time, the realities of life; but, by God's mercy, these illusions didn't last long. The only true glory, I soon learned to realise, is the glory that lasts for ever; and, to win that, you don't need to perform any dazzling exploits—you want to live a hidden life, doing good in such an unobtrusive way that you don't even let your left hand know what your right hand is doing.[2] That happened, for example, when I read stories about heroic Frenchwomen like the Venerable Joan of Arc, who loved their country so well. How I longed to imitate them; how strong it seemed to beat in me, this heroic ardour of theirs, this sense of divine inspiration! And it was in that connexion that a great grace came to me; one of the greatest, I always think, I have ever received in my life —because in those days I seldom had those lights in prayer which latterly have been showered upon me. I felt that I was born for greatness; but when I asked myself how I was to achieve it, God put into my mind that ideal which I've just mentioned. The glory which was reserved for me was one which didn't reveal itself to human eyes; I must devote myself to becoming a great saint. That sounds conceited, of course, when you consider how imperfect a creature I was, and still

[1] Literally, "The Divine Prisoner's little flower."
[2] Matthew 6, 3.

am, after eight years in religion. But this daring ambition of aspiring to great sanctity has never left me. I don't rely on my own merits, because I haven't any: I put all my confidence in him who is virtue, who is holiness itself. My feeble efforts are all he wants; he can lift me up to his side and, by clothing me with his own boundless merits, make a saint of me. I didn't realise, then, how much suffering it had got to cost, this road to sanctity; but God lost no time in assuring me of that, by sending me the trials I have been telling you about.

Chapter XI

PREPARATION FOR FIRST COMMUNION

IT'S TIME, now, to pick up the thread of my story where I left it. Three months after my recovery, Papa took us to Alençon; it was the first time I had been back there. How glad I was to revisit them, the scenes where my earliest years had been passed; above all, to say my prayers at Mamma's grave, and ask her to go on protecting me. God, in his mercy, has given me little knowledge of the world; only just enough to make me despise it and want to keep away from it; and I suppose I really saw it for the first time during this stay at Alençon. So much opportunity to enjoy myself and be happy there; everybody entertained me, petted me, admired me; in fact, for a whole fortnight I trod the primrose path. And all this, I confess, had its attractions for me; how rightly does the Book of Wisdom warn us that the sorcery of the world's vanities can bewitch even unworldly minds![1] At ten years old, one's mind is easily dazzled, and I look upon it as a great grace that we didn't stay longer at Alençon. Our friends there were worldly people, who had the knack of serving God and at the same time enjoying, to the full, the good things of earth. The thought of death seldom crossed their minds; and yet death has come to so many of them, these people who were so young, so rich, so happy when I knew them! It intrigues me to go back, in memory, to the enchanted world they lived in, and to wonder where they are now—what satisfaction do they derive now from the châteaux and the parks where I used to see them enjoying all that life had to give them? It makes you realise that there's nothing but frustration and labour lost, here under the sun;[2] that nothing is worth while except loving God with your whole heart and being poor in spirit as long as this life lasts.

Perhaps our Lord wanted to prepare me for his first visit to

[1] 4, 12.
[2] Ecclesiastes 2, 11.

77

my soul in the Blessed Sacrament, by shewing me what the
world was really like; in pledging myself to follow him, I
was to make a real choice between two paths. I associate my
first Communion with a period in my life when the sun
shone unclouded. I don't think I could have been in better
dispositions; and meanwhile all disquietude of soul had left
me—for nearly a year, our Lord wanted me to experience the
greatest happiness that's possible to us in this vale of tears.
You can't have forgotten, dear Mother, the exquisite little
treatise you composed for me three months beforehand? It
helped me so much to make a preparation which was orderly
in method, and yet concise. Of course, I'd been preparing
my mind for a long time beforehand, but it needed a fresh
impetus—it had to be garnished, as it were, with fresh
flowers, to make our Lord feel at home. The flowers were so
many pious practices* which I adopted at the time; only the
buds from which they sprang were the aspirations and acts
of love, even more numerous, which you'd written down for
daily use in my little book.

And then, each week you wrote a letter that stirred my
soul to its depths, and helped me to persevere in a better way
of life. I needed it badly; here was I, your own daughter, de-
prived of the happiness Céline had—that of sitting on your
knee, night after night, to make my preparation. When my
turn came, it was Marie who had to do duty, instead of
Pauline; I sat on her knee instead, and drank in every word
she spoke; and the great generosity of her heart passed into
mine. Just as a great soldier will teach his children the use
of arms, she told me about the conflicts life had in store for
me, and the palm which is the prize of victory. She told me,
too, about the imperishable riches which lie strewn about our
path from day to day; what a tragedy that we should pass by
without the energy to put out a hand and pick them up! And
then she explained to me how saintliness was to be achieved
by fidelity over quite tiny things, and gave me that leaflet
about renunciation which became a favourite subject for my
thoughts. How eloquent she was, this dear godmother of
mine! I thought it such a pity that this profound teaching
of hers had no audience, apart from me; I argued, in my
simple way, that if I was so moved by it there was no reason

why hardened sinners shouldn't have been equally moved, and given up the perishable goods of earth to win treasure in heaven.

Up to this time, nobody had taught me the art of mental prayer; I should have liked to know about it, but Marie was satisfied with my spiritual progress as it was, and kept me to vocal prayer instead. One day, one of my mistresses at the Abbey asked what I did with myself on holidays, when I was left to my own devices. I told her that I got behind my bed, where there was an empty space in which you could shut yourself away with the curtains, and there . . . well, I used to think. "Think about what?" she asked. "Oh," I said, "about God, and about life, and eternity; *you* know, I just think." The dear nun made a great joke of this, and later on she used to remind me of my thinking days, and ask me whether I still thought. I can see now that I was practising mental prayer without realising what I was doing; God was teaching me the art in some secret way of his own.

How quickly they passed, those three months of preparation! And now it was time for me to go into retreat, which meant becoming a boarder like the older girls and sleeping at the Abbey. I can find no words to describe the pleasant memories this retreat has left in my mind; if the life of a boarder brought plenty of distress with it, I had no reason to complain—the unspeakable happiness of those days spent in waiting for our Lord more than made up for it. You couldn't, I suppose, have such an experience except in a religious community; only a few of the girls were there at the time, so that it was possible to give individual attention to each, and oh, what motherly love they devoted to us, these mistresses of ours! They took more trouble about me than about any of the others. Every night, the head-mistress would come along with her lantern, to give me a loving kiss as I lay there in bed. This touched me so deeply that, one night, I said I was going to tell her a secret; and then, with a great air of mystery, I took out the precious little book which lay there under my pillow and shewed it to her, my eyes shining with joy.

In the mornings, it felt rather grand to imitate the other girls when they woke and got up in the morning; only I

wasn't accustomed to dressing without somebody to help me
—no Marie there, and how was my hair going to be curled?
Very shyly, I had to hand over my comb to the mistress in
charge of the dressing-room, who was highly amused to find
a girl of eleven not knowing how to look after herself. However, she did comb my hair for me; not half so gently as my
godmother did, only I didn't dare to utter the little screams
which usually accompanied the morning ceremony. All
through my retreat I felt that I was being spoilt as few
children are, motherless children especially. Every day, Marie
and Léonie came to see me, brought round by Papa, who
petted me enormously, so that I didn't feel the lack of family
life—there was no cloud on the bright horizon of my retreat.
You may be sure I listened attentively to the instructions
which the Abbé Domin gave us, and made an abstract of them,
though I didn't keep any record of my private meditations,
feeling sure (and quite rightly) that I should be able to
remember them.

I thoroughly enjoyed attending the whole of the office
with the community. I made myself rather conspicuous by
wearing a large crucifix (a present from Léonie) in my belt,
as the missionaries do; the nuns were very much taken with
it, and thought I must be trying to imitate my sister at Carmel.
And, sure enough, I was thinking a great deal about you,
because I'd been told that Pauline would be in retreat too.
Only I was asking our Lord to give himself to me, whereas
she was giving herself to him. It made those days of solitude
and expectation doubly precious to me.

One morning, I remember, I was sent to the infirmary
because I had a bad cough. Ever since my illness, the nuns
had taken great care of me; whenever I had a slight headache,
or looked paler than usual, I was either sent outside to get
some fresh air, or to rest in the infirmary. And then dear
Céline came in; she had got leave to come and see me, though
I was in retreat, so as to present me with a picture which
delighted me hugely—what do you think it was? The little
flower at the door of the Tabernacle. How wonderful to have
that as a present from Céline. How often my thoughts have
gone back, lovingly, to her!

On the eve of the great day, I received absolution, my

second absolution.[1] My general confession left my soul
utterly at peace; God didn't want any cloud to overshadow
me. And, that afternoon, the whole family came to see me,
and I asked for their pardon—at least, I had no language
but tears, so deeply was I moved. There was, of course, no
Pauline, but I knew she was with me in spirit; hadn't she
sent me, through Marie, a lovely picture which I admired so
much and wanted everybody else to admire too? I had, by
the way, written to Père Pichon asking for his prayers, telling
him that I was soon going to be a Carmelite, and then he'd be
my director. (And it happened, sure enough, four years
later; it wasn't till I went to Carmel that I opened my conscience to him.) When Marie actually gave me a letter from
him, my cup was full; everything conspired to make me
happy. And, best of all, he said in his letter: " To-morrow I
shall be saying Mass for you and Pauline "—Pauline and I
drawn closer together than ever on that day, the eighth of
May in the calendar, as if our Lord couldn't make up his
mind which of us was to receive the greater outpouring of
his grace.

[1] Children, at this date, were not always given absolution after
their confessions, owing to a doubt whether they were yet capable
of committing a deliberate sin.

Chapter XII

FIRST COMMUNION AND CONFIRMATION

AT LAST the day came, that greatest of all days for me; even the tiniest details of that visit to heaven have left their imprint on my memory, not to be described. To what gladness I awoke; how gently and how reverently they embraced me, the mistresses and the older girls who were there! The big room, and the dresses laid out there, white as snowflakes, which we put on, one after another. . . . And above all the chapel, and that lovely hymn, chanted in the fresh morning air, " O altar of God, where the angels are hovering." But I don't want to go into details; there are scents which you can't expose to the air without their losing their fragrance, and there are experiences of the soul which you can't express in human language without losing their inner meaning, their heavenly meaning. They are like that white stone given to the faithful warrior, on which a name is written, known only to him who receives it.[1] What comfort it brought to me, that first kiss our Lord imprinted on my soul! A lover's kiss; I knew that I was loved, and I, in my turn, told him that I loved him, and was giving myself to him for all eternity. There were no demands on me; there had been no struggles, no sacrifices. It was a long time since we had exchanged looks, he and I, insignificant though I was, and we had understood one another. And now it wasn't a question of looks; something had melted away, and there were no longer two of us—Thérèse had simply disappeared, like a drop lost in the ocean; Jesus only was left, my Master, my King. Hadn't I begged him to take away my liberty, because I was so afraid of the use I might make of it; hadn't I longed, weak and helpless as I was, to be united once for all with that divine Strength?

[1] Apocalypse, 2. 17.

So deep was my joy, so overpowering, that I couldn't contain myself; before long, tears of happiness were pouring down my cheeks to the astonishment of my companions. "What was she crying about?" they said to one another afterwards. "Something on her conscience perhaps? No, it must have been because she couldn't have her mother there, or that sister she's so fond of, the Carmelite." They didn't realise what happens when all the joys of heaven come flooding into a human heart; how difficult it is for that heart, still in exile, to stand the strain of the impact without finding relief in tears. No, I wasn't regretting Mamma's absence on that first Communion day; all heaven was in my heart, and she, who had gone to heaven long since, was present to me when our Lord became present to me, giving me her blessing and rejoicing in my happiness, like the loved mother she was. And I shed no tears, either, about the absence of Pauline; I should have been glad indeed to have her at my side, but this sacrifice was one which I had long since accepted; I had no room for any feeling but joy, and felt closer to her than ever; wasn't she just giving herself up, irrevocably, to him who came so lovingly and gave himself to me?

That afternoon, it was I who recited the act of consecration to our Lady; it was only fair that I, who had lost my earthly mother so young, should talk to my heavenly Mother in the name of the rest. And that is what I tried to do, talk to her; give myself up to her, like a child throwing its arms round its mother and asking for her protection. I think she smiled down at me from heaven, unseen; hadn't she smiled down visibly at me, and given life to the little flower that seemed to be fading away? And now she had brought her own Son to birth in me, the wild rose on the lowland plain, the wild lily on the mountain slopes.[1] On the evening of that wonderful day, there was an earthly reunion with my family. Already after Mass, I had held Papa and those others who were near and dear to me in my embrace; but the real reunion

[1] Canticles II, 1. The Saint here uses the Rose and the Lily as titles of our Lord himself; but in the original they refer to the bride, who thus describes herself out of a humility which is entirely Theresian.

was when he took my hand and went with me to Carmel. It was then that I saw my own Pauline, betrothed now to Jesus, wearing a veil as white as mine, and a crown of roses.* Don't think that I wasn't touched by the family party which was held that evening; I was delighted with the lovely watch Papa gave me. But it was a restrained happiness; there was a peace in my soul which nothing could disturb. Marie took me to sleep with her on the night of that wonderful day; for our happiest times on earth must end in darkness. It's only the first experience of our final, eternal communion in heaven that can be a day without sunset.

The day after my first Communion was still one of happiness, but overcast with melancholy. Marie had given me such a lovely dress, and I had lots of other presents, but these things didn't satisfy me; I couldn't be content with anything less than our Lord's presence. How I longed for the day when I should be able to receive him again! About a month later, when I went to get shriven for Ascension-tide, I took my courage in both hands and asked if I might go to Communion. To my surprise, the priest consented, and I found myself kneeling at the Holy Table between Papa and Marie. This second Communion, too, has left touching memories behind it; I was shedding tears still, but with an indescribable sense of consolation, and I kept on repeating to myself those words of St. Paul: "I am alive; or rather, not I; it is Christ that lives in me."[1] From then on, my longing for our Lord's presence continued to increase, and I got permission to communicate on all great feasts.

On the eve of every such occasion, Marie would still take me on her knee and prepare me for it. Once, I remember, she talked to me about suffering, and told me that it was a path I probably wouldn't have to tread—I would always be carried like a little child in the arms of God's mercy. Her words came back to me after Communion next day, and thereupon I felt a great desire for suffering spring up in my heart, together with the conviction that our Lord had a lot of crosses in store for me. I was carried away on a tide of happiness which I shall always look upon as one of the greatest graces I ever received. Suffering was now the magnet

[1] Galatians 2, 20.

which drew me to itself; it had a charm which thrilled me, although I had never experienced it. Oh yes, I had suffered, but without any love of suffering; it was only then that I was conscious of a real attraction for it: God alone claimed my love, and I must find enjoyment only in him. Often, at Communion, I found myself repeating those words from the *Imitation*: "Jesus, sweet to the taste beyond all our telling, turn all earthly consolations into bitterness for me."[1] That prayer came quite naturally from my lips, without any effort on my part; I felt as if I were repeating them automatically, like a child repeating a formula heard on the lips of some grown-up person she's fond of. Later on, dear Mother, I must tell you how our Lord has seen fit to satisfy this longing of mine, and has, all the time, killed my taste for any other kind of consolation; if I went on about it now, I should have to anticipate things, because I've still got a lot to tell you about my girlhood.

Soon afterwards, I was in retreat again, for my Confirmation. To receive a visit from the Holy Ghost—that meant very careful preparation; I could never understand why people didn't take more trouble about it, this sacrament which was all centred in love. In the ordinary way, you only spent a single day in retreat to prepare for it: I was lucky, because the Bishop couldn't manage to come on the date fixed, so I had two whole days to myself. By way of passing the time, our mistress took us to the hill near-by which we called Monte Cassino; and there I picked great handfuls of marguerites, against Corpus Christi Day. There was room for nothing but joy in my heart; that I should have the happiness of waiting for the Holy Spirit to come down, just as the Apostles did! Only a few hours now, and I should be a Christian fully formed; above all, I was fascinated by the mysterious sign of the Cross which the bishop traces on your forehead, to remain there for all eternity.

It came at last, the moment I so looked forward to. My experience when the Holy Spirit came to me was not that of a strong wind blowing; it was more like that "whisper of a gentle breeze" which Elias heard on Mount Horeb.[2] I was

[1] *Imitation of Christ*, III, xxvi, 3.
[2] III Kings 19, 13.

granted, that day, the strength to suffer; the ordeal was to begin. It was dear little Léonie who stood godmother for me, so moved by the ceremony that she couldn't keep back her tears from the beginning to the end of it. She and I received Communion together; and so the happiness of that wonderful day was crowned for me by a fresh union with our Lord.

Chapter XIII

BACK AT SCHOOL

AFTER THESE days of rejoicing, so delightful to me, so unforgettable, I went back to the common round—which meant, now, life at school, with all the discontent which accompanied it. At the time of my first Communion, I was glad enough to be among girls of my own age, all full of good intentions because they had resolved, like me, to take life in earnest. Now, I found I had to associate with school-fellows of a very different kind; to my great distress, they were worldly, and always ready to disobey the rules. My own natural disposition was happy enough, but I didn't take kindly to the games one plays at that time of life; so that in recreation I was often to be found leaning up against a tree* and indulging in graver thoughts. One game I had invented for myself which I did enjoy, and that was burying the little birds we found lying dead under the trees; plenty of the others helped me, and our cemetery was quite a pretty sight, all set about with tree-shoots and tiny flowers, to match the size of our feathered friends. I was fond, too, of telling stories to the others, making them up out of my head as I went along; they would crowd around me, deeply interested, and sometimes the older girls would come and join my audience. The same story would last two or three days, because I tried to make it more circumstantial when I saw, from the looks of my school-fellows, that I was holding their attention. But after a while the mistress in charge put a stop to my career as an orator; play-time, she considered, was meant to exercise our muscles, not our wits.

In class, I found it easy to remember the gist of what was taught me, not so easy to learn things by heart. When we were doing Catechism, in the year before my first Communion, I asked leave nearly every day to learn it up during recreation time; this got over the difficulty, and I always came out top. If I forgot a word, and lost my place at the head of the class, the result was a flood of tears which poor Abbé Domin had no idea how to stop! He was quite pleased with me (when I wasn't crying), and used to call me his little " Doctor," because my name was Thérèse. I remember one occasion when the girl next me couldn't think of the question she ought to be asking the girl next her; it went all round the class, and then the Abbé said to me: " Now we shall see if you deserve to be at the top." What a humble, modest creature I was![1] I was only waiting for that; I got up as cool as a cucumber and, to the general surprise, repeated it without a single mistake. Even when I'd made my first Communion, I had a love of the Catechism which lasted to the end of my school days.

I did well at my lessons, and nearly always came out top; history and essay-writing were my best subjects. But if my mistresses regarded me as a very promising pupil, that opinion wasn't shared in my uncle's family, where I had the reputation of a little dunce, well-behaved and good-natured, to be sure, and sound in my principles, but clumsy and incompetent. It wasn't surprising if that was the impression my uncle and aunt had, and no doubt still have; I was too shy to talk much, and when I put anything down on paper, my horrible scrawl and my spelling, which can only be described as original, didn't make it very attractive. When I did bits of sewing and embroidery, the result was all right and satisfied the nuns, but the awkward, ungainly way in which I held my work justified the low opinion people had of me. I thank God for it; he wanted my heart to be entirely devoted to him; hadn't I prayed him to turn all earthly consolations into bitterness for me? And it was a discipline I needed; I shouldn't have been proof against compliments. As it was, I got accustomed to hearing a lot about other people's intelligence and nothing about my own, so I concluded that I hadn't got any and did my best to get on without it.

I had a sensitive, affectionate nature, and I might easily have squandered my affections on other people, if I'd found anybody who could appreciate the depth of my feelings. I did try, sure enough, to start up friendships with girls of my

[1] It looks as if the Saint was being ironical at her own expense. The phrase " in my profound humility," underlined by herself, would otherwise be irrelevant to the context.

own age, two of them especially. I was fond of them both,
and they were fond of me, too, as far as they were capable of
it; but the love bestowed on us by our fellow-creatures is so
limited, so fickle! It wasn't long before I realised how little
they understood me. One of them had to go home for a
bit; how constantly I thought of her while she was away, how
carefully I kept a little ring she'd given me! And I was delighted when she came back a few months later, but found, to
my chagrin, that I only got cold looks in return. Well, there
was no appreciation there, and I wasn't prepared to go about
asking for affection when there was no disposition to give it.
All the same, God has given me a constant nature; when I
love with a pure intention, I go on loving, and I still pray
for my old school-fellow, she is my friend still.

Céline had formed a special friendship with one of our
mistresses, and I would have been glad to follow her example;
but I had no knack of winning other people's good graces, so
nothing came of it. Lucky for me that I had so little gift of
making myself agreeable; it has preserved me from grave
dangers. I shall always be grateful to our Lord for turning
earthly friendships into bitterness for me, because, with a
nature like mine, I could so easily have fallen into a snare and
had my wings clipped; and then how should I have been able
to " fly away and find rest?"[1] I don't see how it's possible for
a heart given over to such earthly affections to attain any
intimate union with God. I can't speak from experience,
because this immoderate love of creatures is a poison-draught
which has always been kept away from my lips, but I'm sure
I'm right about this—I've seen so many souls go that way.
They're like the poor moths; dazzled by the lure of this rush-
light, they fly into it and burn their wings, only to come back
later into the soft radiance of that true love which is divine.
They need fresh wings, brighter and more nimble than ever,
if they're to fly back to our Lord, the divine Fire that burns
without consuming what it burns. He knew, evidently, that
I was too weak to be exposed to such temptations; if once I'd
allowed this false light to dazzle me, it might have burned
me outright.

If that didn't happen, if I only found bitterness where other
souls find attraction, and have to resist the attraction by

[1] Psalm 54. 7.

fidelity to grace, that was no credit to me. It was only God's
mercy that preserved me from giving myself up to the love
of creatures; without that, I might have fallen as low as St.
Mary Magdalen did. I find such comfort in those penetrating
words of our Lord to Simon the Pharisee: "He loves little,
who has little forgiven him."[1] But I, you say, owed him
little? On the contrary, I owe him more than the Magdalen
herself; he remitted my sins beforehand, as it were, by not
letting me fall into them. Oh dear, I wish I could explain
exactly what I feel about it. Put it like this—a clever doctor
has a son who trips over a stone, falls, and breaks a limb. His
father is at his side in a moment, picks him up tenderly, and
treats his injuries with all the skill he has. Thanks to him, the
boy is completely cured before long; and the father, sure
enough, has done something to earn his love. But now,
suppose the father sees the stone in his son's path, runs ahead
of him and takes it out of the way, without calling any attention to what he is doing. At the time, the boy is unconscious
of the danger he would have run, but for his father's foresight; is less grateful, less moved to affection, than if a cure
had been performed. But if he learns afterwards what risks
he has been spared, the boy will love him more than ever.
And that's what God's loving providence has done for me.
When he sent his Son into the world, it was to ransom
sinners, not the just[2]—yes, but, you see, in my case he has
left me in debt to him not for much but for everything. He
hasn't waited to make me love him much, like the Magdalen;
he's made me realise what I owe to his tender foresight, to
make me love him to distraction, as I do. When I'm told that
an innocent soul can't love as a repentant soul does, how I
long to give that sentiment the lie!

Off at a tangent again! Let me return to my story. Nearly
a whole year passed, after my first Communion, without any
interior trials; it was only when the anniversary came round,
and I went into retreat, that I became subject to that dreadful
affliction—scruples. It's an ordeal you can't understand unless
you've been through it, so it's no use trying to explain what
I went through during the next year and a half. My lightest
thoughts, my simplest actions, troubled my conscience afterwards; and I could only find relief in telling Marie about them

[1] Luke 7, 47.   [2] Luke 5, 32.

—not that I liked that, because it meant explaining to Marie the exaggerated opinion I had formed of her. Once I had got it off my chest, I felt at peace for the moment, but the moment was like a flash of lightning; the next, my troubles had started again. And dear Marie listened to me so patiently, without a sign of being bored! As soon as I got back from the Abbey she would set to, curling my hair for the next day —Papa insisted that his little princess should always have her hair in curl, to the surprise of the other girls, and still more of the nuns, who thought they'd never seen a girl so spoilt by her parents. And there I would sit, in tears all the time, telling her about my scruples. At the end of the year Céline finished her schooling and went home. I was so unhappy at going back to school alone that I fell ill at once. Céline and I had been inseparable, and I felt like an orphan, staying on there without her; the only attraction of school life was gone.

Chapter XIV

MARIE ENTERS CARMEL

I LEFT SCHOOL, then, at the age of thirteen: but I went on with my education by taking several lessons every week with Madame Papinau. She was a good-hearted woman and very well educated, with a touch of faded charm about her. She lived with her mother, and they made a delightful household between the three of them—three, because a cat was a member of the family, and I had to let her sit on my copybooks, and to say nice things about her figure. I became thus intimate with the family, because Les Buissonnets was a long walk for ageing legs, so I had my lessons at their house. How well I remember the drill of it—old Madame Cochain looking at me with wide blue eyes; her quiet, precise voice: "Madame Papinau! Mademoiselle Thérèse is here," and the answer, coming in child-like tones: "Here I am, Mamma." And so lesson-time would begin.

Apart from what I learned in the course of them, these lessons had the added advantage of improving my knowledge of the world. You could hardly believe it; here was this room full of old-fashioned furniture, with books and bundles of paper lying about everywhere, and yet visitors kept on coming in, priests, old ladies, young girls, and so on, to see the family. Madame Cochain did the honours of conversation as much as possible, to let her daughter get on with the lessons; but I didn't learn much on days like that. There was I, my nose in my book, hearing everything that was said, and some of it none too good for me—vain thoughts come to the mind so easily! Here was one lady talking about my lovely hair, and another, just going out of the door and thinking I couldn't hear, wanting to know who that very pretty girl was. Compliments are at their best when you aren't meant to hear them; and the thrill of pleasure I felt made me realise that I was full of pride.

I'm always ready to sympathise with the people who lose their souls;—after all, it's so easy, once you begin to stray along the primrose path of worldliness. To be sure, once your soul has been raised up, even in a small degree, above the common level, you see bitterness in all the pleasures the world has to offer, and the longings of your heart are too large to be contented with ephemeral praise. But if God hadn't called me from the first, to something higher, if the world had lavished its smiles on me all along, what mightn't have become of me? When I tell the story of his mercies to me, I find such great cause for thankfulness! As the Book of Wisdom says, he caught me away from the world "before wickedness could pervert my thoughts, before wrong-doing could allure my heart."[1]

The Blessed Virgin, too, kept good watch over the little flower that was dedicated to her; she didn't want to see it tarnished with the stains of earth, so she took care to plant it high up, in her own mountain air, before it opened. That happy moment hadn't yet arrived, but already my love for my heavenly Mother was growing all the time; and I now went out of my way to prove it. It's a long story, but I *must* tell you about it in brief. As soon as I went to school, I joined the Association of the Holy Angels; I loved all the prayers we had to say, because I had a special devotion to the Holy Angels, above all, to the Angel God had appointed to be my guardian here. Soon after my first Communion I took a further step, and a new ribbon announced that I had become an "aspirant" to fuller dedication as a Child of Mary; only I had to leave school before I actually joined the Association. And now, as I hadn't finished my schooling at the Abbey, I found I wasn't allowed to enter it on the strength of being an old girl. That wouldn't have worried me much, only all my sisters had belonged, and I wanted to have the same right to call myself our Lady's child as they had. So I pocketed my pride, and asked if I might join the Association at the Abbey. The headmistress didn't like to say No, but she made the condition that I must come round two afternoons in the week, so that they could judge whether I was worthy to be admitted. Other older girls, who had made a special confidante among

[1] Book of Wisdom 4, 11.

the mistresses, would have welcomed the chance to go and have a chat with her, but the permission was worse than useless to me. All I could do was to go up and say good afternoon to the mistress, and work there in silence till the sewing-lesson was over; then, as nobody took any notice of me, I used to go up to the tribune in the chapel, and stay there in front of the Blessed Sacrament till Papa came to take me home. That was my only consolation; but indeed, what more could I want? Our Lord was my only real Friend, the only Person I could really talk to; I found human conversation cloying, even when it was about holy things. Talking *to* God, I felt, is always better than talking *about* God; those pious conversations—there's always a touch of self-approval about them.

Well, if I went to the Abbey, it was only for our Lady's sake. Sometimes I felt very lonely, just as I did when I was at school. In those days, when I wandered about the big court feeling depressed and ill, I'd often repeated to myself a line of poetry which brought peace and strength back into my soul: it runs, " Time's but a ship that bears thee, not thy home."[1] Those words cheered me up when I was quite small; and even now, when so many of my childhood's impressions have disappeared with the passage of the years, that image of the ship appeals to me, and helps me to bear this life of exile. After all, it's just what the Book of Wisdom says: " The ship that ploughs the angry waves, what trace is left of her passage?"[2] Thoughts like this take me out of my depth; it's as if I was already reaching the shores of eternity, with our Lord offering me his embrace, and the Blessed Virgin coming to greet me—Papa, too, and Mamma, and those four innocents! It's as if I was already starting on that life which will mean eternal reunion with them.

But, before that final reunion, there were plenty of partings to come. In the very year when I became a child of Mary, she carried my own Marie off to Carmel—Marie, my only support, to whom I looked for guidance and consolation and a pattern of right living, the oracle to whom I always appealed. Oh, no doubt Pauline had still the first claim on my affections, but then Pauline was at a distance, such a distance

[1] *Réflexion*, by Lamartine.   [2] Book of Wisdom 5, 10.

from me! It had been terrible, trying to get accustomed to living without her, but there was a barrier between us you couldn't cross, and you had to admit it; Pauline was lost to me as if she'd been dead. She went on loving me, praying for me: but I thought of her as a kind of Saint, quite cut off from earthly interests, so that the difficulties I had nowadays would have come as a shock to her, perhaps estranged her from me. And I couldn't, in any case, exchange confidences with her now as I used to at home—Marie had the run of the parlours, but Céline and I were only let in at the last moment, a tantalising moment.

Marie, then, was really all I had; you may say that I couldn't do without her. My scruples, for example—she was the only person I confided them to, and even my confessor never knew that I suffered from this distressing complaint because I only mentioned to him the sins Marie had told me I might confess,* you'd have thought I hadn't a scruple in the world, when in reality I was as bad as I could be. Marie, in fact, knew every thought which passed through my mind; she understood all about wanting to enter Carmel. I loved her so much, how was I to live without her? My aunt used to ask us to come and stay with her every year at Trouville, in batches; I should have enjoyed going there, but only with Marie; it was no fun without her.

I'm wrong, I do remember one pleasant time I had at Trouville, the year Papa went off to Constantinople. Céline and I couldn't bear his being such a long way away, so Marie sent us both to the seaside, to take our minds off it. And I did enjoy myself; after all, Céline was there, and my aunt gave us all the treats she could think of, donkey-rides and shrimping* and so on. I was still very young, at twelve and a half; I can remember my delight when my aunt gave me sky blue hair-ribbons, and how I mentioned it in confession at Trouville, because I regarded my childish pleasure as a sin. It was while we were there that I had, one evening, a disconcerting experience. My cousin, Marie Guérin, was a permanent invalid, and cried a good deal,* which made my aunt fuss over her and call her all sorts of pretty names—but it was no use, she went on crying and complaining of her headache. I had a headache myself nearly every day, without complaining of it; so one evening I thought I'd imitate Marie, and sat down to have a good cry* on an armchair in a corner of the room. Jeanne and my aunt soon rallied round to find out what was the matter with me, but when I answered, like Marie, that I'd got a headache, I found it didn't work; there must be some other reason, they thought, for my tears. So they talked to me as if I were a grown-up, and Jeanne scolded me for not being more open with my aunt—she thought I must have something on my conscience.

Well, I had bought my experience cheap; no more imitating other people for me. I understood, now, the fable about the donkey and the pet dog;[1] I was just like the donkey, seeing how the dog was made much of, and putting his great clumsy hoof on the table in the hope that some of the kisses would come his way. If I wasn't beaten as he was, I was paid out all the same, and the payment I got cured me, for life, of any desire to attract attention; one experiment was quite enough! Next year, the year in which my dear godmother left for the convent, my aunt asked me again, but alone this time; and I was so homesick that I fell ill and after a few days had to be taken back to Lisieux. They had thought I was seriously ill, but I was only pining for Les Buissonnets; I recovered the moment I put my foot inside it. That's the kind of girl I was; and now God was going to take away from me the one person on whom I depended for support!

As soon as I heard of Marie's resolution, I made up my mind that I mustn't look for enjoyment in this world any longer. Here was my room, Pauline's old studio, which I'd adopted and furnished to suit my taste; it was a real jumble, a collection of pious objects and curiosities, with a garden and an aviary thrown in. At the far end was a large plain black cross, and a few drawings I liked; on another side-wall, a basket done up with muslin and pink ribbon, devoted to grasses and flowers, on the other, a portrait of Pauline at ten reigned in solitary majesty. Under this portrait was a table, supporting a cage with a lot of birds in it; their chirping made visitors put their hands to their ears, but I was too fond of them for that. Then there was the little white book case, with my lesson-books and note-books on it; that also had to hold a

[1] La Fontaine, *Fables*, IV, 5.

statue of our Lady, with fresh flowers in vases, and some candles round it; let alone a quantity of other holy statues, little baskets in shell-work, cardboard boxes, and heaven knows what.

And then there was my garden, hanging in front of the window, where I kept flowers in pots, the rarest kinds I could lay hands on; but there was a flower-stand inside what I called my museum, which was really the place of honour. Right in front of the window was my own table with a green cloth over it, in the middle of which I had deposited an hour-glass, a small statue of St. Joseph, a watch-case, some flower-vases, an ink-stand, and so on. A few rickety chairs, and a lovely doll's cot belonging to Pauline—there you have the complete inventory of my furniture. A plain attic room, but to me it stood for the whole world—I could have written a *Voyage autor de ma Chambre* like de Maistre. It was here that I liked to be left alone for hours on end, to get my work done, and to think my own thoughts with this charming prospect in front of me.

Well, when I got the news that Marie was leaving us, this room of mine lost all attraction for me. I couldn't leave her alone for a moment, this dearly-loved sister who was so soon to take her flight. Goodness, how I must have tried her patience! Every time I passed her door, I knocked till she opened it and smothered her with kisses, as if I were laying up a store of them for all the years in which I should have to do without them. A month before she entered Carmel, Papa took us to Alençon again; but this visit was nothing like the earlier one—it was all gall and wormwood to me. How hopelessly I broke down and cried at Mamma's grave, simply because I'd picked some corn-flowers for it and forgotten to bring them with me! Really, in those days I could make a tragedy of anything. It's so different now, when by God's grace I never let myself be got down by the troubles of the moment: looking back, I'm overcome with gratitude at the heavenly favours I've received: I don't seem to be the same person at all. No doubt I longed, even then, for the grace to have the free control of my own action, the mistress, not the slave of my impulses; those words of the *Imitation*[1] had a

[1] III. xxviii, 1.

profound effect on me; but I still needed a long apprentice-ship before the coveted gift was granted me. At the time I was still a child, and seemed to have no will of my own; a weak character, they said at Alençon.

Chapter XV

THERESE GROWS UP

IT WAS while we were at Alençon that Léonie tried to become a Poor Clare; this unexpected departure of hers saddened me, because I was very fond of her, and hadn't had the chance of kissing her good-bye before she went. I shall never forget the kindness, and the embarrassment, with which Papa broke the news to us about Léonie: she had taken the habit as a Poor Clare already. He was as much surprised as we were,* but he didn't like to say so, because he could see that Marie was taking it badly. When we went round to the convent, it gave me a stifled sort of feeling I'd never had anywhere else: it wasn't a bit like Carmel, where your heart went out to everything you saw; the nuns, too, didn't attract me, and I wasn't in the least tempted to stay there. Only Léonie was very touching in her new habit; she said we must have a good look at her eyes, because we wouldn't see them again—the Poor Clares always lower their eyes in public. As a matter of fact, God was content with the sacrifice she had made after two months of it; she came back home, and we saw those blue eyes of hers again, often wet with tears.

But when we left Alençon, I imagined she would stay on there, and it was with a heavy heart that I left the gloomy Rue de la Demi-lune. Only three of us now, and Marie was going to leave us so soon! On the fifteenth of October the day of parting came, and only the two youngest were left, out of all that big, happy family at Les Buissonnets. The doves had flitted from the nest, and even the two who remained would have liked to follow suit, only their wings weren't strong enough yet for the journey. God lost no time in giving me such strength, though I was the youngest and the weakest of all. Why did he call me before Céline? She was more worthy of the call; but he likes to make us conscious of his mercy and his power by using the tool that seems less

99

apt. Our Lord knew how feeble I was, and that's why he hid me away in the cleft rock[1] out of my turn.

At the time when Marie entered Carmel, I was still a mass of scruples, and now that I had lost my earthly confidante, I could only have recourse to heaven. Those four innocent souls that had made their way to heaven before me—surely they, who had never lived to know earth's troubles and fears, would be sorry for this sister, sorely tried on earth? To them, then, I addressed myself, with all the simplicity of a child; reminding them that I'd always been the darling, the spoilt child of the family, because I was the youngest, and if they'd lived they'd have been just as kind to me as the rest. No reason to forget me because they were in heaven; on the contrary, with all its resources at their disposal, they could easily win me the peace of mind I wanted, and prove that love doesn't end with death. I didn't have to wait for my answer; before long, a delicious sense of peace flooded into my soul, and I realised that there were people who loved me in heaven too. Ever since then, this devotion of mine towards my little brothers and sisters has grown stronger; I have often sought out their company, to tell them what a sad thing exile is, and how I long to join them soon in my true country.

If heaven showered its graces on me, that was not because I had done anything to earn them; I was still full of imperfections. True, I was burning with desire to do good, but I set about it in a very odd way. Here's an instance. Being the youngest, I'd never learned to look after myself; it was Céline who looked after the room we slept in, and I never did a hand's turn. But when Marie went into Carmel, it came into my head that I ought to be going out of my way to please God; so I would make the bed sometimes, or fetch Céline's flower-pots in from the garden* while she was out. That was all right, but as my sole object was to please God, I ought to have been indifferent to any mark of gratitude from human creatures. Instead of that, if poor Céline omitted to look happy and surprised about these good deeds of mine, I was miserable about it and burst into tears. Really, my touchiness in those days was quite unbearable. If I'd given some slight annoyance to anyone I was fond of, without in

[1] Song of Songs 2, 140.

the least meaning to, it was obvious that crying about it only
made things worse, but could I control myself? No, I wept
like the Magdalen herself; and as soon as I had begun to
cheer up about what I'd done, I started crying about having
cried over it. Arguments were unavailing; nothing would
cure me of this unpleasant habit.

Yes, I was still in my swaddling-clothes; how did I find
the freedom of movement to want Carmel? God had to
perform a miracle on a small scale to make me grow up;
grow up all in a moment. And the occasion he chose for it
was Christmas, that night of illumination which somehow
lights up for us the inner life of the Blessed Trinity. Our
Lord, newly born, turned this darkness of mine into a flood
of light; born to share my human weakness, he brought me
the strength and courage I needed. He armed me so well,
that holy night, that I never looked back; I was like a soldier,
winning one vantage-point after another, like a "great
runner who sees the track before him."[1] My tears dried up at
their source; they flowed, now, only at long intervals and with
difficulty. Somebody had once said to me: "If you cry like
that when you're small, you'll have no tears left later on";
and it was true.

Yes, it was on December the twenty-fifth, 1886, that I was
given the grace to leave my childhood's days behind; call it, if
you will, the grace of complete conversion. We'd just got back
from Midnight Mass, in which our Lord had come to me
with all his strength and vigour. On such occasions, there was
a treat in store for me at Les Buissonnets—I would go off to
find my Christmas boot* in the chimney corner; we'd
loved this so much in our childhood that Céline went on
treating me as if I were a baby, as being the youngest. Papa
was always so fond of seeing my happiness, and listening to
my cries of delight as the magic boot revealed, one after
another, my surprise presents, and part of my enjoyment was
the pleasure he took in it. But this time, our Lord meant to
shew me that I ought to be getting rid of my childish defects;
so this innocent joy was denied me, and he allowed Papa to be
the means of my disappointment. He, Papa, was tired after
the Midnight Mass, and the sight of my boots in the chim-

[1] Psalm 18, 6.

ney corner annoyed him. Imagine my distress when I overheard him saying: "Well, thank goodness it's the last year this is going to happen!"

I was going upstairs at the moment, to take off my hat; Céline, who knew how touchy I was, saw my eyes shining with tears and was ready to cry herself; in her loving sympathy, she knew exactly what I was feeling. "Oh, Thérèse," she said, "don't go down just yet; it'll only make you miserable looking inside your boots now!" But she didn't know the Thérèse she was dealing with; our Lord had changed me into a different person. I dried my tears and went down at once; my heart was beating fast, but I managed to get hold of my boots and put them down in front of Papa, and as I took out my presents you would have thought that I was as happy as a queen. Papa smiled, his good humour restored, and Céline thought she must be dreaming. But no, it was a sublime reality; little Thérèse had recovered the strength of mind which she'd lost at four and a half and recovered it for good.

With this night of illumination, the third period of my life begins, the best of all, the richest in heavenly graces. In a single instant, our Lord brought about the change which I'd vainly tried to achieve these ten years past; I'd tried, and that was enough for him. I was in the same position as the Apostles, when they said: "Master, we have toiled all night, and caught nothing"; in my case, he was still more merciful; he took the net himself, threw it, and brought it back loaded with fish. He did more; he made me "a fisher of men."[1] I felt a great desire to work for the conversion of sinners: a desire which had never before been so vividly present to me; to put it quite simply, charity had found its way into my heart, calling on me to forget myself and try to bring happiness to others; and since then I've been as happy as the day is long.

There was one particular Sunday when I was looking at a picture of our Lord on the Cross, and was struck by the sight of the blood flowing from one of those divine hands. How pitiable that it should be allowed to fall on the ground unheeded, instead of being jealously hoarded up! I would take up my stand, in spirit, at the foot of the Cross, and

[1] Luke 5, 5 and 10.

gather up this saving balm that distilled from it, always with the intention of applying it to the needs of souls. And again, that cry of our Lord's on the cross, "I'm thirsty," went on echoing in my heart; and they kindled in me a zeal which I'd never known before—how could I allay his thirst for souls, except by sharing it? I wasn't thinking, as yet, about his priests, only about praying for obstinate sinners, threatened with eternal flames—how I burned with the longing to save them!

God gave me some encouragement about this, to assure me that my ambitions were acceptable to him. I'd been told about an abandoned wretch who'd just been condemned to death* for his appalling crimes; and there was every reason to think that he would die impenitent. He must be saved from hell! I tried everything; there was nothing I could do myself, but I could offer to God our Lord's infinite merits, and all the treasury of his Church; and I got Céline to have a Mass said for me—I didn't like to ask for it myself, because I was shy about owning up that it was for Pranzini, the wretched man I'm speaking of. I'd rather not have told Céline, but she questioned me so eagerly and so lovingly that I had to tell her my secret. And she didn't make fun of me; on the contrary, she wanted to give me her help in converting my sinner (as she called him). I was only too thankful; I would have liked all creation to join with me in praying for the grace that was needed. In my heart, I felt certain we shouldn't be disappointed; but by way of encouragement in this practice of praying for sinners, I did ask for a sign. I told God I was sure he meant to pardon the unfortunate Pranzini, and I'd such confidence in our Lord's infinite mercy that I would cling to my belief even if Pranzini didn't go to confession, didn't make any gesture of repentance. Only I *would* like him to shew some sign of repentance, just for my own satisfaction.

My prayer was answered, and to the letter. Papa didn't allow us to read the newspapers, but I thought there could be no harm in following up the story of Pranzini. The day after his execution I came upon a copy of *La Croix*; I lost no time in opening it, and what I read brought the tears to my eyes, so that I had to hurry away and conceal my emotion. Pranzini didn't go to confession; he went up on to the scaffold, and was just preparing to put his head between the bars of the guillotine, when a sudden inspiration came to him. He availed himself of the crucifix which the priest was holding out to him, and kissed, three times, the sacred wounds. And with that, his soul went to receive its award, from those merciful lips which told us that " there will be more rejoicing in heaven over one sinner who repents, than over ninety-nine souls that are justified, and have no need of repentance."[1]

Well, there was my sign: and it fitted in exactly with the pattern of that grace which had moved me to pray for sinners. The thirst for souls had come to me upon sight of the precious blood flowing from our Lord's wounds; this was to be the cordial draught that would heal their ailments. And here was this man, the first child of my prayers, as you might call him, dying with those sacred wounds pressed closely to his lips. What a courteous answer was this! After that special grace, my longing to save souls grew from day to day; it was as if I heard our Lord saying to me what he said to the Samaritan; " Give me some water to drink."[2] Lovers are fond of exchanging presents. On my side, I offered to our Lord souls that were revivified, now, by the dew of his precious blood. And the more I did that, the more he, on his side, increased in my imperfect nature the thirst for souls, better than any draught his love could have bestowed on me.

[1] Luke 15, 7.   [2] John 4, 7.

Chapter XVI

INTERIOR PROGRESS

HITHERTO, MY LIFE had been moving within the limits of a narrow circle, and now God had found the means to extricate me from it. It's with heart-felt gratitude that I look back over the way he made me travel; but even now, it has to be admitted, although I'd taken the big step forward, there were plenty of things I'd got to leave behind me. Here was I delivered from scruples, cured of that deplorable touchiness I've spoken of; but by now my mind was opening out. The sublime, the beautiful, had always appealed to me, but it wasn't till this period of my life that I was seized with a great desire for knowledge. Lessons and exercises were all very well, but they weren't enough for me; I took to reading on my own, especially in the two departments of history and science. Other subjects left me cold, but these two really gripped me, and in quite a short time I had amassed more knowledge than had come my way in the whole course of my schooling. Oh, it's quite true that this was "frustration and lost labour, all of it";[1] that chapter of the *Imitation*[2] where it talks about unnecessary curiosity was always coming back to my mind, but I went on all the same, persuading myself that I was of the right age for study, so there couldn't be any harm in it. And indeed, however much waste of time there may have been, I don't think God grudged it me; I was always careful to devote so many hours to reading and no more. so as to keep my itch for acquiring information within due limits.

The fact is, I was at the dangerous moment of girlhood, but God was looking after me. He might have applied to me the words he addresses to Jerusalem in the prophecy of Ezechiel: "Who but I came upon thee, as I passed on my way? And already thou were ripe for love; my troth I plighted to thee, and thou wert mine. Cloak of mine should be thrown about

[1] Ecclesiastes I, 14.　　[2] Probably III, x, 3.

thee; oil I brought to anoint thee, clad thee with embroidery; a collar for that neck, on thy head a crown magnifical. Of wheat and honey and oil was thy nourishment; matchless beauty was thine, such beauty as brought thee to a throne."[1] Yes, that's what our Lord did for me; I could take up every word of what I've just written, and show how appropriately it describes his treatment of me; but the graces I've already mentioned are sufficient proof of it. Let me only say something about the *nourishment* he gave me, and gave me in such good measure.

For a long time past, what had kept me going was the wholemeal bread you get in *The Imitation of Christ*: I found nothing else really useful, until I began to discover the treasures hidden in the gospels. Dear *Imitation*! I knew nearly all the chapters by heart, but nothing would part me from my little book; it lived in my pocket during the summer, and in my muff during the winter, so that it had become quite an institution; it was a favourite joke at my aunt's to open it at random and " put me on " at the first chapter you came to. But I was fourteen now, and developing a taste for wider reading; and God saw fit to supplement this dry bread with " oil and honey " that would content me. I got that from Abbé Arminjon's book, *Fin du monde présense et mystères de la vie future*. The dear Carmelites had lent this book to Papa; I didn't ordinarily read his books, but I made an exception in this case and got his leave to have a look at it. Here was another great grace in my life; I can still see myself reading it at the window of the room where I did my lessons, but the impression it made on me was something so intimate, so exquisite, that I can't attempt to describe it.

All the tremendous truths of religion, all the mysteries of eternity, came flooding into my soul with a feeling of happiness that had nothing to do with this world. I was getting a foretaste, already, of " the welcome God has prepared for those who love him "[2]—yes, heart can feel what eye has never seen; and realising that there is no proportion between those heavenly rewards and the cheap sacrifices we make in this life, I longed to love our Lord, love him passionately, shew him, while life still offered its unique chance, a thousand proofs of my love. I copied out several passages, about per-

[1] Ezechiel 16, 8-13.   [2] Corinthians 2, 9.

fect love, and about the welcome God means to give us at that moment when he himself becomes our rich, eternal reward; I repeated to myself, again and again, the tender words which had so entwined themselves round my heart.

Céline was by now the privileged confidante of my thoughts. Ever since Christmas we had been able to understand one another; the difference of age didn't matter, because I'd grown so much in size and still more because I'd grown so much in grace. In earlier days, I'd often complained because she wouldn't tell me her secrets, and she assured me I was too tiny; I'd have to grow "by the whole height of that stool" before she could trust me. I was fond of getting up on to the magical stool in question, close to her side, and asking her to talk to me in confidence; but all my pains were wasted— there was still a barrier between us. But now our Lord wanted us to go forward side by side, so he united us by a bond closer than any ties of blood; we were to be sisters in spirit. We were like the maidens in the Canticle of St. John of the Cross, where the Bride cries out to her Lover:

> " Tracking your sandal-mark,
>   The maidens search the roadway for your sign,
>   Yearning to catch the spark
>   And taste the scented wine
>   Which emanates a balm that is divine."[1]

Light of foot we followed in our Lord's footsteps: the sparks of love which he spread so generously in our souls, the strong satisfying wine which he gave us to drink, made transitory things vanish from our sight; our lips breathed tender aspirations which he, no other, had communicated to us.

Those were wonderful conversations we had, every evening, upstairs in the room with a view. Our eyes were lost in distance, as we watched the pale moon rising slowly above the height of the trees. Those silvery rays she cast on a sleeping world, the stars shining bright in the blue vault above us, the fleecy clouds floating by in the evening wind—how everything conspired to turn our thoughts towards heaven! How beautiful it must be if this, the obverse side of it, was so calm and clear! Perhaps it's silly of me, but that opening-up

[1] Stanza 25 (translated by Roy Campbell).

of our hearts has always reminded me of St. Monica and her son at Ostia, rapt in ecstasy as they contemplated the wonderful works of their Creator.[1] I feel as if we'd received graces belonging to the same high order as some of those bestowed on the great Saints: as the *Imitation* says, God has two ways of making himself manifest; he shews himself to some people in a blaze of light, to others under a considerate veil of symbols and figures.[2] Well, of course it was only this second kind of revelation he saw fit to give to Céline and me, but how light and transparent it seemed, this veil which hid him from our sight! How could there be room for doubt, how could there be any need of faith or hope? It was love that taught us to find, here on earth, the Bridegroom we searched for. " He came upon us alone, and greeted us with a kiss: henceforward we need fear no contemptuous looks."[3]

Graces like these, as you would expect, bore abundant fruit in our lives; so that the path of holiness came easy and natural to us. At first, there would sometimes be a struggle, and I would make a wry face over it; but gradually that feeling disappeared, and I could renounce my own will, from the first, without difficulty. " If a man is rich," our Lord says, " gifts will be made to him, and his riches will abound."[4] And so it was with me; if I would only correspond faithfully with each grace that was given me, a multitude of others would follow. He gave himself to me in Communion, at the time I'm speaking of, oftener than I'd have dared to hope. I made a rule of going whenever my confessor would let me, but allowing him to judge for himself, not asking it of him as a favour. (Nowadays, I should be more plucky, and take the opposite line; I'm quite sure that if a soul feels drawn towards frequent Communion, the confessor ought to be told about it. After all, our Lord doesn't come down from heaven every day just to wait there in a gold ciborium* he has found a much better heaven for his resting-place; a Christian soul, made in his own image, the living temple of the Blessed Trinity.)

Anyhow our Lord, finding me so eager and so well-disposed,

---

[1] St. Augustine's Confessions, IX, 10.   [2] III, xliii, 4.
[3] A composite quotation from Canticles VIII, 1, and *Imitation of Christ* IV, xiii, 1.
[4] Matthew 13, 12.

saw to it that my confessor should encourage me to make my Communion four times a week all through that May; and when May was over, he raised it to five times in any week when a great feast came along. It was with tears of happiness that I left the confessional; our Lord himself, I felt, was determined to be my Guest. You see, I'd had a short shrift, I never said anything of my interior dispositions; why should I need any other guidance than his, when the way by which he led me was so direct, so clearly lit up? Directors, after all, were only faithful mirrors, to reflect our Lord's will in the conduct of souls; what if God meant to deal with me personally, without making use of any intermediary?

When a gardener takes a great deal of trouble with some fruit he wants to ripen before its time, he doesn't mean to leave it hanging on the tree; it must be served up at a banquet. And it was on the same principle that our Lord lavished his graces on such a tender plant as I was. Once, while he was on earth, he cried out in a transport of joy: "Father, I give thee praise that thou hast hidden all this from the wise and the prudent, and revealed it to little children."[1] And now, just because I was so helpless and insignificant, he saw in me the opportunity for a startling exercise of his mercy. He brought himself down to my level, and taught me, all unobserved, the lesson of love. Oh dear, those learned people who spend a whole lifetime in getting up their subjects! How surprised they'd have been to hear that there was a secret which all their scientific method couldn't discover for them, the secret of perfection! It wasn't to be understood except by the poor in spirit; and here was a girl of fourteen who was able to tell them about it.*

[1] Matthew 11, 25.

Chapter XVII

FIRST STEPS TOWARDS CARMEL

St. John of the Cross says in his Spiritual Canticle[1] that he had

> " No other light
> Except for that which in my heart was burning.
>
> It lit and led me through
> More certain than the light of noonday clear
> To where One waited near,
> Whose presence well I knew."

For me, the place where our Lord waited was Carmel; but before I could find, in him, " cool shade to rest under,"[2] I had many ordeals to undergo. It didn't matter; God's call was so urgent that I would have passed through fire to prove my loyalty. As it was, I could only find one living soul to encourage me in my vocation, and that was my own Pauline. Every beat of my heart woke an echo in hers, and it was only through her that I reached the coveted shore—the ground of Carmel, so enriched with the dew of heaven, which had welcomed her five years earlier. For five years, dear Mother, I thought you were lost to me; but no sooner did my trials begin than your hand was there to point me along the road I must follow.

And I needed all the encouragement I could get. My visits to the parlour at Carmel made me miserable nowadays; I had only to mention my Carmelite ambitions to find myself cold-shouldered. Marie, who thought I was too young, did all she could to put me off; and even you, Mother, sometimes tried to damp my ardour, to see if I was really in earnest. If I hadn't had a real vocation, I should have been discouraged from the start; as soon as I made any move to answer our

[1] Stanzas 3 and 4 (translated by Roy Campbell).   [2] Canticles II, 3.

110

Lord's call, I found nothing but one obstacle after another. I didn't like to tell Céline about wanting to enter so young; and that made it worse, because I hated having any secrets from her. But these regrets only lasted for a short time; it wasn't long before dear Céline got to know of my resolve, and, instead of trying to deter me, accepted the sacrifice God asked of her with heroic courage. I say heroic, because by now we were so closely united, animated as it were by a single soul. For several months we'd been living the sort of life a young girl dreams of; everything about us was to our liking, we had all the liberty we wanted; in a word, it was a sort of earthly paradise. And now, before we'd had a real taste of it, it was to be abandoned deliberately; and dear Céline didn't repine for an instant. Besides, our Lord wasn't calling her first, and she might have made a grievance of that; she had the same vocation, and it was her turn. But no; you might have thought yourself back in the age of the martyrs, when those who were left behind in prison gave the kiss of peace to those brothers of theirs who were the first to be tried out in the arena; comforting themselves with the thought that perhaps *they* were being reserved for a greater test of courage. Céline said good-bye to Thérèse, and was left alone to face the high and terrible ordeal for which our Lord, as a mark of his love, had destined her.[1]

Once she was in my confidence, once she knew the whole position about my difficulties and discouragement, she behaved exactly as if her own vocation had been the point at issue; there was nothing to fear from Céline. But how was I to tell Papa? He'd already given his three eldest daughters to religion; how to break it to him that he must say good-bye to his favourite? I had to wrestle with my own feelings for some time before I had the courage to speak out. But I'd got to go through with it; I was nearly fourteen and a half; it was only six months, now, to Christmas, and I'd set my heart* on entering religion at the same holy hour at which I'd received my grace the year before. In the end I chose Pentecost as the date for making my disclosure; all through the day I was asking the Apostles to pray for me, so that I might find the

[1] Referring to the terrible break-down in the mental health of their father, M. Martin. This happened soon after Thérèse's entry into Carmel; he died shortly before Céline's entry, six years later.

right words to use. After all, it was up to them to help me overcome my timidity: the Carmelite vocation which God had marked out for me meant evangelising, by prayer and acts of sacrifice, the Church's evangelists.

It wasn't till the afternoon, when we got back from Vespers, that I found the opportunity of speaking to him, this well-loved father of mine. He had gone outside and was sitting by the well, the wonderful book of nature spread out before him. The sun, though its rays had lost their power, still picked out the tree-tops with gold, and the birds were still at their vespers, high up in the branches. On his handsome face there was an expression of heavenly calm, and you could see that his soul was utterly at peace. I went up and sat there beside him without saying a single word, but my eyes were wet with tears. He looked down at me ever so tenderly, and pressed my head close to his heart: "What's the matter, little princess?" he said. "Tell me about it." Then he got up, as if to disguise his own feelings, and began to walk up and down, still holding me close to his side.

When I told him about my longing to enter Carmel, his tears came out to meet mine, but he didn't say a word to discourage my vocation. He only suggested that I was still very young to take such a serious resolution. But I put up such a good case for myself that Papa, with his honest, straight-forward nature, was quick to see the will of God in these promptings of mine; and so deep was his faith that he cried out: "What an honour God is doing me, in asking me like this for the gift of one daughter after another!" Our walk didn't come to an end all at once; my heart went out to his, in gratitude for the kindness with which he'd received my confidences. What a wonderful father to have! He seemed now to be experiencing the calm and the happiness which are the reward of making a sacrifice. It was like talking to a Saint; how I wish that I could recall his words and put them on paper! But it is all a faint memory, laid up in lavender; I cannot give any account of it, and I'll only mention one thing which stands out in my memory—an action of his which was symbolic, though it wasn't meant to be.

There were some little white flowers, rather like lilies, growing on a low wall close by. He picked one of these flowers and gave it me, pointing out how it was God's care that had fostered this plant and kept it in being. As I listened to him, I felt I was listening to the story of my own life; so close was the analogy between them, the insignificant flower and the insignificant Thérèse! I took the flower from him as if it had been the relic of a Saint, and in doing so I noticed that, instead of picking it, he had pulled it out by the roots, which were quite uninjured—as if it were meant to take fresh life in some new soil, richer than the soft moss in which it had first awakened. Wasn't that exactly what Papa had done for me a few minutes ago, when he gave me leave to find a home on Mount Carmel, far from the lowland walks of childhood? I put the flower between the leaves of my *Imitation*, marking the chapter on the duty of loving God above all things: and there it remains, only the stalk has broken off now, close to the roots, as if God meant to tell me that he's going to sever my connexion with this earth before long, instead of leaving me to fade away gradually.

When I'd got Papa's consent, I imagined that it was all plain sailing; but no, there were plenty of wearisome obstacles still in the way, to test the genuineness of my vocation. I was trembling all over when I told my uncle about the decision I had reached. He couldn't have been kinder, but he flatly refused to give me his permission—I wasn't to raise the subject of my vocation with him till I had turned seventeen. It would be the height of imprudence, he said, to admit a child of fifteen to the life of Carmel, which by general consent was a life of mature reflection, whereas I had no experience of the world. What *would* people say? He assured me that nothing short of a miracle would induce him to let me go. I could see that argument would be useless, so I left him with a sense of overwhelming disappointment, and took refuge in prayer. What could I do but ask our Lord to perform this miracle which was the condition of my answering his call?

I couldn't raise the question with my uncle again all at once; I shrank from the effort of going to see him. At the time, I thought he'd dismissed it from his mind, though I found out later that the acute distress I shewed had told in my favour. Before any rift appeared in the clouds, I went through an ordeal which lasted three whole days, as if to make me realise something of the grief felt by our Lady and St. Joseph when they had to go in search of the Child Jesus. It was a pilgrimage through the desert; or let's say, rather, that my soul was like a cock-boat with no pilot on board, at the mercy of the storm. Oh yes, I knew that our Lord was there, a Passenger on my frail barque, but I couldn't catch sight of him. There wasn't so much as a lightning-flash to pierce the clouds—if only the storm would have burst, to let me see him for a moment even by that ominous light! But no, it was night everywhere, a deep night enfolding my soul; I felt, like our Lord in his Agony, that I was quite alone, without anything in heaven or on earth to console me; God himself seemed to have abandoned me. All those three days nature itself seemed to be in tune with my state of mind; there was never a ray of sunshine, and the rain fell in torrents. At all the critical moments of my life, I've found that nature seemed to be the mirror of my own soul's condition: heaven shed tears in sympathy with mine, and a cloudless sun shone brightly on my days of happiness.

The fourth day came, a Saturday (our Lady's day), and I went round to see my uncle. To my surprise, he looked hard at me and took me into his study before I'd had time to suggest it. He began by rallying me gently on being afraid of him: then he said there was no need to go on praying for a miracle—he'd asked God to make up his mind for him, and his prayer had been answered. And, sure enough, I stopped praying for a miracle, because the miracle had already happened; by uncle was a different person. Nothing about prudence now; he said I was a flower God had decided to pick while it was still in the bud, and he wasn't going to stand in the way. That was his considered answer, and it was worthy of him; for the third time, he'd allowed one of the nieces he loved like daughters to bury herself away from the world; his was the faith of the first Christians. My aunt, too, how grateful I was for her kindness and tact! All through this difficult time she never said a word to make things worse; and yet when she added her consent to my uncle's, she betrayed in a hundred ways what a grief it really was to her. And they didn't know, then, that they'd be called upon to make the same sacrifice twice more. But God, when he asks for these sacrifices, never comes empty-handed; he makes a present to his friends of the strength and courage they need. But I mustn't let my feelings run away with me; I must return, as best I can, to my story.

Light of heart, I made my way back to Les Buissonnets, under a sky no longer clouded. The night was over; our Lord had woken and brought joy into my heart again, stilling the roar of the waves. I felt as if a light breeze now filled my sails, and it couldn't be long before I reached the shore that was in full sight. Sure enough, he hadn't deserted me; but there were still storms to be encountered—storms that would hide the friendly blaze of the lighthouse and threaten me with the prospect of drifting away altogether from the shore I longed to reach. It was only a few days after my uncle had given his consent that I went round to see you, dear Mother, and give you the glad news that all my trials were at an end. Imagine my surprise and disappointment when you told me that the priest who was ecclesiastical superior of the convent wouldn't admit me before I was twenty-one!

Here was the most resolute opposition I had to meet with, and it came from an unexpected quarter. But I didn't lose my courage; I went round with Papa and Céline to see Father Superior myself, in the hope that I could move him to pity by shewing that I really had got a Carmelite vocation. He received us rather coldly, and nothing could be got out of him, even when Papa—how splendid he was!—came out in support of my apppeal. No, there was no danger in delay; I could perfectly well lead a Carmelite life at home; I wouldn't be able to take the discipline, perhaps, but that wouldn't mean that all was lost. He ended up by saying that he was only the Bishop's delegate; if the Bishop approved of my entering Carmel he, personally, would have nothing more to say. I left the presbytery in a flood of tears, glad to find that it was now raining heavily, and I could hide my face with my umbrella. Papa didn't know how to comfort me; he could only promise to take me to Bayeux whenever I wanted. I was so determined to carry my point that I said I'd go to the Holy Father himself if the Bishop wouldn't let me enter Carmel at fifteen.

Chapter XVIII

THE VISIT TO THE BISHOP

MEANWHILE, a good deal was happening, although externally my life was much the same; I went on with my studies, and had drawing lessons from Céline, a clever mistress, who found me an apt pupil. But all the time I was growing up: above all in the love of God. I was conscious of new stirrings in my heart—sometimes, real transports of love. I remember one evening when I was at a loss to tell our Lord how much I loved him, and wanted him to be honoured and loved; how terrible, I thought, that no act of love is ever made in hell! And I told God that I was ready to go there myself, if it pleased him to contrive, in that way, that for all eternity there should be one loving soul in that abode of blasphemy. I knew really, of course, that it wouldn't do; that nothing glorifies him except what fulfils his desire for our happiness; but lovers can't get on without these fond expressions. The point was, not that I didn't long for heaven; but Love was the heaven I looked forward to, and I felt sure, like St. Paul,[1] that nothing could separate me from the divine Person who inspired it.

Before I left the world, God gave me an opportunity which the youngest of a family doesn't often get—that of first-hand acquaintance with the souls of little children. It came about in a tragic way; a relation of our maid died quite young, leaving a family of three babies; and during her illness we took in the two little girls, the elder of them not yet six. I took charge of them all day, and was delighted by the simplicity with which they drank in the things I had to tell them. What deep roots they strike, these theological virtues which baptism implants in us! Even at that age we're ready to make sacrifices for the sake of a reward in the world to come. When I wanted to persuade my two babies to be nice to one another,

[1] Romans 8, 39.

I didn't promise them toys or sweets to make them come down off their high horse: I just told them about the Child Jesus in heaven and the rewards he had waiting for good little girls there. Whereupon the elder, who was beginning to reach the age of reason, looked at me with shining eyes, asked me all sorts of questions about the Child Jesus and Heaven, and readily undertook to let her sister always have her own way. All her life, she said, she'd never forget what the " tall young lady " had told her.

Seeing these innocent souls at close quarters, I realised what a mistake it is not to train them from the very start, when they are like wax to receive impressions for better or worse: I saw what our Lord meant about hurting the conscience of " one of these little ones."[1] There are so many souls which would attain sanctity, if only they were well directed. True, God doesn't stand in need of our help. But he gives a clever gardener the chance and the skill to raise some rare and delicate plant, even though the growth comes from him: why shouldn't our Lord do the same with souls? A clumsy gardener who tried to go in for grafting without knowing the plants he was dealing with, and tried to make roses grow on a peach-tree, would merely be spoiling a good tree. And it *is* important to find out from the first what claim God is making on this or that soul, and follow up the action of his grace without hurry or neglect.

Children learn the secret of holiness—that is, the song of divine love—from those who are entrusted with their education just as birds learn to sing by listening to the parent bird. I had a canary once that sang to perfection; and at the same time I had a linnet which I tended with great care because I'd taken charge of it before it could fly. Born to captivity, it had no parents to learn from; but when it heard the canary trilling all day, it tried to follow suit. Not easy for a linnet; his gentle voice wasn't up to the shrill notes of his music-master. It was touching to witness his efforts, but they succeeded in the end; without losing the sweetness of his voice, he sang in canary fashion. Dear Mother, it was you who taught me to sing, from childhood upwards, it was your voice that thrilled me; and it's splendid, nowadays, to hear people

[1] Matthew 18, 6.

say that I remind them of you! Not that I'm in the least like you really; but I do hope, with all my disabilities, to join my song with yours in eternity.

But I mustn't linger any more over the experiences I had or the bad times I went through before entering Carmel. Let's get back to the story of my vocation. On the appointed day, the 31st of October, I went off to Bayeux alone with Papa, in high hopes, but appalled at the idea of calling on a Bishop—a Bishop, when I'd never paid a call without my sisters in my life! In a general way, I could always keep quiet until I was asked questions; this time, I'd got to explain what I'd come about, set out in full my reasons for wanting to enter Carmel; shew proof, in fact, that my sense of vocation rested on solid ground. What wouldn't I have given to get out of it! But God must have given me special grace to overcome my shyness. And it's true, of course, that "Love never pleads inability: to Love, everything seems possible and everything seems allowable":[1] it was only love of our Lord which enabled me to surmount these difficulties, and those subsequent difficulties which were the high price I paid for my vocation. A high price, I say; but now that I'm inside Carmel, under the cool shade of the presence I have longed for so eagerly,[2] I realise that I've bought my happiness ever so cheap: and I'd be prepared to go through any number of further trials if it was still to be won.

We reached Bayeux in torrents of rain: Papa wasn't going to let his little princess knock at the Bishop's door with her best clothes wringing wet, so we took an omnibus to the Cathedral. Our bad luck started at once; the Bishop and his clergy were assisting at a big funeral, and the church was full of ladies in mourning; and there was I in a light-coloured dress and a white hat, with everybody looking round at me. There was no question of leaving the church while it was raining like that; and, to make things worse, Papa, with a kind of patriarchal simplicity, took me right up to the front. To save his feelings, I had to follow him with the best grace I could, and I'm afraid I was a severe distraction to the pious folk of Bayeux, whom I never wanted to see again. In the end I did find a chapel right behind the high altar, where I could breathe freely: here I spent my time praying hard till

[1] *Imitation of Christ*, III, v, 4.   [2] Canticles II, 3.

the rain stopped and allowed us to get away. Papa called my attention to the beauty of the church as we passed through it and it did look much more splendid now that it was empty; but I was in no mood for admiring things.

We went straight round to find M. Révérony, who was expecting us, because he'd fixed the date himself, but was out at the moment. I didn't think much of the streets in which we wandered about, nor did I do much justice to the skill of the cook in a fine hotel where Papa entertained me, close to the Palace.* Dear Papa, he was so sweet to me, telling me not to worry, because the Bishop was sure to do what I wanted. So we rested a bit, and made a fresh start to find M. Révérony; this time, there was another gentleman waiting on the doorstep; but he was asked, with the Vicar-General's compliments, to wait a bit, and we went in first. (Poor man, he must have had a tiresome wait; ours wasn't a short interview.) M. Révérony was kindness itself, but he seemed rather surprised at the reason for our visit: he looked at me with a smile and put several questions to me, then he said: " Come this way, and I'll introduce you to his Lordship." And then, seeing the tears starting to my eyes, he added: " Now then, no diamonds, please; his Lordship wouldn't like to see that." So he took us through several enormous rooms, hung with episcopal portraits; the size of them made me feel no bigger than an ant, and I wondered what on earth I was going to say to the Bishop.

There he was, talking to two priests in a long gallery; a word or two passed between him and the Vicar-General, and then they came back together to the study where we were waiting for them, with three huge armchairs in it that faced a blazing fire. As his Lordship came in, Papa knelt down beside me to receive his blessing; then they sat down, one on each side of the fireplace. What was to be done about the armchair in the middle? I was polite enough to refuse when M. Révérony offered it to me, but he insisted; wasn't I there to shew that I knew how to obey orders? So I sat down without thinking about it any more, and was horrified to see him take an ordinary chair, while I was ensconced in an armchair that would have held four people of my size quite comfortably—not that I felt comfortable in the least. I hoped that Papa would set the ball rolling, but he told me to explain the purpose of our visit for myself. You may be sure that I laid on all the eloquence at my disposal; but the Bishop had been treated to plenty of eloquence before, and didn't seem much impressed by my arguments. If only I could have produced a word of support from the Superior, it would have done more good, but I couldn't; and opposition from that quarter told heavily against me.

The Bishop asked me if it was a long time since I first thought of becoming a Carmelite: "Oh, yes, *Monseigneur*," I replied, "a long, long time." "Oh, come," said M. Révérony, laughing, "you're not going to tell us it was as long as fifteen years." I smiled back at him as I answered: "That's true, but there aren't many years to count out; you see, ever since the age of reason I've wanted to be a nun, and I've set my heart on Carmel ever since I got to know it well, because I felt sure it was the place where my soul's longings would be set at rest." (I can't answer for the actual words I used, Mother; I expect I put it even worse than that, but I've given you the general sense.) The Bishop, meanwhile, was looking at it from my father's point of view; surely I ought to stay at home and be a comfort to him for several years yet? You can imagine how astonished and how impressed he was when Papa took my side, pleading for me to be allowed to leave home at fifteen! But of course it was all no use; before he made up his mind, the Bishop said, he must have a talk with the Father Superior; nothing could be done without that.

This was the worst news I could have had; I was up against a brick wall there. Regardless of what M. Révérony had said, I not only let his Lordship see the diamonds in my eyes, I treated him to a shower of them. He was touched, I could see that; he put his arm round my neck and let my head rest on his shoulders, petting me with a fondness he'd never shewn, I was told, for anybody else. After all, there was hope yet; he thought it was a good idea my going to Rome, because it would help to strengthen my resolution; I'd much more to be cheerful about than to cry over. He'd be going to Lisieux the following week, and he'd see the Curé of Saint-Jacques about me: his answer would reach me in Italy without fail. With that I had to be content; even if there'd been any use in

further remonstrances, I'd none to make; all my treasured
eloquence had dried up.

The Bishop took us back as far as the garden, and was
hugely amused when Papa told him I'd put my hair up for
the occasion, to make myself look older. This wasn't forgotten; the Bishop never talked about "that little daughter of
mine" without telling the story about my hair. M. Révérony
went with us to the end of the garden: "It's unheard-of," he
said, "a father being as eager to sacrifice his daughter as she
is to sacrifice herself." Papa asked him several questions
about the pilgrimage; how did one dress for the audience, for
example? I can still see him turning round in front of M.
Révérony and asking: "Would I do like this?" He had
told the Bishop, by the way, that if he didn't let me enter
Carmel I would ask leave from the Holy Father instead. All
Papa's words and gestures were quite unstudied, but he was
such a fine figure of a man, with so much natural dignity
about him, that the Bishop couldn't help being impressed.
(He, the Bishop, was accustomed to meet people with good
drawing-room manners; but it was something new for him
to meet "the King of France and Navarre" with his little
princess!)

Back in the street, I started crying again; not so much over
my own disappointment as over Papa's unsuccessful journey
—he'd set his heart on sending a telegram to Carmel to
announce the Bishop's favourable reply, and now he was
coming home with nothing to report. That was a bad time
with me: all my plans for the future seemed wrecked; the
more I got to grips with the situation, the worse things went.
A time of great sadness, but of peace all the same: I wanted
God's will, nothing else.* Once I was at Lisieux, I went to
Carmel for consolation, and it was you, Mother, who gave it
me. I shall never forget what you've suffered by your sympathy with me; if I wasn't afraid of being irreverent, I'd
apply to you what our Lord said to the Apostles before his
Passion: "You . . . have kept to my side in the hour of trial."[1]
And my dear sisters, what a comfort they were!

[1] Luke 22, 28.

Chapter XIX

THE JOURNEY TO ITALY

THREE DAYS after this, I had a much longer journey to make, all the way to Rome. What a journey! It taught me more clearly than I could have learned from long years of study how this world we live in is a world of shadows, lost labour all of it, here under the sun.[1] Not that I didn't see sights of great beauty, wonderful legacies of art and piety: nay, I was privileged to tread the same holy ground as the Apostles, ground that had been drenched in the blood of the martyrs, and all this contact with sacred things widened the horizons of my soul. I'm very glad I went to Rome; but at the same time I can quite understand how worldly-minded friends came to imagine that Papa had taken me on my travels to make me think better of leaving the world—it might easily have shaken a less determined resolution. You see, the pilgrims mostly belonged to the world of high society, which was a quite new experience for Céline and me. But we weren't dazzled by it at all, these titles and handles to people's names, we felt, were so much smoke. At a distance, I'd sometimes been taken in by these pretensions, but on a close view all wasn't gold that glittered; I could understand what the *Imitation* means when it says: " Don't be taken up with the shadow of some name that once was great, or with having a long visiting-list, or with enjoying the intimacy of any human being."[2] I realised that true greatness lies in the dispositions of your soul, not in the name you inherit; after all, doesn't Isaias tell us that God will find a new name for his elect?[3] Doesn't St. John say the same thing: " Who wins the victory? I will . . . give him a white stone, on which stone a new name is written, known to him only who receives it?"[4] It's only in heaven that we shall be given our patents of nobility. It's then that each of us will receive his due award

[1] Ecclesiastes 2, 11.   [2] *Imitation of Christ*, III, xxiv, 2.
[3] Isaias 65, 15.   [4] Apocalypse 2, 17.

from God;[1] poverty and neglect endured here for the love of Christ will make a man take high rank there, make him noble and rich.

Another discovery I made: about priests. I'd never been in close touch with them, and I'd been puzzled about the chief object for which the Reformed Carmelites exist. Pray for sinners by all means, but why priests? Surely their souls were like flawless crystal already: it bothered me. Well, that journey to Italy justified itself, if only by throwing a side-light on my vocation. I mean, I lived for a month among a lot of good holy priests, and came to realise that although their high office makes them take rank above the angels, they have their frailties and their weaknesses like other men. And these were good holy priests, "the salt of the earth"; if such people need our prayers, and need them badly, what about the priests who have gone slack? "If salt loses its taste," our Lord asks, "what is there left to give taste to it?"[2] I see now, Mother, what a wonderful vocation it is to aim (as we Carmelites do) at preserving the tang of the salt which is going to preserve men's souls. To evangelise the evangelists—that's the chief object of all the prayers we offer and all the sacrifices we make: we've got to pray for them while they're busy bringing souls to Christ by their preaching, and still more by their example. Well, I mustn't go on about that: I should never stop.

And now, dear Mother, I'm going to tell you traveller's tales; too many of them, I dare say, and I can't answer for it that they won't bore you—I can't plan out what I'm going to write beforehand, because it all has to be done at odd moments in my free time. Thank goodness there'll be plenty of time in heaven to tell you about all the mercies that have been granted to me; we shan't be interrupted then, and you'll be able to see the whole thing at a glance. In the meanwhile, as I've got to use this clumsy earth-language, I'll tell you the story as it comes to me, like a child which knows that its mother is going to make a good audience.

The pilgrimage didn't start from Paris till the seventh of November, but Papa took us there a day or two ahead of time, to see the sights. I was more asleep than awake as we passed through Lisieux at three o'clock in the morning, but there were thoughts racing through my brain, about going out into the unknown, and the adventures that awaited me there. Papa was in excellent spirits: when the train started, I remember he began singing the old-fashioned refrain:

> "Here we spin on the broad highway
> Spanking along in my old chay."

Sight-seeing began as soon as we reached Paris; dear Papa would spare no effort to amuse us, and it looked as if we should have worked through all the wonders of the capital in no time. There was only one of them that really took me out of myself, and that was Notre Dame des Victoires. I can't describe what I felt, kneeling in front of the statue; I was so full of gratitude that it could only find its outlet (just as on my first Communion day) in tears. Our Lady gave me the assurance that she really had smiled at me, really had effected my cure; I knew then that she really was watching over me, that I was her child—I began calling her "Mamma," because "Mother" didn't seem intimate enough. Oh, I prayed so hard that she would go on looking after me, and would make my dream come true before long by taking me under the protection of her stainless robe. I'd wanted that, from my earliest years, and as I grew up I'd come to realise that, for me, Carmel was the only place where that shelter could be found.

This, too, I asked of our Lady of Victories, that she would keep me clear of anything that might tarnish the purity of my mind. I realised that on a long journey like this I might come across sights and sounds capable of disturbing my conscience. I dreaded the encounter of evil things which were still a closed book to me; I had yet to be taught by experience that nothing can be unclean for those who have clean hearts;[1] a simple upright soul doesn't find harm in anything, because the harm lies in our own guilty consciences, not in the senseless objects that surround us. I prayed to St. Joseph with the same intention; I had a devotion towards him which was closely bound up with my love for our Lady; so I said, each day, the prayer which begins, "St. Joseph, father and guardian

[1] Titus 1, 15.

of virginity," and felt that I could undertake my long travels
without fear under such patronage.

We started early on the morning of the 7th, after visiting
the basilica of Montmartre and consecrating ourselves there to
the Sacred Heart. It wasn't long before we got to know our
fellow-pilgrims; I was usually shy and tongue-tied in the
presence of strangers, but this tiresome disability seemed to
have disappeared completely. To my surprise, I found myself
talking quite freely to society ladies, to priests, and even to
the Bishop of Coutances himself; it was as if I'd always lived
in a world like that. I think we were generally popular;
Papa seemed proud of his two daughters, and on our side we
were equally proud of him; there was no finer figure of a
man in the company. He liked to have Céline and me with
him; and when, at some halt on the journey, he saw me at a
distance, he would call me to him and give me his arm as if
we were back at Lisieux. As for M. Révérony, he kept a
shrewd eye on all that I did; I'd see him looking at me from
a distance, and when I wasn't facing him at table he'd
manage to lean forward and get a look at me, or listen to
what I said. His curiosity was natural; he wanted to know if
I really was fit for the Carmelite life, and I think he must
have given me good marks, because by the end of the
journey he was on my side (though he didn't do me much
good in Rome, as you shall hear).

Rome was our goal, but there were plenty of wonderful
experiences on the way there. Switzerland, where the moun-
tain-tops are lost in cloud, with its graceful pattern of water-
falls, its deep valleys where the ferns grow so high and the
heather shews so red! How deeply it affected me, this lavish
display of natural beauty! That God should have seen fit to
squander such masterpieces on a world of exile, an ephemeral
world like this! I was all eyes as I stood there, breathless, at
the carriage-door; I wished I could have been on both sides of
the compartment at once, so different was the scenery when
you turned to look in the other direction. Now we were on
the mountain-side, with a bottomless chasm beneath ready to
engulf us; now we would pass some delightful village, its
chalets and its church-tower covered with a soft canopy of
snow-white cloud, or a wide lake at evening, with its calm

surface reflecting at once the blue sky and the glow of sunset, till it had all the beauty of fairyland. Far away on the horizon we could see the great mountains, shadowy in outline except where their snow-clad tops shewed dazzling in the sun, to complete the splendour of the view.

The sight of these beauties made a deep impression on my thoughts; I felt as if I were already beginning to understand the greatness of God and the wonders of heaven. I saw the religious life, too, as it really is—the surrender of your own will, the unregarded sacrifices you make on a small scale; how easy it must be to get wrapped up in yourself and lose sight of your high vocation. "Later on," I thought, "when the testing time comes, I shall be shut up within the four walls of Carmel, and my outlook will be restricted to a small corner of this starry sky. Very well, then, I shall be able to remember the sights I'm looking at now, and that will give me courage. I shall find it easier to forget my own unimportant concerns as I contemplate, in the mind's eye, the greatness and power of the God whom I try to love above all things. No attraction for me about the puppet-shows of earth, now that I've had this foretaste of what our Lord has in store for those who love him."

So much for the sight of God's power in creation; and now we were to admire the capacities with which he's endowed his human creatures. Our first stop in Italy was at Milan, where we explored every nook and cranny of the marble cathedral, manned by a whole army of statues. Céline and I had no inhibitions at all; we were always in front, at the heels of the Bishop, determined to see all there was to be seen of the relics, and listen to all that was said about them. Even when he said Mass at the tomb of St. Charles we were there, with Papa, close behind the altar, leaning our heads against the coffin where the Saint lies in all his pontificals. It was like that everywhere, except where places unsuitable to a Bishop's dignity were in question; then we had the sense to leave him alone. We were among the intrepid pilgrims who climbed up the very highest of the marble towers, while the nervous ladies stopped at the first stage and put their hands over their eyes; it was wonderful to see the whole of Milan at your feet, with all the passers-by looking no bigger than ants. And so we came down from those dizzy heights, to start on a round of carriage expeditions which were to go on for a month—it quite cured me of all desire to spin easily along the broad highway!

We found ourselves even more delighted with the Campo Santo. They looked all the better, these white marble statues, brought to life by the artist's chisel, for being strewn haphazard up and down the huge cemetery. You felt you wanted to offer them your sympathy, these men and women of stone; so life-like were they, so calm and resigned in the expression of grief. How the thought of immortality must have dominated their minds, the artists who could produce such masterpieces! That child over there, throwing flowers on the grave of its parents, you would swear that the marble had lost all its weight, so lightly do the petals seem to slip through his fingers. You would swear that the wind was scattering them as they fell, just as it seems to blow back, here a widow's veil, there the ribbons that bind the hair of a young girl. Papa shared our delight; in Switzerland he had been rather tired, but now his good spirits had returned, and he could enjoy the beauty of the scene as much as we did. He had the soul of an artist, and there was no mistaking the devout admiration which lit up his handsome features.

One old gentleman, and a Frenchman at that, seemed to have less poetry about him; he looked askance at us, as if to say he was sorry he couldn't share our appreciation, and said in a very ill-tempered voice: "Really, the way these French people lose their heads!" Poor old gentleman, I think he would have done better to stay at home, because he didn't seem to enjoy his travels a bit. We often found him near us, and always with a complaint on his lips; he didn't like the carriages, the hotels, the people he met, the towns we went through—nothing was good enough for him. Papa, generous as usual, was always trying to cheer him up by offering to exchange places and so on; he, Papa, knew how to make himself at home everywhere, in complete contrast with this disagreeable neighbour of ours. One saw so many different sides of human character: what a fascinating study the world is, when you are just going to say good-bye to it!

When we got to Venice it was a complete change of scene: the bustle of great towns was left behind us, and the silence was only broken by the cries of gondoliers and the plashing of their oars. Venice, for all its charm, struck me as a melancholy place. Even the palace of the Doges, its huge rooms with their treasures of gold and carved wood and marble, with their masterpieces of painting, has something melancholy about it—so many years now, since those vaulted rooms echoed with the sentence of life or death passed by those stern rulers! Poor prisoners, they no longer have to suffer in those cells, those dungeons buried away underground! When we went round these horrible places of confinement, it carried me back to the days of the martyrs; and I would gladly have stayed there for a bit to see what it was like. But no, it was time for us now to cross the Bridge of Sighs—sighs of relief, we were told, when these wretched men exchanged their underground prisons for the welcome alternative of death.

We left Venice for Padua, where we venerated the tongue of St. Antony, and Bologna, where the body of St. Catherine still shews the mark of the kiss the Child Jesus imprinted on it. But if I stopped to mention all the interesting features of all the towns we visited, all the details of our pilgrimage, I should go on for ever; I must confine myself to the chief landmarks of our journey.

St. Thérèse

Thérèse's writing desk

Thérèse (left) doing the washing

...me sentir le courage de parler !... Cependant il fallait me décider, j'allais
avoir quatorze ans et demi, six mois seulement nous séparaient encore de la
nuit de Noël où j'avais résolu d'entrer à l'heure même où l'année précédente
se fit ma grâce [1]... Pour faire ma grande confidence je choisis le jour de la
Pentecôte. toute la journée je suppliai les Sts Apôtres de prier pour moi, de m'in-
spirer les paroles que j'allais avoir à dire... N'était-ce pas en effet qui devaient
enfant timide que Dieu destinait à devenir l'apôtre des apôtres par la prière
et le sacrifice !... Ce ne fut que l'après-midi en revenant des Vêpres que je trouvai
l'occasion de parler à mon petit Père chéri, il était allé s'asseoir au bord de la
[...] là, les mains jointes, il contemplait les merveilles de la nature. le soleil d[ont]
les rayons adoucis perdaient leur ardeur dorait le sommet des grands arbres, où les
petits oiseaux chantaient joyeusement leur prière du soir. La belle figure de Pa[pa]
avait une expression céleste, je sentais que la paix inondait son cœur ; sans
dire un seul mot j'allai m'asseoir à ses côtés les yeux déjà mouillés de larmes, il me
regarda avec tendresse et prenant ma tête il l'appuya sur son cœur, me di-
sant : "Qu'as-tu ma petite reine ?... confie-moi cela ... ." Puis se levant, comme pour
cacher sa propre émotion, il marcha lentement tenant toujours ma tête sur
son cœur. A travers mes larmes je lui confiai mon désir d'entrer au Carmel, alors
ses larmes vinrent se mêler aux miennes, mais il ne dit pas un mot pour me
détourner de ma vocation se contentant simplement de me faire remarquer que
j'étais bien jeune pour prendre une détermination aussi grave. Mais je défend-
is si bien ma cause, qu'avec la nature simple et droite de Papa, il fut bientôt
persuadé que mon désir était celui de Dieu lui-même et dans sa foi profon-
de il s'écria que le Bon Dieu lui faisait un grand honneur de lui de-
mander ses enfants. nous continuâmes longtemps notre promenade, mon cœur sou-
lagé par la bonté avec laquelle mon incomparable Père avait accueilli ses confidenc[es]

Thérèse's handwriting

Chapter XX

SIGHT-SEEING IN ROME

I WAS GLAD to leave Bologna; it was entirely spoilt for me by
the University students who crowded its streets and hedged
us in whenever we went about on foot—especially by a brief
encounter I had with one of them.[1] It was a great relief to
find ourselves on the way to Loreto; no wonder our Lady
chose this spot for the resting-place of the Holy House, a
town in which peace and joy and poverty reign undisturbed.
The women there keep up the old national dress, instead of
imitating Paris fashions as they do in other towns. Altogether,
Loreto appealed to me, and as for the House, I can't tell you
how deeply I was moved to share the same roof, as it were,
with the Holy Family. On these walls our divine Redeemer
had gazed; on this ground the sweat had fallen from Joseph's
brow; here Mary had carried, in and out, the Child of her
virginal womb. To have seen the little room in which the
angel greeted her, to have put down my rosary-beads for a
moment in the bowl from which the Child Jesus had eaten—
those are things you can't remember without a thrill.

Best of all, we received our Blessed Lord there in his own
house; became his living temples on the very spot which had
been consecrated by his earthly presence. The Italian custom
is to have the Blessed Sacrament reserved on one single
altar, which is the only one at which you can make your
Communion. Here at Loreto, where the basilica is only a
marble casket in which the Holy House reposes like a precious
diamond, the Blessed Sacrament altar is outside the sacred
enclosure. This wouldn't do for Céline and me; we wanted
to go to Communion inside. So we left Papa to do as the
rest of the world did, like the gentle soul he was, and went off
to find a priest belonging to our party who had got special
leave to say Mass in the Holy House itself; it was just a matter

[1] When she arrived at Bologna, Thérèse was lifted down from the
train to the platform by one of these students, to her great disgust.

129

of getting him to put two small Hosts on the paten, and
there were we, fortunate enough to make our Communion on
this hallowed ground. This was a blessing straight from
heaven; no words can do justice to our feelings. It was a foretaste of that moment when we shall be made one with our
Lord in that other, eternal dwelling-place of his; when our
joy will be unending, when there will be no more sadness
of saying good-bye, no need to scrape* a fragment or two
from walls sanctified by a divine presence, because his home
will be our home for all eternity. He just lets us have a look
at his earthly home, to make us love poverty and the hidden
life; what he keeps in store for us is his heavenly palace,
where we shall no longer see him hidden under the form of
a little child, or of a consecrated Host, but as he really is, in
all the splendour of his majesty.

It remains for me to say something about Rome, the goal
of our journey; Rome, where I had hoped to find consolation,
and found only a cross. We got there at night, and were
woken by the porters shouting: "Roma, Roma!"—no, it
wasn't a dream, we were really there. We spent our first day
outside the walls, and in some way it was the most enjoyable;
round the city, the ruins keep the stamp of antiquity, whereas
in the centre it's all big shops and hotels, just like Paris. That
drive through the Campagna is a cherished memory; but I
mustn't attempt to give any account of the places we visited,
which are all in the guide-books; I must be content to record
the chief impression I carried away. One of these was the
thrill of setting eyes on the Colosseum; the arena in which so
many martyrs had shed their blood for Christ—at last I should
be able to kneel and kiss that holy ground! But a cruel disappointment awaited me; the centre of the building is no
better than a mass of fallen masonry, which the unfortunate
pilgrim has to contemplate from behind a barrier—and indeed
it is such a litter of ruins that there's not much temptation to
do anything else. Was I to come away from Rome without
ever going down into the arena of the Colosseum? No, I
couldn't bear the idea; the guide's explanations fell on deaf
ears—I must get down, get down. I even thought of asking a
workman who was passing by to lend me his ladder; it was
lucky I didn't, because he'd have thought I was raving.

We're told in the gospel that the Magdalen looked down

into the tomb several times before the two angels appeared to her.[1] It was the same with me; baulked of my hopes, I kept on looking down into the ruins and (without seeing any angels) found at last what I wanted: "Quick, Céline," I shouted happily, "we can get down here!" In a moment we had clambered over the barrier, at a point where the fallen masonry reached right up to it; and there we were climbing down across the ruins, which gave at every step, while Papa looked on, astonished at our daring. It wasn't long before he told us to come back, but the two truants were out of earshot; like soldiers buoyed up by the thought of danger, we were encouraged by the bruises we got in the process. Céline had had the sense to listen to the guide, and heard him describe a particular bit of criss-cross pavement as the place where the martyrs actually suffered; before long she found it, and we were kneeling beside it, twin souls with a single thought. How fast my heart was beating as my lips touched the dust that had been consecrated by the blood of those first Christians! I asked for the grace to bear a martyr's witness to our Lord, and felt deep in my heart that the prayer had been granted.

The whole thing didn't take long; we picked up a stone or two, and then we were back at the foot of the crumbling wall, starting out again on our adventurous climb. We were so obviously happy that Papa didn't like to scold us; indeed, I could see that he was rather proud of our enterprise. Heaven was manifestly on our side, because the other pilgrims hadn't noticed our absence; they had passed farther along, and were no doubt gazing up at the splendid arches, with the guide calling attention to the little cornices carrying figures of Cupids—neither he nor our clerical friends could guess the secret of our happiness.

I have gracious memories, too, of the Catacombs; they came up to all the expectations I had formed of them in reading the lives of the martyrs. We spent a good deal of the afternoon there; but the atmosphere of the place is so charged with associations that I felt as if we'd only been there for a

[1] The statement that the Magdalen looked down into the tomb several times is perhaps a reminiscence of some sermon or some devotional treatise. The gospel account (John 20, 11-12) hardly seems to justify it.

few minutes. Of course we couldn't leave the Catacombs without taking away a souvenir; so we waited, Céline and I, till the procession had moved on a bit, and crept down right to the bottom of the tomb where St. Cecilia was buried, to carry off some of the earth which was hallowed by her presence. Until I made this pilgrimage to Rome, I'd never had any special devotion for St. Cecilia; but now I had the chance of visiting her house, which has become a church, the actual scene of her martyrdom. Now I learned the real reason why she had been proclaimed the patroness of music—it wasn't a question of her beautiful voice, or of her talent as a musician, but in memory of the chant she sang in the depths of her heart to the heavenly Bridegroom who dwelt concealed there.

So now I felt something more than a special devotion for St. Cecilia, a real bond of friendship with her. She became a favourite, a confidante to whom I entrusted my secrets. Everything about her attracted me, but above all the way she gave herself up into God's hands, the boundless confidence which enabled her to inspire souls hitherto so fond of worldly enjoyments with her own ideal of virginity. St. Cecilia reminds me of the bride in the Canticles; " a song in an armed camp " is such a good description of her.[1] Her whole life was a melodious song that rose above all the trials she endured; and no wonder, because she " carried the holy gospel printed on her heart "[2]—her heart, in which the divine Lover had found a resting-place.

And of course our visit to the Church of St. Agnes had a friendly meaning for me; here was a Saint who had been my friend ever since childhood, and now I was to see her in her own home. I said a great deal to her about somebody who bears her name; and I did everything I could to secure some relic of her which I could take back to you, dear Mother, at Lisieux. But the only one I managed to get was a little red stone which had somehow come loose from a rich mosaic— dating back to the time of St. Agnes, so that her eyes must

[1] The reference is to Canticles VII, 1, where, however, a dance is referred to rather than a song, apparently named " The Dance of the Two ' Camps'," or possibly " of Mahanaim."
[2] Responsory after the third lesson of St. Cecilia's feast.

often have rested on it. Dear Saint, how charming of her to
make me a present of the exact thing we were looking for, a
relic, when it was against all the rules that we should have
one! I've always thought of it as a delicate attention on her
part; a proof of the love with which this kindly Saint looks
down on my dear Mother, and protects her.

Chapter XXI

THERESE AT THE VATICAN

THEN, WHEN we'd spent six days doing the round of all the other wonderful sights in Rome, on the seventh I was taken to see the greatest of them all, Pope Leo XIII. How I looked forward to that day, and how I dreaded it! It might make all the difference to my vocation; no news had come from the Bishop, and you'd told me in a letter that I wasn't quite so much in his good books as I had been; what chance had I now, unless I could get the Holy Father's permission? And that meant asking for it; and that meant summoning up my courage to talk to the Pope! The very thought made me tremble all over—God knows what I went through awaiting that audience; nobody else does, except dear Céline. I shall never forget how she helped me through this time of trial; it might have been her own vocation that was at stake. The priests who were with us commented on the affection we shewed for one another; I remember an evening when a whole crowd of us had foregathered, and there was a shortage of chairs, so that I had to sit in Céline's lap. We made such a perfect pair that one of the priests said: "Look at those two girls, so fond of one another; they're inseparable!" Yes, we were fond of one another, but our love was so unselfish and so strong that the thought of separation didn't worry us —we knew that if we lived in separate continents we should be near one another still. It didn't cost her a pang to see me in my little cock-boat, nearing the shore of Carmel; she would stay afloat on the treacherous waves of the world as long as God wanted her to, sure of making harbour when her turn came.

On Sunday the 20th of November we put on our cere-monial dress—black, with a lace mantilla, and a large Papal medal on a ribbon of blue and white—and made our way through the Vatican to the Pope's own chapel. Eight o'clock came, and we were deeply touched to see him come in vested

134

for Mass. He gave his blessing to all the pilgrims present, then went up to the altar and said Mass with a devotion worthy of Christ's Vicar on earth—a holy father, and no mistake. How fast my heart beat, how fervently I prayed, as our Lord came to rest on earth in the hands of his own High Priest! And at the same time I had a great feeling of confidence; there were those splendid words in the gospel for the day: " Do not be afraid, you, my little flock. Your Father has determined to give you his kingdom ";[1] and could I doubt that in a short time the kingdom of Carmel would be mine? I had forgotten those other words of our Lord's about allotting a kingdom to his disciples just as his Father had allotted a kingdom to him:[2] that meant, surely, that they could only prove themselves worthy of their ambition by enduring crosses and trials. It was to be expected (he told them) that Christ should undergo sufferings, and enter so into his glory;[3] no sitting at his side until they had drunk of his own cup.[4] Well, I was to drink the cup the Holy Father gave me, a cup of bitterness, not without tears.

A second Mass followed, one of thanksgiving; then the audience began. The Pope sat in a big armchair, in a white cassock and cape, wearing a zucchetta. I got a general impression of cardinals and archbishops and bishops standing round him, but I didn't try to distinguish because I had eyes for nothing but the Holy Father himself. We passed before him one by one, each pilgrim kneeling, kissing first his foot and then his hand, and receiving his benediction; then two members of the noble guard touched him lightly on the shoulder as a warning to get up—touched the pilgrim, I mean, not the Pope; how badly I tell my story! Before I went in, I had fully resolved to speak out; but my courage began to desert me when I found M. Révérony, of all people, standing close to his right hand! And at the same moment word was passed round, as from M. Révérony, that nothing must be said, because the interview was long enough as it was. I turned round to consult dear Céline and she said: " Speak out." A moment later, there I was at the Holy Father's feet, kissing his shoe: but when he held out his hand, I clasped mine together and looked up at him with the tears starting to my

[1] Luke 12, 32.   [2] Luke 22, 29.   [3] Luke 24, 26.
[4] Matthew 20, 22.

eyes: "Most Holy Father," I said, "I've a great favour to ask of you." He bent towards me till his head was nearly touching my face, and his dark, deep-set eyes seemed to look right down into the depths of my soul. "Most Holy Father," I said, "in honour of your jubilee, I want you to let me enter the Carmelite order at fifteen." My voice must have been indistinct through emotion; so he turned to M. Révérony, who was looking at me in surprise and disapproval, and said: "I can't quite understand." If it had been God's will, M. Révérony could easily have made things all right; but no, it was all cross for me this time, no crown. "This child here," said the Vicar-General, "is anxious to enter Carmel at fifteen, and her superiors are looking into the matter at this moment." The Holy Father looked at me with great kindness, but all he said was: "Very well, my child, do what your superiors tell you." I put both my hands on his knees, and had one more try: "Yes, but if you'd say the word, Most Holy Father, everybody would agree." He fixed his eyes on me, and said, emphasising every syllable as he uttered it: "All's well, all's well; if God wants you to enter, you will." He spoke with such earnestness and such conviction that I can still hear him saying it.

His kindness gave me courage, and I wanted to go on; but the two members of the noble guard, finding that I paid no attention to their ceremonial touch, took me by the arms, and M. Révérony helped them to lift me up; I kept my arms on the Pope's knees, and they had to carry me away by main force. As they did so, His Holiness put his hand to my lips, and then raised it in blessing; he followed me with his eyes for quite a long time.* As for my own eyes, they were full of tears, and M. Révérony got quite as many diamonds as he'd had at Bayeux. Well, they carried me off (you might say) to the door, where another noble guard gave me a Papal medal. Céline, who came next to me, had witnessed the whole thing, and was almost as much distressed as I was, but she managed to ask the Holy Father to give Carmel his blessing. "Carmel has had its blessing already," said M. Révérony disapprovingly, and the Holy Father repeated, much more kindly: "Yes, Carmel has had its blessing."

When Papa had his interview, among the men of the party, M. Révérony couldn't have been nicer: "Here," he said, "is the father of two Carmelite nuns." The Pope expressed his approval by putting his hand on our dear father's head, as if marking him out for some special destiny in his Master's name. Well, he is in heaven now, the father of four Carmelite nuns; our Lord's own hand, not that of his Vicar on earth, has been laid on his forehead, not foreshadowing unhappiness, but bestowing eternal glory on his faithful servant. He, Papa, was much distressed to find me in tears at the end of my interview, and tried, without much success, to comfort me. I felt, to be sure, a great sense of peace deep down in my heart; I had done everything to satisfy God's claim on me. But on the surface I felt only disappointment; our Lord made no sign, it was as if he had withdrawn his presence altogether. Here was another day without sunshine; the blue skies of Italy were overcast with cloud, and wept with me. It was all over now; I could take no interest in my journey now that my errand was unsuccessful. And yet the Holy Father's parting words ought to have consoled me, prophetic as they were; in spite of all obstacles, God's will was accomplished—his will, not that of his creatures.

For some time past, I had indulged the fancy of offering myself up to the Child Jesus as a plaything, for him to do what he liked with me. I don't mean an expensive plaything; give a child an expensive toy, and he will sit looking at it without daring to touch it. But a toy of no value—a ball, say—is all at his disposal; he can throw it on the ground, kick it about, make a hole in it, leave it lying in a corner, or press it to his heart if he feels that way about it. In the same way, I wanted our Lord to do exactly what he liked with me: and here, in Rome, he'd taken me at my word. . . . In Rome the child Jesus made a hole in the ball to see what was inside it, and then, satisfied with that, threw the ball away and went to sleep. Who's to tell us what the child was dreaming about, while the ball lay there neglected? Perhaps he dreamed that he was still playing with it, first dropping it and then picking it up, letting it roll a long way away and then pressing it to his heart, to make sure that it never slipped from his hand again. Yes, he can do just what he likes; but you see, Mother, it's a depressing sensation to feel you're like the ball that's been thrown on one side.

Chapter XXII

THE RETURN JOURNEY

ALL THE SAME, I went on hoping against hope. A few days after the audience, Papa went to see Brother Simeon;[1] another visitor was M. Révérony, who was very gracious to him. Papa rallied him about having done nothing to help me over my difficulties, and then started telling Brother Simeon all about me. The holy old man seemed deeply interested, even taking notes of the story, and saying, in a voice full of emotion: "You don't get Italian girls like that." I think this interview must have had a considerable effect on M. Révérony, who shewed signs, from then on, of being at last convinced about my vocation. Next day, we started early in the morning for Naples and Pompeii. Vesuvius obliged us by keeping up a regular cannonade all day, and producing a thick column of smoke. There's something terrifying about the traces of its activity left on Pompeii; what a proof of God's power! "A glance from him makes earth tremble; at his touch, the mountains are wreathed in smoke."[2] But there was no opportunity of taking a solitary walk among the ruins, and meditating on the uncertainty of our human lot: too many tourists about, so that the melancholy effect of the ruined city was spoilt. Things were better at Naples; there were plenty of two-horsed carriages waiting to take us up, in style, to the monastery of San Martino, set on a hill which dominates the town. But oh dear, the horses! They kept on taking the bit between their teeth, and several times I felt as if my last moment had come. It was no use the coachmen repeating the magic formula: "Appipau, appipau!" which seems universal in Italy; the poor horses still did their best to upset the carriage, and it was only the help of our guardian angels which brought us safe to our magnificent hotel.

[1] Brother of the Christian Schools, a prominent figure at this time among the French colony in Rome.
[2] Psalm 103, 32.

I should explain that all through our journey we were put up at first-class hotels: I've never enjoyed so much luxury in all my life. But, as we all know, there are things money can't buy; if only I could have felt certain of Carmel, I could have been happy enough in a thatched cottage, but there was no balm for a bruised heart in gilded ceilings, marble staircases, and silk hangings! I don't need to be told that happiness lies in the depths of the heart, not in outward circumstances; a prison or a palace, it makes no difference. How much more contented I am here in Carmel, with all the inward and outward trials such a life involves, than I could be in the world with all the advantages it has to offer, and, not least, the charms of home!

I was going through a bad time, but I didn't show it, because I still imagined that the petition I'd made to the Holy Father had gone unnoticed. I found out before long that I was mistaken about this. Céline and I were left alone in the carriage at a halt on the journey, and the other pilgrims had gone off to the refreshment-room, when suddenly M. Legoux, the Vicar-General of Coutances, put his head in and asked: "How's our little Carmelite getting on?" I realised, then, that everybody was in the secret, but mercifully they didn't talk about it; and they all looked so sympathetic that I felt my appeal to the Pope had made anything but a bad impression. Do you know, at Assisi, I actually shared M. Révérony's carriage—an honour which was never granted to any of the ladies on the pilgrimage!

It happened like this. We'd been round all the scenes that are still fragrant with memories of St. Francis and St. Clare, and finished up with the convent of her sister, St. Agnes.* I'd been having a good look at the Saint's head, and was one of the last to leave. There! If I hadn't lost my belt! I went about among the crowd looking for it, and a kind priest found it for me; but he left me still hunting, because the buckle wasn't there and it was no good without that. Well, at last I saw the glint of it in a corner, and it didn't take me long to pick it up and fix it to the belt, but the hunt had been a slow business. and when I got outside the church I was surprised to find myself quite alone. All the other carriages had disappeared except M. Révérony's. What on earth was I to do? Run after the other carriages, at the risk of missing

the train and making Papa anxious about me? Or ask for a
seat in M. Révérony's fine coach? That was the course I
decided on: it meant putting on my most gracious manner
and appearing as much at ease as I could. In spite of my great
shyness, I managed to explain my awkward situation. It was
rather an embarrassment really, for him, because he'd got his
carriage full of the most important people on the pilgrimage;
no room anywhere. Fortunately a very polite gentleman came
to my rescue by getting out and letting me take his place: he
himself sat ignominiously next the driver.

I felt like a caged squirrel; you could hardly have expected
me to feel completely at my ease, with so many important
people round me, and above all that redoubtable figure opposite me. But he was very kind, breaking off his conversation
with the company now and again to say a word or two to me
about Carmel. When we got to the station, all the notabilities
started getting out their fat leather purses, to tip the cabman;
but M. Révérony wouldn't allow me to contribute any small
change out of the tiny purse I carried; he insisted on giving
a large tip for both of us. Another time, when I found
myself next to him on the omnibus, he was even more
gracious, and promised to do all he could to get me into
Carmel. Incidents of this kind did soothe my feelings a bit,
but I must admit that the journey home was a less pleasant
affair than the way out, when I was buoyed up by hopes of
what the Holy Father could do for me. I was out in the
wilderness again, with no prospect of human aid; I had to fall
back on my trust in God, realising now that it's safer to have
recourse to him than to any human agent of his.

Not that my low spirits prevented me from taking a lively
interest in the holy places we visited. At Florence I had the
happiness of seeing the body of St. Mary Magdalen de' Pazzi,
in the choir of the Carmelite church—the Carmelites actually
threw open the large grille to let us see it. We hadn't been
expecting this, and there was a general rush to touch the
Saint's tomb with our rosaries. I was the only person there
whose hand was small enough to get through the grille, and
everybody had to hand their rosary-beads to me; it was a
proud moment. I was always for touching things. At Holy
Cross church in Rome we venerated several relics of the
true Cross, as well as two of the Thorns and one of the Nails,

all enclosed in a magnificent gold reliquary with no glass in it. So when my turn came I managed to put my little finger through one of the holes, and actually touched one of the Nails which had been bathed in the precious Blood. Was it presumptuous of me? Well, God sees into the depth of our hearts, and he knew that my intentions were good, that I'd have done anything rather than offend him. I claimed the privileges of a child, that doesn't bother about asking leave, but treats all its Father's treasures as if they were its own.

I still can't understand why it's so easy for a woman to get excommunicated in Italy! All the time, people seemed to be saying: "No, you mustn't go here, you mustn't go there; you'll be excommunicated." There's no respect for us poor wretched women anywhere. And yet you'll find the love of God much commoner among women than among men, and the women during the Passion showed much more courage than the Apostles, exposing themselves to insult, and wiping our Lord's face. I suppose he lets us share the neglect he himself chose for his lot on earth; in heaven, where the last will be first, we shall know more about what God thinks. Anyhow, on this pilgrimage I was determined to be first here and now, without waiting till I got to heaven. I remember visiting a house of Carmelite friars, where everybody else kept to the outer passages, but I made my way boldly into the central cloisters. It wasn't long before I saw a dear old Carmelite making signs to me from a distance to clear out. But was I going to? No. I came up closer and pointed to the pictures round the cloister, telling him by signs how pretty they were. Well, I had my hair down and I suppose I looked rather young, so he decided that I was only a child and cleared out himself, with the kindliest of smiles. If only I had known Italian, I should have liked to tell him that I was going to be a Carmelite myself; but the tower of Babel defeated me as usual.

We went on to Pisa and Genoa, and so made our way back to France. The scenery we passed through was really magnificent; the railway ran close to the sea part of the time, and it looked as if the waves were coming right up to us—there was a storm going on, and it was late evening, which made the whole thing more impressive. Elsewhere, you saw whole fields full of orange-trees with the fruit hanging ripe on them,

green olive-trees with their fairy-like leaves, the graceful outline of the palms. After sunset, all the tiny seaports shone out
with lights, just as the first stars began to come out in the
sky. I was full of poetic thoughts at the sight of these
wonders which I was looking at for the first and last time. But
not of regrets; my heart was set on wonders greater than
these. I had seen earth's beauties, now I had no eyes but for
the beauties of heaven; and if it would help other souls to
share these with me, I was ready to shut myself away in a
prison.

Chapter XXIII

LAST DAYS AT LES BUISSONNETS

HAPPY IMPRISONMENT, how I longed for it! But the door wasn't standing open for me yet; there were to be further efforts, more frustration. I quite realised that when I got back to France, but my courage was high; I still hoped that I should be allowed to enter on Christmas Day. As soon as we reached Lisieux, our first visit was to Carmel; and what a visit that was! We had so much to say to one another after a month of absence which seemed much longer than a month; indeed, I felt years older in experience. Dear Mother, what happiness it was to see you again, to lay bare the miseries of a bruised soul to you, who understood me so well, who only needed a word or a look to tell you all my feelings! Well, there it was, I was resigned now; I'd done all I could, even talked to the Holy Father about it; I didn't know what my next step ought to be. You told me to write to the Bishop and remind him of his promise; so I did that as best I could, but my uncle thought what I'd written was too child-like, so he wrote it for me. Then, just as I was going to post it, I had a letter from you suggesting that I shouldn't write yet; I'd better wait a few days; so I did what I was told—left to myself, I felt I should go wrong. Only when time was getting on, ten days before Christmas, was the letter sent.

The answer, surely, couldn't be long in coming? Every day after Mass I went off with Papa to the post-office, thinking to find there my order of release, but each morning brought a fresh disappointment. Still my faith was unshaken; I kept on asking our Lord to set me free, and he did set me free, but not in the way I expected. Christmas Day came round, and still he gave no sign; he was like the child that lies alseep, with its toy left unnoticed on the ground.

It was with a heavy heart that I went to Midnight Mass; I had so counted on being able to hear it from behind the grille of Carmel. Yes, it was a severe trial to my faith, but our Lord's heart is still waking when he seems asleep,[1] and he gave me some light on my situation. Where there is faith " like a grain of mustard-seed," he will grant miraculous signs, will move mountains to and fro, by way of bolstering up this faith that is so weak;[2] but when it comes to his closest friends—his Mother, for example—he tests their faith by keeping them waiting for the miracle. He allows Lazarus to die, when Martha and Mary have sent warning that he is sick;[3] at Cana of Galilee, when our Lady puts the difficulties of their host before him, he tells her that his time has not come yet.[4] But what a reward he has in store for them, water turned into wine, Lazarus raised to life! Why shouldn't our Lord treat me in the same way, by keeping me waiting first and then satisfying all the dearest wishes of my heart?

I had a good cry that afternoon, Christmas Day though it was; and afterwards I went round to visit the Carmelites. What was this? The first thing I saw when the grille opened was a charming figure of the Child Jesus, carrying a ball in his hand with my name written on it. And as he lay there silent, the nuns sang in his name a lovely poem, written by my own dear Pauline, every word of which brought welcome consolation with it. I shall never forget this fresh instance of your unvarying kindness. I cried again, but this time from happiness, as I thanked the nuns; then I told them about another surprise, which dear Céline had arranged for me when I got back from Midnight Mass. There in my room I found a bowl with a tiny ship floating on it; on this the Child Jesus lay asleep, with a toy ball close beside him. On the white sail, Céline had written the words: " I lie asleep, but oh, my heart is wakeful," and on the ship itself the single word, " Self-Abandonment." No word for me from our Lord himself, his eyes were shut as far as I was concerned: but how he revealed himself to me in these human comforters, trained in the school of his considerate love!

On New Year's Day of 1888, our Lord had a fresh cross for me to bear, but this time I had to bear it by myself, and that was all the more difficult because I couldn't in the least understand what lay behind it. I was told* that the Bishop's letter,

---

[1] A reference to what the Bride says in Canticles V, 2.
[2] Matthew 17, 19; this interpretation of the passage is not the common one.   [3] John 11, 3.   [4] John 12, 4.

giving his consent, had been received on the 28th, Holy Innocents' Day; but I hadn't been told about it at the time, because it had now been decided that I shouldn't be admitted till after Lent.[1] It brought tears to my eyes, the thought of waiting so long—you see, this was a new kind of ordeal for me altogether. The difficulty up to now had been to cut loose from the world; now I had broken my bonds, only to find that God's Ark itself was shut against the homeless dove! I know it must have seemed very unreasonable of me, to repine at the prospect of three months spent in exile, instead of accepting it willingly; but it really was an ordeal, though it may not have seemed so, and it helped a great deal to develop in me the practice of self-abandonment, and of other qualities as well.

How did I pass those three months, a time, as it proved, so full of graces? My first thought was that perhaps I'd better give up living by a rather strict rule, as my habit had been of late; after all, why worry about that now? But before long I came to realise that this respite was a precious opportunity, and decided to give myself up, more than ever, to a recollected and mortified way of life. When I say "mortified," I don't mean to suggest that I went in for penitential practices of any kind. That's a thing, I'm afraid, I've never done; I've heard so much about saintly people who took on the most rigorous mortifications from their childhood upwards, but I'd never tried to imitate them—the idea never had any attractions for me. I expect that comes from cowardice on my part; I had Céline's example in front of me, and I could easily have devised, as she did, a hundred minor ways of making oneself uncomfortable. Instead of that, I'd allowed people to wrap me up in cotton wool, to treat me like a bird that's being fattened for the market, as if there were no need for penance in my life at all. What I did try to do by way of mortification was

[1] The manuscript of the Life here reads, literally: "You wrote to tell me that the Bishop's letter had been received on the 28th, Holy Innocents' Day, but you hadn't informed me about it at the time, because you had decided that I shouldn't be admitted till after Lent." An erasure in the text shows that this is a correction of what the Saint wrote. The use of the word "you" is designed to make it appear that Mother Marie de Gonzague, Superior in 1888, is the person addressed in Note-book A; really, of course, it was Mother Agnes.

to thwart my self-will, which always seemed determined to get its own way; to repress the rejoinder which sometimes came to my lips; to do little acts of kindness without attracting any attention to them; to sit upright instead of leaning back in my chair. That wasn't much, was it? But I did make these insignificant efforts to make myself less unworthy of a heavenly Bridegroom; and this period of apprenticeship has left tender memories behind it.

Three months are soon passed, and all in good time the day came—the day I had been looking forward to so eagerly. The actual date fixed for my reception into Carmel was Monday the ninth of April, when they were keeping the feast of the Annunciation, postponed that year because Lady Day had fallen in Lent. The night before, the whole of my family gathered round the table at which I was to sit for the last time. How harrowing they are, these farewell gatherings between close friends! Just when you'd like to fade out and be forgotten, there's a whole wealth of loving words and tender embraces, which only serve to remind you of the sacrifice which such a parting involves.

Papa hardly said a word, but his eyes rested on me with deep affection. My aunt had a fit of crying now and again; my uncle said any amount of nice things which shewed how fond he was of me. My cousins, Jeanne and Marie, were full of considerate kindness; especially Marie, who took me aside and begged my pardon for all the unhappiness she had caused me, which only existed in her imagination. And, to complete the company, there was my dear Léonie, who had come back some months before from her first effort to try her vocation with the Visitation nuns; kissing me and embracing me still more tenderly than the others. I haven't mentioned Céline, but you can imagine, dear Mother, how lovingly that night was passed, the last night on which we were to share the same room.

And so, on the morning of the great day itself, I took a last look at Les Buissonnets, the beloved cradle of my childhood's years, which I was never to see again. And then, with dear Papa giving me his arm, I set out to climb the hill-side of Carmel.

Chapter XXIV

FIRST IMPRESSIONS OF CARMEL

TO-DAY, AS YESTERDAY, the whole family was there; we all heard Mass and went to Communion. Together, we made our Lord welcome in his sacramental presence; there was sobbing all around me, nobody but myself was dry-eyed. My own sensation was a violent beating of the heart which made me wonder whether I'd find it possible to move when we were beckoned to the convent door. I did just manage it, but feeling as if it might kill me; it's the sort of experience one can't understand unless one's been through it. There was no outward sign of all this; all the other members of the family kissed me good-bye, and then I knelt down and asked for a blessing from the best of fathers, who knelt down too, and blessed me with tears in his eyes. I think the angels smiled down on us, rejoicing at the sight of an old man giving up his daughter, in the very spring-time of life, to the service of God.

A few moments more, and then the doors of God's Ark shut behind me, and I was being embraced by those dear sisters who had so long been mothers to me, whose example I was to take henceforward as my rule of living. No more waiting now for the fulfilment of my ambitions; I can't tell you what a deep and refreshing sense of peace this thought carried with it. And, deep down, this sense of peace has been a lasting possession; it's never left me, even when my trials have been most severe. Like all postulants, I was taken off to the choir as soon as I'd entered; the light there was dim, because the Blessed Sacrament was exposed, and I was conscious of nothing at first except a pair of eyes—the eyes of dear, holy Mother Geneviève resting upon me. I knelt for a moment at her feet, thanking God for the grace of being allowed to know a Saint; and then I went on with Mother Marie Gonzague.

In all the different parts of the convent, everything charmed me; it seemed so completely cut off from the world; and

147

above all, how I loved my[1] little cell! But there was nothing
agitating about this delight I experienced, it was quite calm;
as if the breeze was too light to rock my little boat on the
water's surface, the sky too bright to admit of a single cloud.
All that difficult time I'd gone through had been worth it
after all, and I could go about saying to myself: "I'm here
for good, now, here for good!" There's nothing transitory
about joy of this kind; it doesn't fade away with the honey-
moon illusions of the noviciate. And indeed, I'd no illusions at
all, thank God, when I entered Carmel; I found the religious
life exactly what I'd expected it to be. The sacrifices I had
to make never for a moment took me by surprise—and yet, as
you know, Mother, those first footsteps of mine brought me
up against more thorns than roses! Suffering opened her
arms to me, and I threw myself into them lovingly enough.
In the interrogation which is made before a nun is professed,
I declared in the presence of the sacred Host that I'd come
there to save souls, and above all to pray for priests. Well, if
you want to secure any object, no matter what it is, you've got
to find the right steps for attaining it. And our Lord let me
see clearly that if I wanted to win souls I'd got to do it by
bearing a cross; so the more suffering came my way, the more
strongly did suffering attract me.

For the next five years, it was this way of suffering I had to
follow, and yet there was no outward sign of it—perhaps it
would have relieved my feelings a bit if other people had
been conscious of it, but they weren't. There'll be a lot of
surprises at the Last Judgement, when we shall be able to see
what really happened inside people's souls; and I think this
way of suffering by which God led me will be a revelation to
the people who knew me. Indeed, I can prove it; two whole
months after I entered, our director, Père Pichon, came down
for the profession of Sister Marie of the Sacred Heart; and
he told me then that he was astonished at God's dealings with
my soul; he'd been looking at me the evening before when I
was praying in choir, and got the impression that my fervour

[1] "My," literally "our"; the Carmelites by way of emphasising
religious poverty, talk about "our room," etc., because it really
belongs to the community. In the present translation, "my" is used
throughout, for fear that this gracious habit of speech should create
confusion.

was still the fervour of childhood, and the way by which I was being led was one of unruffled calm.

I derived a great deal of comfort from my interview with this holy priest, but it was through a mist of tears, because I found it so difficult to explain the state of my soul to him. All the same, I made my general confession, the most thorough-going I'd ever made; and at the end of it he used an expression which echoed in my inward ear as nothing else ever had. " In the presence of Almighty God," said he, " and of the Holy Virgin, and of all the Saints, I assure you that you've never committed a single mortal sin." Then he added : " You must thank God for the mercy he's shewn you : if he left you to yourself, you wouldn't be a little angel any longer, you'd be a little demon." I'd no difficulty in believing that; I knew well enough how weak and imperfect I was. But my gratitude knew no bounds; I'd always been terrified that I might, somehow, have soiled the robe of my baptismal innocence; and an assurance like this, coming from a director after St. Teresa's own heart, so wise, so holy, seemed to me to come straight from our Lord himself. Some other words of his remained deeply imprinted on my heart : " My child, there's one Superior, one Novice-master you must always obey— Jesus Christ."

As it proved, that's what happened; and our Lord had to be my Director as well. I don't mean that I kept the state of my soul a secret from those who had charge of it; on the contrary, I wanted it to be an open book to them. But Reverend Mother was often ill, and couldn't devote much time to me. I know she was very fond of me, and said the nicest things about me; but God saw to it that she should treat me very severely without meaning to. I hardly ever met her without having to kiss the ground in penance for something I'd done wrong; and it was the same on the rare occasions when she gave me spiritual direction. This was a grace beyond all price; quite unmistakably, God was acting like this through his earthly representative.* I don't know what would have become of me if I'd been treated as the pet of the community—which is what the outside world naturally supposed. Instead of learning to see my superiors as the expression of our Lord's will, I might have become interested in them as persons, and so my heart, which had always been fancy-free when I was in the world, might have been entangled by human attachments in the cloister. From all that I was mercifully preserved; actually I was very fond of Reverend Mother, but my affection for her was quite disinterested, pointing always upwards to the claims of a divine lover upon my soul.

Our Novice-mistress was a real saint, of the type they produced in the early days of Carmel. I was with her all day, because she had to teach me my work, and she was kindness itself to me; but somehow I could not open out to her. It was always an effort to me to take spiritual advice, simply because I'd no practice in talking about the affairs of my soul, and had no idea how to express what was going on inside me. One of the older nuns put her finger on this when she said to me with a smile, one day at recreation: "Dear child, I can't imagine you have a great deal to confide to your superiors." "What makes you say that, Mother?" "Why, there's such a simplicity about your soul. Of course, the nearer you approach perfection, the simpler you will become; nearness to God always makes us simple." I think she was right, but my difficulty in opening out, whether it arose from simplicity or not, was a great trial to me. I realise that now, having become, since then, not less simple, but more capable of giving expression to my thoughts.

I said just now that our Lord was also my Director. Immediately upon entering Carmel I came to know the priest who was meant to help me in this way, but he'd scarcely had time to take me under his charge when he was sent overseas, and I lost him as soon as I'd found him. All I could do was to write a letter to him once a month, and get a letter back once a year. No wonder if I turned to him who is the Director of all those entrusted with the direction of souls and learned from him that secret which he hides from the wise and prudent, and reveals to little children.[1]

How was it to thrive, this little wild flower planted out on the hill-side of Carmel? Only under the shadow of the Cross, watered by our Lord's tears and his precious blood, with his adorable Face for its sun, that Face overcast with sorrow. Till then, I'd never realised the depth of meaning

[1] Matthew 11, 25.

there was in devotion to the Holy Face; it's to you, Mother, that I owe my fuller knowledge of it. Just as you were the first of us to join Carmel, so you were the first of us to sound the mystery of that love which the face of Jesus Christ conceals and reveals; and now you called me to your side, and I understood it all. I understood the true object of human ambition; our Lord hadn't wanted any kingdom in this world, and he shewed me that " if you want to learn an art worth knowing, you must set out to be unknown, and to count for nothing: "[1] you must find your satisfaction in self-contempt. If only my face could be hidden away, like his, pass unrecognised by the world;[2] to suffer and to remain unnoticed, that was all I longed for. God has always shewn such mercy in the paths by which he has led me; he has never inspired me with a wish and left it unfulfilled—that's why the bitterest cup he puts to my lips always tastes delicious.

[1] *Imitation of Christ*, I, ii, 3.   [2] *Ibid*, III, xlix, 7.

Chapter XXV

M. MARTIN'S BREAK-DOWN

MAY WAS a month of happy festivities; it was then that dear Marie made her profession and took the veil. She was the eldest of the family, and here was the youngest of the family crowning her with her bridal wreath. And now it was the turn for fresh trials. Just a year before, Papa had had a paralytic stroke affecting his legs, and we had been greatly alarmed; but his splendid constitution soon pulled him round, and our fears were forgotten. On the pilgrimage to Rome, we did notice more than once that he easily got tired, and wasn't in his usual spirits. Another thing which I noticed about him was the progress in his spiritual life; like St. Francis of Sales, he managed to overcome the irritability which was natural to him, and you would have said he had the sweetest temper in the world. The cares of life hardly seemed to ruffle the surface of his mind; he rose superior to all its rebuffs. Meanwhile, God was filling him with a sense of consolation; the tears he used to shed, the look of heavenly contentment that shone in his face, when he made his daily visit to the Blessed Sacrament! When Léonie came back without finding her vocation with the Visitation nuns, he didn't seem downcast, didn't complain that his prayers for her perseverance hadn't been answered; it was with a light step that he went to bring her home. And as for myself, how splendidly he bore that parting! This was how he broke the news to his friends at Alençon: "Dear friends, that little princess of mine, Thérèse, entered Carmel yesterday. It's the sort of sacrifice only God could ask of one. No, don't offer me any sympathy; my heart is overflowing with happiness."

It was time, now, that this faithful servant should receive his wages; it was fitting that they should be paid in the same currency in which God rewarded, here on earth, his only Son.

152

Papa had just presented him with an altar,[1] and he was the first victim chosen to be offered on it in union with the sacrifice of the Lamb. You remember well enough, Mother, our heart-rending experiences in the month of June, 1888, especially on June the 24th. These experiences are so deeply imprinted on our hearts that there is no need for me to recall them. We suffered cruelly, and still we were only at the beginning of our ordeal.

Meanwhile I was due to take the habit. I was duly received by the Chapter; but was it possible, in the circumstances, to make a ceremony of it? There was talk of giving me the habit without any appearance in public, and then it was thought best to wait. Quite unexpectedly, Papa recovered from his second attack, and the Bishop chose January the 10th as the date of the ceremony. The relay had been a trying affair, but what a day of happiness it was! Nothing was wanting, not even snow. I forget if I've already mentioned what an attraction snow always had for me; even when I was quite tiny I loved to see the whiteness of it, and took delight in going for a walk when the flakes were falling on me. I wonder what was the reason for it? Perhaps because I was a winter flower myself, and nature was all dressed in white when I first looked out through the eyes of childhood. Anyhow, I'd always hoped that when I dressed in white to take the habit it would be in a white world; and now here was the eve of the great day, and nothing to be seen but a grey sky and a drizzle of rain at intervals, with a mildness in the air that held out no hopes of snow; next morning came and there was no change.

Yet, as I say, it was a day of great happiness, and the best part of it all was dear Papa, who had never seemed to me so handsome or so distinguished; everybody looked at him in admiration. And indeed this was his day of achievement, the last day of festivity he was to enjoy here on earth. He'd now given all his children to God; Céline had just told him about her vocation, and he'd wept for joy and gone off with her to thank God for the honour of having all his children taken away, one after another. At the end of the ceremony, the

[1] The reference is to an altar in the Church of St. Peter at Lisieux which was the gift of M. Martin.

Bishop intoned *Te Deum*; and although one of the priests there pointed out that this was only the custom at professions, the great hymn of thanksgiving had started now and had to be sung through to the finish. It was right, surely, that the feast should be rounded off in this way, summing up, as it did, the whole cycle of our family history.

So, for the last time, I kissed Papa good-bye, and went back into the enclosure. The first thing I saw when I got into the cloister was my favourite statue of the Child Jesus dressed in pink, smiling at me among the flowers and the lights; and then, immediately afterwards—snow-flakes! The cloister-garth was white all over, just as I was—a proof, surely, of our Lord's considerateness, that he should give me snow as a betrothal present. No mortal lover would be in a position to humour his bride in such a way—a useful reflection, perhaps, for our neighbours in the world, who regarded the whole thing as a minor miracle, and were lost in astonishment. To be sure, it was an odd taste of mine to be so fond of snow; but then, that's all the better proof of the extraordinary condescension he shewed, this Bridegroom of mine who makes his choice of the snow-white lilies.

After the ceremony, the Bishop came in, and shewed me all the kindness of a father; he was really proud, I think, of my perseverance, and described me everywhere as his little daughter. It was always like that when he came to visit the convent; I remember especially the day when he came to us for the centenary of St. John of the Cross. He took my head between his hands and petted me in all sorts of ways; I had never felt so honoured! At the same time, I had the grace to cast my mind forward, and think of the welcome God will give us later on in the presence of his Angels and his Saints; an earthly foretaste like this, however remote, was not without its consolations.

This tenth of January, as I say, was Papa's day of achievement. It makes me think of our Lord's entry into Jerusalem on Palm Sunday, a single day of triumph, followed by all the miseries of his Passion. And that Passion was not for himself alone; it was to pierce, like a sword, the soul of the Mother of God. Our hearts, in the same way, were to echo the sufferings of one whom we loved better than anything else on earth. I remember saying, at the time of our first ordeal in June

1888: "It's a time of great suffering, but I feel that I've got the strength to bear worse trials than this." I'd no idea, then, of the trials which were actually in store for us; I never dreamed that on the 12th of February, only a month after I'd taken the habit, our dear Father would have to undergo such a wretched, such a humiliating experience. This time, I no longer talked about being prepared to put up with worse. I'm not going to try and describe what our feelings were; words couldn't do justice to them.

One day, in heaven, we shall take pleasure in recalling these trials we had the honour of undergoing; and indeed, even now, we can take pleasure in the fact that we underwent them. Because, after all, those three years of Papa's cruel torment were years of great value, of great spiritual profit to his family;* no ecstasies or revelations could have been so well worth having—a spiritual opportunity the Angels themselves might have grudged us! For myself, I found as usual that a full measure of suffering only gave me an appetite for more, and before long my soul, like my heart, was ill at ease. Dryness in prayer became a daily experience with me; and yet, when I was thus robbed of all consolation, I counted myself the happiest of creatures,* because all my longings were satisfied.

Dear Mother, how joyfully we ought to look back on a time of unhappiness which could wring nothing from our hearts but sighs of love and of gratitude, a time when all those five daughters of his were speeding on together towards a more perfect life! Léonie and Céline, in their exile at Caen, were still in the world, but were of the world no longer. Dear Céline, what great things this ordeal did for her soul! All the letters she wrote at this time bore the stamp of loving resignation. And those meetings in the parlour! Instead of keeping us apart, the grille of Carmel seemed to unite us more closely than ever, unite us in our thoughts, in our aspirations, in our love of Christ and of souls. When I was talking to Céline, the things of this world never intruded on our conversation for a moment; it was all of heaven. We were back in that sunny room at Les Buissonnets, dreaming of what eternity meant, and choosing for ourselves, in the hope of eternity, nothing better than suffering and neglect for our earthly lot.

Chapter XXVI

THE EVE OF PROFESSION

So THE days wore on, the days of my betrothal, and a long engagement it seemed to me! At the end of the statutory year I was warned[1] not to think, at present, of asking to be professed, because the Father Superior was certain to refuse his consent; I must wait another eight months. Here was a sacrifice which didn't, at first sight, seem easy to make; but it wasn't long before I saw things in a clearer light. At that time, I remember, I was using as my meditation-book Père Surin: *On the Foundation of the Spiritual Life*. And it was borne in upon me during my prayer that this eagerness to make my profession was mixed up with a good deal of self-love. After all, I'd given myself over to our Lord for his pleasure, his satisfaction, not mine; and here was I trying to see if I could get him to do my will, not his. Another thing occurred to me too; a bride's got to have a trousseau against her wedding-day, and what sort of trousseau had I got? So I told our Lord: "I'm not going to ask you to hurry on my profession; I'm ready to wait just as long as you want me to; only it mustn't be through any fault of mine that this union between us has to be put off. In the meantime, I'll work hard at trying to make myself a lovely wedding-dress, all set with jewels; and when you see that it's ready, I know quite well that nothing in heaven or earth will prevent you from coming to me, and making me, once and for ever, your bride."

Ever since taking the habit, I'd been seeing my way much clearer towards perfection, especially where the vow of poverty is concerned. While I was still a postulant, it didn't

[1] As before, our present text of the autobiography reads, not "I was warned," but "you warned me." The original writing has been erased, and an alteration made, so as to look as if Note-book A had been addressed to Mother Marie de Gonzague.

worry me, always having the best of everything for my use and finding everything I wanted close to hand. Our Lord was directing me, and he let all that go on, because in the ordinary way he doesn't let us into the whole of his secret at one blow, he illuminates our minds gradually. In the early days of my own spiritual life, when I was about thirteen or fourteen, I used to wonder what further heights there could still be for me to climb; I didn't see how I could possibly get a clearer idea of what perfection meant. But of course I realised before long that the farther you go along that road, the more conscious you are of the distance between you and the goal, and by now—well, by now I'm resigned to seeing myself always far from perfect; even glad, in a way.

But what was I saying? Oh yes, about the direction our Lord used to give me at this time. One evening after Compline I went to look for my cell lamp on the shelf where such things were kept, and it wasn't there; the Great Silence had started, so there was no chance of getting it back; obviously one of the other sisters had picked it up by mistake for her own. I needed it badly, but somehow I didn't find myself repining over the loss of it; I counted it as a privilege, because after all, I said to myself, poverty doesn't mean just going without luxuries, it means going without necessities. All was dark around me, but there was a fresh infusion of light within. It was at this time that I developed a positive taste for ugly things and inconvenient things, so that I was really delighted when somebody took away the pretty little jug that used to stand in my cell, and replaced it by a big one that was badly chipped. I resisted, too, not without effort, the temptation to make excuses for myself; and it was all the harder for me because I didn't like having any secrets from my Novice-mistress. Here is the story of my first success in that direction, which really did cost me something, though it sounds petty enough. A little vase on a window-sill had got broken, and the Novice-mistress thought I had left it lying around; so she called my attention to it and told me to be more careful another time. And I kept my own counsel, simply kissing the floor and promising to be tidier in future. I was so far from being well grounded in good habits that little humiliations of this sort came difficult to me, and I had to console myself with the reflection that all these things would come out at the Day of Judgement. In the meantime, it appeared, you got no thanks for doing your duty, unless you were prepared to stick up for yourself, whereas the mistakes you made became public property at once!

I tried my best to do good on a small scale, having no opportunity to do it on a large scale; I would fold up the mantles which the sisters had left lying about, and make myself useful in ways of that sort. I had a real love of mortification, but I'm afraid it was a hunger which only came from undernourishment: I wasn't allowed to do anything in that line—when I was in the world, I never rested against the back of the chair I was sitting in, but now I was told this gave me a stoop. I expect if my superiors had prescribed a whole lot of penances for me, I should have lost my enthusiasm in no time. As it was, all I could do was to take such opportunities of denying myself as came to me without the asking; that meant mortifying pride, a much more valuable discipline than any kind of bodily discomfort. The refectory, in which I started work as soon as I had taken the habit,* with always giving me the chance of putting my self-love where it belonged—that is, trampling it underfoot. It's true, dear Mother, that I had the comfort of sharing my work with you, and learning at first hand from your good example; but even this partnership had its drawbacks, because the rule had to be observed, and I wasn't in a position to tell you everything, to open my heart to you, as in the old days; this was Carmel, not Les Buissonnets. Anyhow, our Lady helped me with my wedding-dress, and as soon as it was ready all the obstacles disappeared; the Bishop sent his leave, the community agreed to take me, and the ceremony of my profession was fixed for September the 8th. Of course, dear Mother, all this brief account of myself which I've been giving you would have called for pages and pages if I'd set it out in detail, but those pages will never be written on earth. Before long, I shall be able to tell you about these things when we meet in our Father's house, in the heaven we so long for, you and I.

My wedding-dress was set with jewels, some old, one of

them quite new and sparkling. By jewels I mean trials; Papa's wretched situation was already bad enough, and now it was complicated by a minor set-back as far as I was concerned— a small thing in itself, but a bitter disappointment. For some time dear Papa's health had been a little better; he was taken out for carriage-exercise, and there was even some question of his facing a railway journey to come and see us. Céline, I need hardly say, was all for its happening on the day when I took the veil. "I won't tire him out," she said, "by making him follow the whole ceremony; I'll go and fetch him at the end of it and bring him up quietly to the grille, so that Thérèse can have his blessing." How like dear Céline! "Love never pleads inability; everything seems possible and everything seems allowable"[1]—so different from human prudence, which hesitates at every turn and walks warily! This time, God allowed human prudence to have its way, as a suitable means of chastening me. So I had to go through my wedding ceremony as an orphan; I could only look upwards and appeal, with more confidence than before, to my Father in heaven.

Before mentioning all this, I ought really to have said something about the retreat I made before my profession; it brought no consolation with it, only complete dryness and almost a sense of dereliction. Once more, our Lord was asleep on the boat; how few souls there are that let him have his sleep out! He can't be always doing all the work, responding to all the calls made upon him; so for my own part I am content to leave him undisturbed. I dare say he won't make his presence felt till I start out on the great retreat of eternity; I don't complain of that, I want it to happen. It shews, of course, that there's nothing of the saint about me; I suppose I ought to put down this dryness in prayer to my own fault, my own lukewarmness and want of fidelity. What excuse have I, after seven years in religion, for going through all my prayers and my thanksgivings as mechanically as if I, too, were asleep? But I don't regret it*, I think of little children lying asleep, under the loving eyes of their parents; I think of the surgeons who put their patients under an anæsthetic—in a word, I remember how God knows the stuff of which we are made, and can't forget

[1] *Imitation of Christ*, III, v, 4.

that we are only dust.[1] Anyhow, my profession retreat, like all
the retreats I've made since, was a time of great dryness; and
yet I felt that all the time, without my knowing it, God was
shewing me the right way to do his will and to reach a high
degree of holiness. You know, I always have the feeling that
our Lord doesn't supply me with provisions for my journey
—he just gives me food unexpectedly when and as I need it;
I find it there without knowing how it got there. It simply
comes to this, that our Lord dwells unseen in the depths of
my miserable soul, and so works upon me by grace that I can
always find out what he wants me to do at this particular
moment.

Some days before I made my profession, I had the satisfaction of receiving the Holy Father's blessing. I'd asked for this
favour through kind Brother Simeon, for Papa and for myself; I was very glad to have this opportunity of repaying the
spiritual debt which I owed Papa for my journey to Rome.
When the great day came, my wedding-day, there was no
cloud on my horizon; on the eve of it, my soul had been in
such tumult as I had never before experienced. Till then, I'd
never known what it was to have a doubt about my vocation,
and this was the ordeal I now had to face. That evening, as I
made the Stations of the Cross after Mattins,* my vocation
seemed to me a mere dream a mere illusion; I still saw life
at Carmel as a desirable thing, but the devil gave me the clear
impression that it wasn't for me; I should only be deceiving
my superiors if I tried to persevere in a way of life I wasn't
called to. Darkness everywhere; I could see nothing and
think of nothing beyond this one fact, that I'd no vocation. I
was in an agony of mind; I even feared (so foolishly that I
might have known it was a temptation of the devil's) that if I
told my Novice-mistress about it she'd prevent me taking my
vows. And yet I did want to do God's will, even if it meant
going back to the world; that would be better than doing my
own will by staying at Carmel. Anyhow, I did get hold of
the Novice-mistress, and stood there covered with confusion,
trying to explain what I felt like. Fortunately she knew her
way about better than I did, and set my doubts completely at
rest; indeed, they disappeared the moment I had given ex-

1 Psalm 102, 14.

pression to them—perhaps the devil had hoped I wouldn't bring myself to do it, and was defeated by my act of humility. Meanwhile I was determined that the act of humility should be complete, so I told Reverend Mother about this strange temptation, and she only laughed at me.

Chapter XXVII

PROFESSION: MOTHER GENEVIÈVE

ON THE morning of September the 8th, I seemed to be carried along on a tide of interior peace; and this sense of peace "which surpasses all our thinking" accompanied the taking of my vows. This wedding of my soul to our Lord was not heralded by the thunders and lightning of Mount'Sinai, rather by that "whisper of a gentle breeze"[1] which our father Elias heard there. I set no limit to the graces I asked for that day; I felt that I had the privileges of a queen, who can use her influence to set prisoners free, and reconcile the king to his rebellious subjects; I wanted to empty Purgatory, and convert sinners everywhere. I prayed so hard for you, Mother, for my dear sisters, for all the family, but especially for my poor father, now so sorely tried and still so holy. I offered myself to our Lord, asking him to accomplish his will in me and never let any creature come between us.

(Here, between the pages of the manuscript, is inserted the *billet de profession,* composed by the Saint and worn on her heart, according to custom, when she took her vows.)

September 8, 1890

Jesus, my heavenly Bridegroom, never may I lose this second robe of baptismal innocence; take me to yourself before I commit any wilful fault, however slight. May I look for nothing and find nothing but you and you only; may creatures mean nothing to me, nor I to them—you, Jesus, are to be everything to me. May earthly things have no power to disturb the peace of my soul; that peace is all I ask of you, except love; love that is as infinite as you are, love that has no eyes for myself, but for you, Jesus, only for you. Jesus, I would like to die a martyr for your sake, a martyr in soul or in body; better still, in both. Give me the grace to keep my vows in their entirety; make me understand what is expected

[1] III Kings 19, 12.

of one who is your bride. Let me never be a burden to the community, never claim anybody's attention; I want them all to think of me as no better than a grain of sand, trampled under foot and forgotten, Jesus, for your sake. May your will be perfectly accomplished in me, till I reach the place you have gone to prepare for me. Jesus, may I be the means of saving many souls; to-day, in particular, may no soul be lost, may all those detained in Purgatory win release. Pardon me, Jesus, if I'm saying more than I've any right to; I'm thinking only of your pleasure, of your content.

Well, the great day passed, as all days must, joyful or sorrowful; even in our greatest moments of happiness, there's a morrow to look forward to. But this time, as I laid my wreath down at the feet of our Lady's statue, I did it without any feeling of anti-climax, because I realised that I'd now come into possession of a joy which time couldn't take away from me. Our Lady's Nativity was a wonderful day for my heavenly wedding; you see, everything was to scale—our Lady just born into the world, making the present of a flower still in bud to the Child Jesus, a day of small things. Only there was nothing small about the graces I received, and the sense of peace that went with them; it was with quiet happiness that I looked up that night at the stars glittering overhead, and reflected that before long heaven would open to my eager gaze, and I should be united to this heavenly Bridegroom of mine in joy everlasting.

I took the veil on the 24th, but a veil hangs over the memory of it; it passed in a mist of tears. Papa could not be there to give a last blessing to his little princess. Père Pichon was already in Canada. The Bishop had arranged to come over and go to dinner at my uncle's, but he was ill and couldn't manage it. Altogether it was a sad disappointment; and yet it left an after-taste of peace. Our Lord allowed me to give way to tears that day, which caused some astonishment; I'd learned by then to put up with worse set-backs without crying over them, but that was due to a special grace, whereas on this 24th of September, he left me to my own resources, and very inadequate they proved to be.

Eight days afterwards my cousin Jeanne got married. I can't tell you, dear Mother, how anxious I was to learn, from her example, about all the little attentions which a bride ought to lavish on her bridegroom; I wanted to know all I could about it, because surely my attitude towards our Lord ought not to be less carefully studied than Jeanne's towards her husband—an excellent creature, but only a creature all the same. I even amused myself by sketching out a wedding invitation of my own, modelled on hers; this was the way it ran:

Letter of invitation to the wedding of Sister Thérèse of the Child Jesus and of the Holy Face.

Almighty God, Creator of heaven and earth, Lord of the whole world, and the glorious Virgin Mary, queen of the heavenly court, invite you to take part in the wedding of their Son Jesus Christ, King of Kings and Lord of Lords, to Thérèse Martin, now invested by right of dowry with two freedoms, those of the Sacred Infancy and of the Passion, her title of nobility being derived from the Child Jesus and the Holy Face.

Monsieur Louis Martin, the Heir-in-chief of all Misfortune and Humiliation, and Madame Martin, Lady-in-waiting at the Court of Heaven, invite you to take part in the wedding of their daughter Thérèse to Jesus, the Word of God, Second Person of the Blessed Trinity, now by the operation of the Holy Spirit made Man, and Son of Mary, the Queen of heaven.

Since it was impossible to invite you to the ceremony of the nuptial blessing, to which only the Court of Heaven was admitted, on the 8th of September, 1890, you are asked to be present at their return from the marriage tour, which will take place.

To-morrow, that is, the day of eternal reckoning, when Jesus Christ, Son of God, will come on the clouds of heaven in all the splendour of his majesty to judge the living and the dead.

The hour of this being still uncertain, you are asked to hold yourself in readiness and be on the watch.

And now, dear Mother, have I anything left to tell you? I thought I'd finished, but it occurs to me that I've said nothing about the happiness of knowing Mother Geneviève. That was, surely, an inestimable grace; God, who had given me so much already, allowed me to live under the same roof with a Saint—and not the sort of saint who defies imitation; hers were hidden, unobtrusive virtues. I owe her a debt for many graces received through her. In particular, I remember one Sunday when I went as usual to pay her a short visit; as we weren't allowed to visit the sick three at a time, and she had two sisters with her I just smiled at her and prepared to go out of the room. But she looked at me as if she had some inspired message to convey, and said this: "Listen, my child, I've got a word to say to you. When you come here, you always want a spiritual keepsake to take away with you, and here's one for to-day. Serve God with peace and with joy; remember, always, that our God is a God of peace." Well, I thanked her and went out, but I went out almost in tears, fully convinced that God had revealed to her the state of my soul. All that day I'd been sorely tried, and was on the verge of melancholy, being in such deep spiritual darkness that I even doubted God's love for me. You can imagine, then, what consolation her words brought me. The next Sunday, when I asked Mother Geneviève what revelation had been made to her, she said none at all; and this made me admire her more than ever—I could see that all she did and said really came from our Lord living in her; and that's the truest and the best kind of sanctity, the kind I would most like to attain, because there's no danger of illusion about it.

On the day of my profession, I was greatly encouraged by hearing from Mother Geneviève's own lips that she'd been through exactly the same temptation as I had, before she took her vows. And you, dear Mother, will remember what a comfort she was to us at the time of our greatest distress.* Altogether, it's a fragrant memory that she has left in my heart. On the day when she went to her reward, I was deeply touched by this first experience I had had of a death-bed; a most moving experience.* I was at the foot of her bed, and could watch the slightest movement of the dying Saint. I spent two hours like that, telling myself that I ought to be overcome with feelings of devotion, and yet finding that it was just the other way about—I was quite numb, quite insensible. And then, at the very moment when her soul was re-born into eternity, my whole attitude suddenly changed; I was conscious of a joy and a fervour which I can't describe to you. It was just as if Mother Geneviève had communicated to me a part of the happiness she was experiencing at that moment; I find it impossible to doubt that she went straight to heaven. I remember saying to her one day: "There won't be any Purgatory for you, Mother," and her gentle reply: "It's what I'm hoping for." Hope, tempered by humility, was no doubt the chief quality God saw in her; the favours we've received through her are proof of it.

How eager we were, all of us, to preserve some relic of her! You know what it is that I treasure. During her last agony, I saw a tear shining like a diamond on her eye-lashes, the last she would ever shed. It didn't fall; I could see it still shining there when she lay in choir, and as nobody had removed it, I went in quietly that evening with a piece of fine linen, and took this for my relic—the last tear of a saint. Since then, I've always carried it in the little locket in which my vows are enclosed.

I don't attach much importance to my dreams, and indeed I seldom have any dreams of the kind that could mean anything. Why is it that when I've been thinking about God all day he disappears from my mind during sleep? In the ordinary way I dream of woods and flowers and brooks and the sea; nearly always, I see dear little children about me, and spend my time catching butterflies and strange birds; a poet's dreams, if you like, but as you see not the dreams of a mystic! Only I did have a more comforting experience one night, soon after Mother Geneviève died. I dreamt that she was making her will, and left some keepsake to each of the sisters, but when it came to my turn it looked as if I should get nothing, because there was nothing left. But she raised herself in bed, and repeated three times, in a curiously penetrating voice: "To you, I leave my heart."

Chapter XXVIII

THE INFLUENZA
MOTHER AGNES PRIORESS

A MONTH after this saintly mother of ours left us, an epidemic of influenza broke out among the community*, and only three of us were left on our feet. I saw many new sights, gained many new impressions about life and about this passing world. My nineteenth birthday was marked out by a death, and two others followed before long. By now I was alone in the sacristy, because the senior sacristan was in a very bad way; it was I who had to arrange for the funerals, to open the choir grille at Mass, and so on. God was very good to me in supplying me with the strength I needed; I still can hardly imagine how I shrank so little from the work that came my way. Death seemed everywhere in the ascendant; the worst cases of all had to be nursed by nuns who could scarcely drag themselves across the room, and the moment a sister was dead, her body had to be left unattended. I had a presentiment as I was getting up one morning that Sister Madeleine was dead; finding the passage all dark, and nobody coming or going between the cells, I went into Sister Madeleine's (the door had been left open) and there she was, sure enough, lying on her pallet fully dressed. I wasn't at all frightened; I just went off and got a candle and a rose-wreath for her.

On the evening when our sub-Prioress died, I was alone with the infirmarian; nobody can imagine the state to which the community was reduced, except those of us who kept our feet through it all, and yet, desolate as we were, I felt that God was watching over us all the time. Those who died seemed to pass from this world to a better without the least struggle; immediately after death a look of joy and peace settled on their features, as if they lay comfortably asleep. And so they did; once the fashion of this world has passed away, they will wake up to enjoy, eternally, the happiness of God's elect. While the community was going through these searching trials, I had the unspeakable consolation of making my Communion every day. That was wonderful; and our Lord went on spoiling me even after the epidemic, because I was still allowed to receive him every day when those others, his more faithful servants, no longer had the same privilege. It was also a great happiness to be able to touch the sacred vessels, and prepare the altar linen* for our Lord's coming; I felt that a great deal of devotion was expected of me now, and often repeated to myself the charge given to deacons at their ordination: "Keep yourselves unsullied, you that have the vessels of the Lord's worship in your charge."

I can't say that my thanksgivings after Communion have often brought with them any strong access of devotion; indeed, I don't know that there's any moment at which I experienced so little. But then, that's not to be wondered at; I've been offering myself to our Lord as a hostess ready to receive him, not for her own satisfaction but simply to please him. I picture my soul at such times as a vacant site, with some rubbish lying about, only I ask our Lady to clear all that away; then I ask her to erect a great tent, worthy of the occasion, and furnish it with all the finery she has at her disposal; and then I ask all the Saints and Angels to come and make music there. I think this is all the welcome our Lord expects when he comes to visit my soul, and if he's satisfied I'm satisfied too. Only, of course, all this exercise of the imagination doesn't prevent my being distracted and dozing off over my prayers. When my thanksgiving's over, I realise what a bad one I've made, and resolve to turn the rest of the day into a thanksgiving after Communion.

You can see for yourself, Mother, that the path by which I travel isn't one of scrupulous fear; anything but that. I can always find some reason to be glad of my failures and make the best of them, and our Lord doesn't seem to mind; or why does he encourage me to follow that path? I remember one day when I was rather worried about going to Communion, a thing which very seldom happened to me; I felt as if God found something wanting in me, and I remember saying to myself: "Now, if for some reason I'm only given half of a Sacred Host to-day, it will worry me; I shall take it as a sign that our Lord is coming to me with reluctance." So I went up to the grille and, believe it or not, for the first time in my life I saw the priest take up two Hosts instead of one, two quite separate Hosts, and give them to me. There were tears of joy in my eyes at this providential coincidence.

It was in the year after my profession, about two months before Mother Geneviève died, that I received great graces during the retreat. In the ordinary way public retreats are even more distressing to me than the ones I make by myself, but it wasn't so this time. I'd made a novena beforehand and prayed hard over it, in spite of a conviction that this retreat father was very unlikely to understand me; his reputation was for dealing with great sinners, not so much with religious. But it was God himself who was my Director, and he wanted me to know it; so it was this priest he chose for his instrument, although I think I was the only person who really appreciated the choice. I'd been going through a bad time spiritually in every way, even to the point of asking myself whether heaven really existed. But I didn't feel inclined to say anything about these intimate doubts of mine, because I wasn't sure that I could express them properly. Then I went into the confessional, and immediately my heart opened out. Almost as soon as I'd begun, I felt that the priest understood me, with an insight that was surprising, almost uncanny.

My soul had become an open book, in which this priest who was a stranger to me could read better than I could myself. He launched me in full sail on that sea of confidence and of love on which I'd been afraid to venture, though it attracted me so strongly. He told me that my faults were not such as to merit God's displeasure. " Speaking to you as God's representative," said he, " and in his name, I assure you that he is well satisfied with what you are doing for him." Imagine what a consolation those words were to me—nobody'd ever suggested to me that one could have faults which nevertheless didn't offend God; I could bear all the homesickness of this earthly exile as long as I felt sure of that! And at the same time I was conscious, deep down in my heart, that what he said was true; after all, God is more tender to us than any mother could be, and you, Mother, are always so ready to forgive those little indiscretions of which I am guilty without meaning to be. Again and again I have found that a single caress from you has had more effect on me than any reprimand you could have uttered. I suppose I'm made like that—when I'm frightened, I simply curl up; when I'm appealed to by love, I can go ahead at full speed.

This feeling that love was winging my feet has been with me specially since that golden day when you were elected Prioress—that Pauline should stand, in my life, for our Lord's earthly representative! Not that I hadn't realised, for a long time, what wonderful things our Lord was doing through your influence; your example taught me that it's only through suffering we can achieve spiritual motherhood, and more than ever I could appreciate the hidden force of our Lord's words: "Believe me when I tell you this; a grain of wheat must fall into the ground and die, or else it remains nothing more than a grain of wheat; but if it dies, then it yields rich fruit."[1] What a harvest you've won! You've sowed with tears, but before long you'll see the reward of your labours; you'll come back rejoicing, carrying your sheaves with you.[2] And some where among these abundant sheaves, a little white flower is hidden away; later on, in heaven, a voice will be given me to put on record all the tenderness and the holiness which I've marked in you, day after day, as we passed through the dark and silent days of our earthly exile.

In these last two years, I've been making plenty of discoveries. God has been merciful to me exactly as he was to King Solomon,[3] in granting *all* my wishes; not only my aspirations towards holiness, but my desire for mere earthly shadows as well—and of course I knew they were only that, even before I had the experience of attaining them. You were always my ideal, Mother, and I wanted to be exactly like you; so when I found you could paint lovely pictures, or make up charming poetry, I would say to myself: "How wonderful to have the gift of painting like that, to have the art of expressing oneself in verse, and to help souls in that way." I wouldn't have dreamed of praying for such natural gifts, so that these desires were buried away in the depths of my heart. But then our Lord himself condescends to dwell in the depths of my heart, and he must have welcomed the opportunity of assuring me that "All man does beneath the sun is frustration, and labour lost."[4] To the surprise of the community, I was

[1] John 12, 24.   [2] Psalm 125, 6.   [3] III Kings 3, 13.
[4] Ecclesiastes 2, 11, 17.

told to paint, and God allowed me to make good use of the lessons my Mother gave me; I found myself capable of writing poetry after your model, and making up poems which some people admired. Solomon found, didn't he, that when he looked round at all he had done, that ungrateful drudgery was no better than frustration and labour lost, and I had the same experience. I found that true happiness consists in hiding oneself, in being content to go without any expert knowledge of creatures. I realised that without love nothing we do can be worth anything, even if we dazzle the world's imagination by raising the dead to life, or converting whole nations. So these gifts which came to me unasked haven't encouraged me to be vain; they carry me straight back to him, and I reflect that he alone is unchanging, he alone can satisfy the limitless desires of our hearts.

And there are plenty of quite different ways in which our Lord has seen fit to humour me; I mean, over childish hopes like that wish to have snow on the ground when I took the habit. Flowers, for instance—you know how fond I've always been of them; and when I shut myself up in the cloister at fifteen, I felt I was renouncing for ever the happiness of running about in the fields when they were bright with the treasures of spring. And yet it's a fact that I've never had so many flowers passing through my hands as in these years since I entered Carmel.[1] A bridegroom can always be trusted to make presents of this kind, and our Lord hasn't forgotten me; he's sent me any amount of cornflowers, marguerites, poppies and so on, all the ones I like best. There's even a little flower that goes by the name of corn-cockle, which I'd never managed to find since we moved to Lisieux; and I did so want to see it again, with all its memories of our childhood at Alençon. Well, there it was at Carmel, looking brightly up at me as if to assure me that God repays us a hundredfold, in small things as in great, if we give up everything for him. But there was one wish I cherished beyond all others, and I used to think I should never see it realised.

---

[1] The Saint is referring to bouquets of flowers brought by the faithful to the door of Carmel, especially for the statue of the Child Jesus.

Chapter XXIX

CELINE ENTERS CARMEL
VICTIMS OF LOVE

THIS CHERISHED dream was that Céline should enter Carmel, our Carmel. It seemed like a dream, too good to be true, that I should ever be able to live under the same roof again with my childhood's playmate, share once more her joys and her sorrows. So I'd made a complete cut; I'd entrusted Céline's future entirely to our Lord, quite ready to see her take ship for the other side of the world, if that was her destiny. The only thing I felt I couldn't bear was the idea that she, in her turn, shouldn't become the bride of Christ; I loved her like myself, and the thought that she might give herself to an earthly husband just couldn't find room in my mind. It went to my heart to think of her being exposed to all the spiritual dangers I had escaped; it was a mother's rather than a sister's feeling I had for her since I had joined Carmel. I remember one day when I knew she was going out to an evening party, and it worried me so much that the tears came in torrents, a thing which wasn't usual with me now, and I entreated our Lord to see that she didn't dance. My prayer was heard; in the ordinary way she was an accomplished dancer, but that evening she found it impossible, and the partner who was in attendance on her simply couldn't get her to take the floor. There was nothing for it but to take her back to her place, and there, in some embarrassment, he left her, and didn't come back the whole evening. This extraordinary experience of hers increased my confidence that our Lord had set his seal on her forehead, as on mine.

On the 29th of July last year, God saw fit to release a most faithful servant of his from the bonds of mortality, and when Papa was thus called away to his heavenly reward, it was the signal for Céline's release from the last links which bound her to the world. She had been our representative in looking after the father we all loved so well, and had acquitted herself

like an angel. The Angels, when they have fulfilled the task
God has given them, go straight back to his presence; that is
why we think of them as always posed for flight. And Céline,
like the angel she was, took wing; she would have gone anywhere in obedience to our Lord's call, but, as it proved, she
had only a short journey to take. It was enough for him that
she had given her consent to a sacrifice whose nature was
kept secret for two whole years, greatly to my distress and,
for that matter, to hers.[1] But in the end dear Papa, who was
always for getting things done at once during his life-time,
saw to it that Céline's affairs were quickly arranged, and the
14th of September saw us reunited once more.

I remember one day, when the obstacles seemed quite
insuperable, saying to our Lord during my thanksgiving:
"You know how I long to be reassured that Papa has gone
straight to heaven. I don't ask for a word from you about
this, only for a sign. If Sister A. de J. gives her consent to
Céline being admitted to Carmel, and makes no difficulties
about it, then that will be my answer, I shall know that Papa
went straight to join you." You'll remember, dear Mother,
that this particular Sister thought three of us was quite
enough, and wasn't anxious to admit a fourth. But God holds
our hearts in his hand, and does what he likes with them; he
did so on this occasion. The first person I met after I'd
finished my thanksgiving was this identical Sister, who called
me to her side in a most friendly way and took me up to your
room, where she talked to me about Céline with the tears
standing in her eyes. No, I can never thank our Lord enough
for the way in which he has satisfied all my ambitions.

And now I have no wishes left at all, except the wish to
love our Lord to distraction; those childish desires of mine
seem to have vanished. To be sure, I still enjoy putting flowers
out on the altar of the Child Jesus; but it hasn't the same
importance for me since I realised my ambition of offering
dear Céline, fresh and graceful as a nosegay of flowers, to the
same Master's service. What is there left for me to desire?
Not suffering or death, though both have their appeal for
me; only love really attracts me. It used not to be so; I

[1] Père Pichon, who was on the Canadian mission, wanted Céline
to go out there, but would not let her tell anyone. The plan never
materialised.

thought at one time that to suffer was to skirt along the coasts
of heaven; I made sure that I was to be carried off by an early
death. Now, self-abandonment is my only guide, the only
compass I have to steer by; there's nothing I can pray for
eagerly except the fulfilment of God's will for my soul, un-
hindered by any intrusion of created things. I can say, with
our father St. John of the Cross:

> " Deep-cellared is the cavern
> Of my love's heart, I drank of him alive:
> Now, stumbling from the tavern,
> No thoughts of mine survive,
> And I have lost the flock I used to drive. . . .
>
> My spirit I prepare
> To serve him with her riches and her beauty.
> No flocks are now my care,
> No other toil I share,
> And only now in loving is my duty."[1]

And he writes elsewhere:

> " Since I knew Love, I have been taught
> He can perform most wondrous labours
> Though good and bad in me are neighbours,
> He turns their difference to naught
> Then both into Himself. . . ."[2]

Oh what a comfort it is, Mother, this way of love! You may
stumble on it, you may fail to correspond with grace given,
but always love knows how to make the best of everything;
whatever offends our Lord is burnt up in its fire, and nothing
is left but a humble, absorbing peace deep down in the heart.

I can't tell you how much illumination I've found before
now in the works of that great father of ours, St. John of the
Cross. When I was seventeen or eighteen, it was all the
spiritual food I needed. After that, I found that all spiritual
books left me as dry as ever, and I'm still like that. I've only

[1] Spiritual Canticle, stanzas 26 and 28 (translated by Roy Campbell).

[2] *Glosa a lo divino*, stanza 4 (translated by Roy Campbell).

to open one—even the finest, even the most affecting of them —to find my heart shut up tight against it; I can't think about what I'm reading, or else it just gets as far as my brain without helping me to meditate at all. I can only escape from this difficulty of mine by reading Holy Scripture and the *Imitation of Christ*; there you have solid, wholemeal nourishment. But above all it's the gospels that occupy my mind when I'm at prayer; my soul has so many needs, and yet this is the one thing needful. I'm always finding fresh lights there; hidden meanings which had meant nothing to me hitherto. It's an experience that makes me understand what's meant by the text, "The kingdom of God is here, within you."[1] Our Lord doesn't need to make use of books or teachers in the instruction of souls; isn't he himself the Teacher of all teachers, conveying knowledge with never a word spoken? For myself, I never heard the sound of his voice, but I know that he dwells within me all the time, guiding me and inspiring me whenever I do or say anything. A light, of which I'd caught no glimmer before, comes to me at the very moment when it's needed; and this doesn't generally happen in the course of my prayer, however devout it may be, but more often in the middle of my daily work.*

Dear Mother, after receiving such graces, do you wonder that I should echo the words of the Psalmist: "Give thanks to the Lord; the Lord is gracious, his mercy endures for ever?"[2] I believe that if all creatures had received these same graces, there would be nobody left serving God under the influence of fear; we should all love him to distraction, and nobody would ever do him an injury, not because we were afraid of him but simply because we loved him. Still, I realise that we aren't all made alike; souls have got to fall into different groups, so that all God's perfections may be honoured severally. Only for me his infinite mercy is the quality that stands out in my life, and when I contemplate and adore his other perfections, it's against this background of mercy all the time. They all seem to have a dazzling outline of love; even God's justice, and perhaps his justice more than any other attribute of his, seems to have love for its setting. It's so wonderful to think that God is really just, that he takes all our weakness into consideration, that he knows our

[1] Luke 17, 21.   [2] Psalm 117, 1.

frail nature for what it is. What reason can I have for fear? Surely he who pardons, so graciously, the faults of the Prodigal Son will be equally just in his treatment of myself, who am always at his side.[1]

On the 9th of June this year, the feast of the Holy Trinity, I was given the grace to see more clearly than ever how love is what our Lord really wants. I was thinking about the souls who offer themselves as victims to the divine justice, with the idea of turning aside and bringing upon themselves the punishments decreed against sinners. I felt that this kind of self-immolation was a fine gesture, a generous gesture, but it wasn't at all the one I· wanted to make. The cry of my heart was something different: " My God, why should only your Justice claim victims; why should there be no victims of your merciful Love? Everywhere that Love is misunderstood and thrust on one side; the hearts upon which you are ready to lavish it turn away towards creatures instead, as if happiness could be found in such miserable attachments as that; they won't throw themselves into your arms and accept the gift of your infinite Love. Must this rejected Love of yours remain shut up in your own Heart? If only you could find souls ready to offer themselves as victims to be burnt up· in the fire of your love, surely you would lose no time in satisfying their desire; you would find a welcome outlet, in this way, for the pent-up force of that infinite tenderness which is yours. If your justice, which finds its scope on earth, demands to take its course, how much stronger must be the impetus which impels your merciful love to take possession of souls! Your mercy, we are told, reaches up to heaven itself.[2] Jesus, grant me the happiness of being such a victim, burnt up in the fire of your divine love! "

It was you, dear Mother, who gave me leave to offer myself in this way, and you know all about the streams of grace, or perhaps I ought to say the seas of grace, which have come flooding into my soul since then. Ever since that memorable day, love seems to pierce me through and wrap me round, merciful love which makes a new creature of me, purifies my soul and leaves no trace of sin there, till all my fear of Purgatory is lost. To be sure, no merits of my own could even win me entrance there; it is only for the souls of the re-

[1] Luke 15, 31.   [2] Psalm 35, 6.

deemed. But at the same time I feel confident that the fire of love can sanctify us more surely than those fires of expiation; why should our Lord want us to suffer unnecessary pain? Why should he inspire me with this ambition to become a victim, if he doesn't mean to satisfy it? No, there's nothing that can bring us comfort like this way of love; for me, nothing matters except trying to do God's will with utter resignation.

There, Mother, that's all I can tell you about the life of your youngest sister. You yourself know far better than I do what I am, and what our Lord has done for me, so you won't mind my having compressed my life as a religious within such narrow limits. How it is going to end, this story which I've called the story of a little white flower? Perhaps it will be picked, still fresh; perhaps it will be replanted in some distant soil*, I can't tell. But I know that the mercy of God will always go with me, and that I shall never cease to bless you for giving me to our Lord. For all eternity, I shall rejoice to think that I am one flower in the wreath you have earned; to all eternity I shall echo your song, which can never lose the freshness of its inspiration, the song of love.

The meaning of the coat of arms here attached

THE DEVICE JHS is one which Jesus has given by way of dowry to his unworthy bride; to her who was called in her babyhood "the orphan of the Beresina," but is now known as Thérèse of the Child Jesus, of the Holy Face. Those two titles are all her claim to nobility, all her riches, all her hope. The vine which separates the quarterings is meant to be a fresh symbol to our Lord, who has said: "I am the vine, you are its branches," and told us that he wants us to bear abundant fruit.[1] Those two tendrils of it, one of which frames the Holy Face, and the other the Child Jesus, are meant to symbolise Thérèse herself, whose chief desire on earth is to offer herself up as a grape for the plucking. She is to be utterly at his disposal, a grape which the child Jesus can squeeze to get the juice from it, a grape which can refresh his lips dry with thirst. The harp is the

[1] John 15, 5.

symbol of my desire to sign eternally the music of love; the device FMT includes the names of Marie, Françoise and Thérèse. And because I have called myself our Lady's little flower, a flower is shewn refreshed by the rays of the morning star; the green ground represents the family in which I was privileged to grow up, and in the background is a mountain which stands for Carmel. It's on this side of the shield that I have included the arrow of love, which is all my title to martyrdom until such time as I am allowed actually to shed my blood for the love of Jesus. I would like to repay in kind all he has done for me; but I don't forget that I am only a frail reed (also represented in the coat of arms). Finally, the triangle with its rays is the symbol of the Blessed Trinity, ever lavish in its gifts to my unworthy soul; in thanksgiving for these, I shall always keep the motto in mind, " Love can only be repaid by love."

List of the special graces granted by our Lord to his unworthy bride

Birth, January 2, 1873.
Baptism, January 4, 1873.
Our Lady's smile, May 1883.
First Communion, May 8, 1884.
Confirmation, June 14, 1884.
Conversion, December 25, 1886.
Audience with Pope Leo XIII, November 20, 1887.
Entry into Carmel, April 9, 1888.
Taking of the habit, January 10, 1889.
Our greatest treasure of mortification, February 12, 1889.
Canonical examination.
Leo XIII's blessing, September 1890.
Profession, September 8, 1890.
Taking of the veil, September 24, 1890.
Offering of myself to the Divine Love, June 9, 1895.

BOOK TWO

*Letter to Sister Marie
of the Sacred Heart*

Chapter XXX

LETTER ADDRESSED TO SISTER MARIE
OF THE SACRED HEART

DEAR SISTER, you want me to give you a keepsake of my
retreat, perhaps the last retreat I shall ever make. I have
Reverend Mother's leave, and I welcome this chance of
conversing with you. You are my sister by a double title, and
it was you who lent me your voice long ago, promising in my
name that I would serve our Lord faithfully, when I was not
yet capable of speech. Here then, dear godmother, is the
child you offered to God, speaking to you this evening with
all the love a child can feel for its mother, with a gratitude
which you'll only be able to realise in heaven. But why
should you, Sister, of all people, want to know about the
secrets our Lord reveals to your goddaughter? I feel sure
that he reveals them equally to you; wasn't it you who taught
me how to gather up the threads of the divine teaching?
Anyhow, I'll try to put a few words together in a childish
way, though always with the feeling that human speech itself
is incapable of reproducing those experiences which the
human heart only perceives confusedly.

Don't think of me as buoyed up on a tide of spiritual consolation; my only consolation is to have none on this side of
the grave. As for the instruction I get, our Lord bestows that
on me in some hidden way, without ever making his voice
heard. I don't get it from books, because I can't follow what
I read nowadays; only now and again, after a long interval of
stupidity and dryness, a sentence I've read at the end of my
prayer will stay with me; this for example: "You want a

179

guide to dictate your actions to you? Then you must read
in the book of life, which contains the whole science of
loving."[1] The science of loving, yes, that phrase wakes a
gracious echo in my soul; that's the only kind of science I want
—I'd barter away everything I possess to win it, and then,
like the Bride in the Canticles, think nothing of my loss.[2] It's
only love that makes us what God wants us to be, and for
that reason it's the only possession I covet. But how to come
by it? Our Lord has seen fit to shew me the only way which
leads to it, and that is the unconcern with which a child goes
to sleep in its father's arms. " Simple hearts, draw near me,"
says the Holy Spirit in the book of Proverbs[3] and elsewhere he
tells us that it is the insignificant who are treated with
mercy.[4] In his name the prophet Isaias has revealed to us
that at the Last Day he will "tend his flock like a shepherd,
gather up the lambs and carry them in his bosom."[5] And as
if all this were not enough, the same prophet, penetrating with
his inspired gaze the depths of eternity, cries out to us in
God's name: " I will console you then, like a mother caressing
her son: you shall be like children carried at the breast,
fondled on a mother's lap."[6]

When God makes promises like that, what's left for us
except to keep silence before him with tears of gratitude and
love? Oh dear, if all the weak, imperfect souls in the world
could only feel as I do about it—I, who am really the least
considerable of them all—there'd be no reason why a single
one of them should despair of scaling the hill of charity and
reaching the very top. Our Lord doesn't ask for great achieve-
ments, only for self-surrender and for gratitude. Listen to
what he says: " The gifts I accept are not buck-goats from
thy folds; I own already every wild beast in the forest, the hills
are mine, and the herds that people them; there is no bird
flies in heaven but I know of it. If I am hungry, I will not
complain of it to thee, I, who am master of earth and all
that earth contains. Wouldst thou have me eat bull's flesh,
and drink the blood of goats? The sacrifice thou must offer
to God is a sacrifice of praise; so wilt thou perform thy vows

[1] Words of our Lord to St. Margaret Mary.
[2] Canticles, VIII, 7.   [3] Proverbs 9, 4.   [4] Book of Wisdom 6, 7.
[5] Isaias 40, 11.   [6] Isaias 66, 12 and 13.

to the most High."[1] You see what it is that our Lord claims;
it isn't that he wants us to do this or that, he wants us to
love him. The same God who tells us that he has no need of
us when he is hungry wasn't ashamed to beg for a drop of
water from the Samaritan woman—but then, he was thirsty,
and thirsty for what? It was the love of this one despised
creature that the Maker of heaven and earth asked for, when
he said: "Give me some to drink";[2] he was thirsty for love.

I feel continually more conscious of it, this deep longing
our Lord has. Among those who follow the call of the
world, he meets with nothing but ingratitude and indifference;
and even among his own disciples how few hearts there are
that give themselves to him without reserve, that really understand the tenderness of his infinite love. Dear Sister, you and
I are privileged to share the intimate secrets of our heavenly
Bridegroom; and if only you would write down all you
know about them, we should have some splendid pages to
read. But no, you hold for yourself that "Kings have their
counsel that must be kept secret"; it's only to me that you
say: "He honours God's ways best that proclaims them
openly."[3] I'm sure you're right to keep silence as you do; and
it's only for your pleasure that I'm writing these lines. How
am I to express heavenly mysteries in the language of earth?
And besides, do what I could, I should find that I'd written
pages and pages without ever really getting down to the subject. There are so many wide horizons, so many effects of
light and shade, infinitely varied, that I shall have to wait till
this earthly night has passed away before he, the Divine
Artist, lends me the colours to portray the wonderful vistas
which he opens up, even now, to the eye of my soul.

Still, you've asked me to give some account of that dream
I had, and of what you call the "little doctrine" which I try
to hand on. I've done it in these pages which follow, but so
badly that I can't imagine how you will take in what I've
written. It may be that you'll find some of my expressions
overstrained; if so, you must make allowances and put it
down to my wretched style. I assure you that there is nothing
overstrained about the attitude of my soul; that is all calm
and peace. In what follows, I mean to address our Lord

[1] Psalm 49, 9-14.   [2] John 4, 7.   [3] Tobias 12, 7.

himself; I find it easier to express my thoughts that way. I'm afraid they'll be very badly expressed even so.

Jesus, my well-beloved, how considerate you are in your treatment of my worthless soul; storms all around me, and suddenly the sunshine of your grace peeps out! Easter Day had come and gone, the day of your splendid triumph, and it was a Saturday in May; my soul was still storm-tossed. I remember thinking about the wonderful dreams which certain souls have been privileged to experience, and how consoling an experience it would be; but I didn't pray for anything of the kind. When I went to bed, my sky was still overcast, and I told myself that dreams weren't for unimportant souls like mine; it was a storm that rocked me to sleep. Next day was Sunday, the second Sunday of May, and I'm not sure it wasn't actually the anniversary of the day when our Lady did me the grace to smile on me. As the first rays of dawn came, I went to sleep again, and dreamed.

I was standing in a sort of gallery where several other people were present, but our Mother was the only person near me. Suddenly, without seeing how they got there, I was conscious of the presence of three Carmelite sisters in their mantles and big veils. I had the impression that they'd come there to see our Mother; what was borne in upon me with certainty was that they came from heaven. I found myself crying out (but of course it was only in the silence of my heart): "Oh, how I would love to see the face of one of these Carmelites!" Upon which, as if granting my request, the tallest of the three saintly figures moved towards me, and, as I sank to my knees, lifted her veil, lifted it right up, I mean, and threw it over me. I recognised her without the slightest difficulty; the face was that of our Venerable Mother Anne of Jesus, who brought the reformed Carmelite order into France. There was a kind of ethereal beauty about her features, which were not radiant but transfused with light— the light seemed to come from her without being communicated to her, so that the heavenly face was fully visible to me in spite of the veil which surrounded both of us.

I can't describe what elation filled my heart; an experience like that can't be put down on paper. Months have passed by now since I had this reassuring dream, but the memory of it is as fresh as ever, as delightful as ever. I can still see the look on Mother Anne's face, her loving smile; I can still feel the touch of the kisses she gave me. And now, treated with all this tenderness, I plucked up my courage: "Please, Mother," I said, "tell me whether God means to leave me much longer on earth? Or will he come and fetch me soon?" And she, with a most gracious smile, answered: "Yes, soon; very soon, I promise you." Then I added: "Mother, answer me one other question; does God really ask no more of me than these unimportant little sacrifices I offer him, these desires to do something better? Is he really content with me as I am?" That brought into the Saint's face an expression far more loving than I'd seen there yet; and the embrace she gave me was all the answer I needed. But she did speak too: "God asks no more," she said. "He is content with you, well content." And so she embraced me as lovingly as ever mother embraced her child, and then I saw her withdraw. In the midst of all that happiness, I remembered my sisters, and some favours I wanted to ask for them; but it was too late, I'd woken up. And now the storm no longer raged, all my sky was calm and serene. I didn't merely believe, I felt certain that there was a heaven, and that the souls who were its citizens looked after me, thought of me as their child. What gave more strength to this impression was the fact that, up till then, Mother Anne of Jesus meant nothing to me; I'd never asked for her prayers or even thought about her except on the rare occasions when her name came up in conversation. So when I realised how she loved me, and how much I meant to her, my heart melted towards her in love and gratitude; and for that matter towards all the Blessed in heaven.

Jesus, my Beloved, this was only a prelude to greater graces still with which you'd determined to enrich me. Forgive me if I recall them to memory to-day; it's the sixth anniversary of the day when you took me for your bride. Forgive me, Jesus, if I overstep the bounds of right reason in telling you about these longings and hopes of mine, which overstep all bounds; and heal the hurt of my soul by granting these wishes fulfilment.

To be betrothed to you, Jesus, to be a Carmelite, to become, through my union with you, a mother of souls—surely that ought to be enough for anybody? But, somehow, not for me; those privileges I've mentioned are the stuff of my vocation, but I seem to have so many other vocations as well! I feel as if I were called to be a fighter, a priest, an apostle, a doctor, a martyr; as if I could never satisfy the needs of my nature without performing, for your sake, every kind of heroic action at once. I feel as if I'd got the courage to be a Crusader, a Pontifical Zouave, dying on the battle-field in defence of the Church. And at the same time I want to be a priest; how lovingly I'd carry you in my hands when you came down from heaven at my call; how lovingly I'd bestow you upon men's souls! And yet, with all this desire to be a priest, I've nothing but admiration and envy for the humility of St. Francis; I'd willingly imitate him in refusing the honour of the priesthood. Dear Jesus, how am I to reconcile these conflicting ambitions, how am I to give substance to the dreams of one insignificant soul? Insignificant as I am, I long to enlighten men's minds as the prophets and doctors did; I feel the call of an Apostle. I'd like to travel all over the world, making your name known and planting your cross on heathen soil; only I shouldn't be content with one particular mission, I should want to be preaching the gospel on all five continents and in the most distant islands, all at once. And even then it wouldn't do, carrying on my mission for a limited number of years; I should want to have been a missionary ever since the creation, and go on being a missionary till the world came to an end.

But above all I long to shed my blood for you, my Saviour, to the last drop. Martyrdom was the dream of my youth, and this dream has grown in the sheltered world of Carmel; and yet here too I realise that the dream I cherish is an extravagant one—a single form of martyrdom would never be enough for me, I should want to experience them all. I should want to be scourged and crucified as you were; to be flayed alive like St. Bartholomew, to be dipped in boiling oil like St. John, to undergo all that martyr ever underwent; offering my neck to the executioner like St. Agnes and St. Cecily, and, like my favourite St. Joan of Arc, whispering your name as I was tied to the stake. When I think of what Christians will have to go through in the days of Antichrist, my heart beats fast, and I could wish that all these torments were being kept in store for

me. Dear Jesus, I couldn't put down all these longings of
mine without borrowing from you the book of life, and copy-
ing out all the exploits of all the Saints; I do so want them to
be mine! What are you going to say to all these fond imagi-
nations of mine, of a soul so unimportant, so ineffective?
Why, in consideration of my weakness, you found a way to
fulfil my childhood's ambitions, and you've found a way now
to fulfil these other ambitions of mine, world-wide in their
compass.

I was still being tormented by this question of unfulfilled
longings and it was a real martyrdom in my prayer, when I
decided to consult St. Paul's epistles in the hopes of getting an
answer. It was the twelfth and thirteenth chapters of First
Corinthians that claimed my attention. The first of these told
me that we can't all of us be apostles, all of us be prophets, all
of us doctors, and so on; the Church is composed of members
which differ in their use; the eye is one thing and the hand is
another. It was a clear enough answer, but it didn't satisfy
my aspirations, didn't set my heart at rest. The Magdalen, by
stooping now and again into the empty tomb,[1] was at last
rewarded for her search; and I, by sinking down into the
depths of my own nothingness, rose high enough to find what
I wanted![2] Reading on to the end of the chapter, I met this
comforting phrase: "Prize the best gifts of heaven. Meanwhile, I can shew you a way which is better than any other."

What was it? The Apostle goes on to explain that all the
gifts of heaven, even the most perfect of them, without love,
are absolutely nothing; charity is the best way of all, because
it leads straight to God. Now I was at peace; when St. Paul
was talking about the different members of the Mystical Body
I couldn't recognise myself in any of them; or rather I could
recognise myself in all of them. But charity—that was the key
to my vocation. If the Church was a body composed of different members, it couldn't lack the noblest of all; it must have
a heart, and a heart burning with love. And I realised that this
love was the true motive force which enabled the other
members of the Church to act; if it ceased to function the
Apostles would forget to preach the gospel, the Martyrs would
refuse to shed their blood. Love, in fact, is the vocation which

[1] See note on page 131.
[2] A reminiscence of St. John of the Cross.

includes all others; it's a universe of its own, comprising all time and space—it's eternal. Beside myself with joy, I cried out: "Jesus, my Love! I've found my vocation, and my vocation is love." I had discovered where it is that I belong in the Church, the place God has appointed for me. To be nothing else than love, deep down in the heart of Mother Church; that's to be everything at once—my dream wasn't a dream after all.

Beside myself with joy? No, that's the wrong expression; my feeling was rather the calm, restful feeling which comes when you see the lighthouse which is going to guide you into harbour. The beacon of love now shone bright before me; I could reflect its beams. Oh, I know quite well that I am only a child, with all a child's weaknesses; but that's precisely what emboldens me to offer myself as a victim to your love. Under the old law the Lord of Hosts, the great King, would only accept in sacrifice such beasts as were pure and without spot; only perfect victims could satisfy the divine Justice. But now, the law of fear has been replaced by the law of love. And love has chosen me, weak and imperfect creature that I am, for its burnt-offering; that is the gesture we might have expected. Love cannot be content without condescending—condescending to mere nothingness, and making this nothingness the fuel for its flame.

I know well, Jesus, that love can only be repaid by love; what I've always looked for and found at last is some way of satisfying my feelings by returning love for your love. "Make use of your base wealth to win yourselves friends who will welcome you into eternal habitations": that was the advice you gave to your disciples, after warning them that "the children of this world are more prudent after their own fashion than the children of the light."[1] Well, here was I with this restless ambition to be everything at once, to combine all the vocations which might easily prove to be base wealth, harmful to my soul; as a child of the light, then, I'd better use it to make myself friends in eternity. I thought of the prayer Eliseus made to our father Elias when he asked him for a double portion of his spirit,[2] and in that sense I prayed

[1] Luke 16, 8, 9.
[2] Eliseus, as chief heir, asks for a legacy twice as large as that allotted to others (Deuteronomy 21, 17).

to all the Angels and Saints in heaven. "I'm the most insignificant of creatures," I told them, "and I couldn't be more conscious of my own wretched failings. But I know how generous hearts like yours love to do good to those around them, and I want you, the blessed citizens of heaven, to adopt me as your child. Whatever credit I win by such means will belong to you entirely, but don't despise the rash request I make of you when I ask you to obtain for me a double portion of your love."

Jesus, I don't know how to intensify this petition of mine; if I tried to, I might find myself sinking under the weight of my own presumption. My excuse is that I'm just a child, and children don't always weigh their words. But a parent who is enthroned and has great resources at his disposal is ready to humour the caprices of the child he loves, even to the point of fondness, even to the point of weakness. And here am I, a child, the child of Holy Church, that Mother who is also a Queen because she is a King's bride. Child-like, I'm not concerned with riches or honour, even with the glory of heaven; I quite realise that that belongs to my elder brothers, the Angels and the Saints. The reflection of the jewels in my Mother's crown will be glory enough for me; it's love I ask for, love is all the skill I have. Sensational acts of piety are not for me; not for me to preach the gospel, or to shed my blood as a martyr, but I see now that all that doesn't matter; my elder brothers will do the work for me, while I, as the baby of the family, stay close to the King's throne, the Queen's throne, and go on loving on behalf of my brothers, out on the battle-field.

But this love of mine, how to shew it? Love needs to be proved by action. Well, even a little child can scatter flowers, to scent the throne-room with their fragrance; even a little child can sing, in its shrill treble, the great canticle of Love. That shall be my life, to scatter flowers—to miss no single opportunity of making some small sacrifice, here by a smiling look, there by a kindly word, always doing the tiniest things right, and doing it for love. I shall suffer all that I have to suffer—yes, and enjoy all my enjoyments too—in the spirit of love, so that I shall always be scattering flowers before your throne; nothing that comes my way but shall yield up its petals in your honour. And, as I scatter my flowers, I shall be singing; how could one be sad when occupied so pleasantly? I shall be singing, even when I have to pluck my flowers from a thorn-bush; never in better voice than when the thorns are longest and sharpest. I don't ask what use they will be to you, Jesus, these flowers, this music of mine; I know that you will take pleasure in this fragrant shower of worthless petals, in these songs of love in which a worthless heart like mine sings itself out. And because they will give pleasure to you, the Church triumphant in heaven will smile upon them too; will take these flowers so bruised by love* and pass them on into your divine hands. And so the Church in heaven, ready to take part in the childish game I am playing, will begin scattering these flowers, now hallowed by your touch beyond all recognition; will scatter them on the souls in Purgatory, to abate their sufferings, scatter them on the Church Militant, and give her the strength for fresh conquests.

Yes, Jesus, I do love you; I do love the Church, my Mother. And it sticks in my mind that "the slightest movement of disinterested love has more value than all the other acts of a human soul put together."[1] But is mine a disinterested love? Or are these wide-ranging aspirations of mine no better than a dream, a fond illusion? If so, Jesus, make it known to me; I only want to be told the truth. If my longings are presumptuous, make them fade away; why should I suffer needless torment? And yet, I don't think I shall really regret having aspired to the highest levels of love, even if it doesn't mean attaining them hereafter; unless, after death, the memory of all my earthly hopes disappears by some miracle, that memory will always be my consolation; to have suffered like that, to have been a fool for your sake like that, will be something dearer to me than any reward I could have expected in heaven. Let me go on, during my exile, relishing the bitter-sweet experience of this ordeal. Jesus, if the mere desire to love you can yield such happiness, what must it be like to possess, to enjoy your love?

But then, how can a soul so imperfect as mine ever hope to possess love in its fulness? It is to you, Jesus, my first and only love, that I must come for the answer to such a question.

[1] St. John of the Cross, *Spiritual Canticle*, commentary on Stephen, XXIX.

Surely it would have been better to reserve these vaulting ambitions for the really great souls, that can take their eagle-flight close to the summits! Whereas I think of myself as a chick not yet fledged, and no eagle in any case; only some-how, feeble as I am, the eyes of my heart have caught the eagle's trick of staring at the sun, the sun of divine love. The poor fledgling can't hope to imitate those eagles, the great souls who make straight for the throne of the Blessed Trinity; it can only flap its wings in a pathetic attempt to fly. Nothing left for it, you'd think, but to die of disappointment when it finds itself so handicapped. But no, I don't even worry abour that; by a bold act of self-committal, I stay where I am, keeping my eyes fixed on the sun, deterred by no obstacle; storm and rain and cloud-wrack may conceal its heavenly radiance, but I don't shift my view—I know that it is there all the time behind the clouds, its brightness never dimmed. Sometimes, to be sure, the storm thunders at my heart; I find it difficult to believe in the existence of anything except the clouds which limit my horizon. It's only then that I realise the possibilities of my weakness; find consolation in staying at my post, and directing my gaze towards one in-visible light which communicates itself, now, only to the eye of faith.

Jesus, you've been very patient with me up to now, and it's true that I haven't ever strayed far from you; but I know, and you know, how often in my wretched imperfection I allow myself to be distracted, when I ought to be looking steadily all the time at this Sun which claims all my attention. I must look like a bird, picking up a bit of grain now on this side, now on that, running off to catch a worm, coming across a bird-bath and wetting its half-fledged wings there, even having a look at some attractive flower it comes across. Find-ing that I can't compete with the eagles, I am the more ready to occupy my mind with the trifles of earth. But after all these infidelities I don't rush away into a corner and try to weep myself to death. I turn back to that Sun which is the centre of my love, and dry my bedabbled wings in its rays. I tell God all about my faults, in soft swallow-notes, down to the last detail; I throw myself recklessly on him, as the best way to gain control over myself, and to win a greater measure of his love—hasn't he told us that you came to call sinners, not the just?[1]

And what if God gives no sign of listening to these twitterings of mine; what if the sun seems hidden away as much as ever? Well, I have to put up with the discomfort of those wet wings; I stay out in the cold, and derive satisfaction from being allowed to suffer, even though I know that this time it's my own fault. How lucky I count myself, Jesus, in being the frail, weak thing I am! If I were one of the great souls, I'd be ashamed to present myself before you in prayer, and go to sleep over it. That's what I do; when I want to fasten my eyes on the heavenly Sun, and find that the clouds won't let me see a single ray of it, I go to sleep without meaning to. I'm like a bird that shuts its eyes and puts its head under its wing when darkness comes on; does it dream, perhaps, that it is still in the sunshine? Anyhow, when I recollect myself, I don't get distressed over it; with my heart still at rest, I take up again my task of love. I call upon the Angels and Saints, who fly like eagles straight towards their fiery goal; their protection will defend me against the birds of prey which threaten to devour me. The spirits of evil cannot claim me for their own; I belong only to you, Jesus, you who have your eyrie up there in the sun of love.

Divine Word, worthy of all admiration and all love, you draw me continually towards yourself. You came down into this world of exile ready to suffer and die, so as to bring souls within their true orbit, the bosom of the Blessed Trinity; and now, reascended into that inaccessible light which is evermore your dwelling-place, you still frequent this valley of tears, hidden under the appearance of the sacred Host. You are still ready to feed my soul with your own Divinity, my wretched soul, that would sink back into nothingness at any moment if you did not give it life with a look! Jesus, my gratitude bids me say that you love me beyond reason; when I meet with such fondness from you, how can my heart fail to go out to you, how can my trust in you have any limits? The great Saints, in their eagle strength, have gone close to the verge of folly in the wonderful things they did for you; I am too poor a creature to do anything wonderful, but I must be allowed the folly of hoping that your love will accept me

[1] Matthew 9, 13.

as its victim. I must be allowed the folly of entreating these eagles of yours, my elder brothers, to win me the grace I need, that of flying upwards towards the Sun of Love on the eagle-wings you, and you only, can lend me. As long as it is your will, my Beloved, I am ready to remain without any power to fly, as long as I may keep my eyes fixed on you, fascinated by your gracious regard, the prey of your love. And one day, I hope, you will come down from your eyrie to carry off this poor creature of yours, carry it up to the very centre of love, and consume it in love's furnace, to which it has offered itself as a victim.

Dear Jesus, how I wish I could explain to all the souls that are conscious of their own littleness, how great your con-descension is! I am certain that if, by some impossible chance, you could find a soul more feeble, more insignificant than mine, you would overwhelm it with graces still more extraordinary, provided that it would give itself up in entire confidence to your infinite mercy. But why should I feel any need to tell others about the secrets of your love? You, nobody else, have taught them to me, and can I doubt that you yourself will reveal them to others as well? I know you will, and I implore you to do it; I implore you to look down in mercy on a whole multitude of souls that share my littleness; to choose out for yourself a whole legion of victims, so little as to be worthy of your love.

Written by the least of them, Sister Thérèse of the Child Jesus and of the Holy Face.

BOOK THREE

Manuscript Dedicated to
Mother Marie de Gonzague

Chapter XXXI

ADDRESS TO MOTHER MARIE
DE GONZAGUE

DEAR MOTHER, you have expressed the wish that I should finish my task of putting the Lord's mercies on record with you. When I began it, the inspiration came from a well-loved daughter of yours, Mother Agnes of Jesus, to whom God had entrusted the supervision of my first childish steps. Hers it was to conduct the chant, when I sang of the grace given to a little flower in our Lady's garden during the spring-time; now it's your turn, and my song must be about the happiness which it feels ever since the fugitive glimmer of dawn made way for the burning heat of midday. With you at my side, Mother, and in response to your wish, I must try once more to express what is in my heart, my sense of gratitude towards God and towards you, who for me are his visible representative. Wasn't it through your agency that I gave myself up once for all to him?* Do you remember that day, Mother? A heart like yours, I feel sure, can't have forgotten it. As for myself, I must wait till I get to heaven; here on earth I can't find words to describe what my feelings were on that day of benediction.

But, dear Mother, there has been one day since then which knitted my heart to yours, if possible, more firmly still. I mean the day when Jesus laid upon you, for still another time, the burden of being Prioress. Oh yes, Mother, I know it was a sad day for you; but though you went sowing in tears, you will be full of joy in heaven to find what a precious harvest you have reaped. . . . Mother, do you mind this childish way of talking? Of course not; of course you will let me talk to you quite naturally, without thinking up the sort of things a young religious ought to say to her prioress. I dare say I shan't always keep within the bounds of the respect which is due to a superior; but if you don't mind my saying so, it's your fault, because you will always treat me like a mother, not like a prioress in the least.

Dear Mother, I don't find it difficult to realise that whenever you say anything to me, it is God who speaks through you. Plenty of the Sisters think that you've always spoilt me, that I've never had anything but endearments and compliments from you since I entered the cloister. But that isn't true; my first memoir, which gave an account of my early days, will tell you what I think about the firm, motherly discipline I had from you. I thank you from the very bottom of my heart for not having treated me too gently. Jesus knew well enough that the little flower he had planted was in need of watering; only the waters of humiliation could revive it—it was too weak a plant to take root without being helped in this way. And it was through you, Mother, that this blessing was bestowed.

In the last year and a half, Jesus has seen fit to change his plan for making it grow. He must have seen that it has been watered enough; it needed sun to bring it out now. So I get nothing but smiles from him; and once more, Mother, it is through you that his smile comes. Only gentle sunshine, and it makes the flower grow strangely well instead of withering it up; at the bottom of its cup there are still drops of that precious dew which it met with earlier on, and these are enough to remind it how insignificant, how frail a thing it is. I don't know how it is, but somehow if the whole world began to pay attention to me, and talk admiringly about me, and load me with praises, it couldn't add a single drop of false satisfaction to the true satisfaction I already enjoy. And this true satisfaction comes from realising that in God's sight I am a helpless little nonentity—that and nothing more. I say I don't know why this should be so, but perhaps there is an explanation. All through those earlier days, when my cup hadn't been filled up with the waters of humiliation, no praise was offered me; now the danger is over—my humiliations have reached the brim, and I find that draught so satisfying that I would not, at any price, exchange it for such brackish water as the world's compliments are.

When I say that, dear Mother, I'm not thinking of that love and confidence which you, personally, have shewn me; don't think me so unfilial as to be wanting in gratitude about that. No, I only mean that such kindness on the part of other people has no dangers for me now; I can take pleasure in it, attributing to God's mercy whatever good there is in me because it's he who put it there. If he wants to make me appear better than I am, it doesn't worry me; he is free to do what he likes. He leads souls, doesn't he, Mother, by such different ways. When we read the lives of the Saints, we find that many of them didn't trouble to leave anything behind them when they died, never a keepsake, never a scrap of writing. Others, like our mother St. Teresa, have enriched the treasury of the Church with an account of the splendid revelations made to them; they weren't afraid of betraying these royal secrets of his, in the hope of making him better known and better loved. Which kind does God like best? I don't think he has any preferences; all alike have been faithful to the guidance of his Holy Spirit. "Tell the just man," he says, "that everything is all right";[1] everything, so long as we want nothing but the will of Jesus. And here am I, in my small way, obeying the will of Jesus by trying to do what my dear Mother asks of me.

As you know, dear Mother, I've always wished that I could be a saint. But whenever I compared myself to the Saints there was always this unfortunate difference—they were like great mountains, hiding their heads in the clouds, and I was only an insignificant grain of sand, trodden down by all who passed by. However, I wasn't going to be discouraged; I said to myself: "God wouldn't inspire us with ambitions that can't be realised. Obviously there's nothing great to be made of me, so it must be possible for me to aspire to sanctity in spite of my insignificance. I've got to take myself just as I am, with all my imperfections; but somehow I shall have to find out a little way, all of my own, which will be a direct short-cut to heaven. After all (I said to myself) we live in an age of inventions. Nowadays, people don't even bother to

[1] The Saint is quoting from some French translation of Isaias 3, 10; the word "everything" is not expressed in the original.

climb the stairs—rich people, anyhow; they find a lift more convenient. Can't I find a lift which will take me up to Jesus, since I'm not big enough to climb the steep stairway of perfection?" So I looked in the Bible for some hint about the life I wanted, and I came across the passage where Eternal Wisdom says: "Is anyone simple as a little child?[1] Then let him come to me." To that Wisdom I went; it seemed as if I was on the right track; what did God undertake to do for the child-like soul that responded to his invitation? I read on, and this is what I found: "I will console you like a mother caressing her son; you shall be like children carried at the breast, fondled on a mother's lap."[2] Never were words so touching: never was such music to rejoice the heart—I could, after all, be lifted up to heaven, in the arms of Jesus! And if that was to happen, there was no need for me to grow bigger; on the contrary, I must be as small as ever, smaller than ever.

This was better than anything I had hoped for; my God, how was I to make your mercies known? The Psalm says: "It is thou, God, that hast inspired me ever since the days of my youth, and still I am found telling the tale of thy wonders, now when I am old and grey-headed."[3] Old age—what does that mean in my case? Perhaps it means now; after all, in the Lord's sight two thousand years are all the same as twenty; as a single day, for that matter. No, dear Mother, don't imagine that your child is in a hurry to leave you; why should it be a greater grace to die in the prime of life than in life's evening? I care for nothing, I want nothing, except to do what Jesus wants. It's only that I can't help being glad when he seems to come so close, as if he were beckoning me to the glory of his kingdom. As far as doing good here on earth is concerned, I have long realised that God has no need of any human agent; of me least of all.

Forgive me, Mother, if I am making you feel unhappy; I do so want you to be happy. But don't you think that if your prayers aren't fulfilled on earth as you meant them to be, because Jesus intends to separate mother and child for a little while, they will nevertheless be fulfilled in heaven? You

---

[1] The Latin here has "quite small," probably meaning "a little child." In the original Hebrew, the word used is "simple," without any reference to age. The quotation is from Proverbs 9, 4.
[2] Isaias 66, 12 and 13.   [3] Psalm 70, 17-18.

want me to go on performing, here under your guidance, a particular task, a pleasant and an easy task—don't you think that if I were in heaven I could get it done equally well?

You said to me, as Jesus said to St. Peter long ago: " Feed my lambs." And I told you, in amazement, that I was too insignificant a person to do that; couldn't you take over the charge of the lambs yourself and look after me, feed my soul with grace, among the rest? Dear Mother, you did pay some attention to this reasonable request; you did undertake to look after sheep and lambs alike. But at the same time you wanted me to be constantly with them, down there in the shade, telling them which pasture was the richest and most nourishing, pointing out to them the gay blossoms they ought never to touch, except by trampling them underfoot. Why weren't you afraid, Mother, that I should let your little lambs go astray? Why weren't you put off by my youth and inexperience? I suppose you remembered that God does sometimes see fit to bestow wisdom on the least of us, and that Jesus did once, with transports of joy, thank his heavenly Father for keeping his secrets hidden from the prudent, and revealing them to little children. Of course, the great majority of men use their own short-sighted ideas as a yardstick for measuring the divine omnipotence; everywhere in the world we see exceptions, but God isn't allowed to make them! These people reckon experience simply by age; it's been their habit, time out of mind, or why does King David, in his youth, describe himself in one of the psalms as " young and despised "?[1] All the same, he says quite boldly in another part of the psalm—it's the hundred and eighteenth: " More learning have I than my elders, I that hold true to my charge. . . . No lamp like thy word to shew light on my path. . . . How calm my heart was, once I resolved to do thy will."[2] And you, Mother, once told me openly that God was giving me such light as might have come from many years of experience! It's all right, Mother, I've reached a stage of self-abasement at which I don't feel any vanity about things like that, don't

[1] Psalm 118, 141. The Hebrew word, here translated " young," has perhaps rather the sense of " insignificant."
[2] Psalm 118, 100, 105, 60. In verse 60, the new Vatican edition gives a different sense.

even feel inclined to coin suitable phrases which would make you think I was ever so humble about them. I prefer simply to recognise, like a true daughter of his Blessed Mother, that Almighty God has done great things in me, and the greatest of all is to make me conscious of my own littleness, my own incapacity.

Chapter XXXII

OBSCURATION OF THERESE'S FAITH

DEAR MOTHER, you don't need to be told that God has seen fit to subject my soul to trials of many different kinds. I've had much to suffer since I came into the world, and the only difference is that whereas, as a child, it brought me sadness, it doesn't do that any longer. It brings me joy and peace; suffering is real happiness to me. Mother, if it doesn't raise a smile when I say that, it's only because you know my heart through and through; of course, to judge by outward appearances, nobody has ever had to go through so little as I have. And yet if people could see what I've been suffering during this last year, how it would astonish them! You, Mother, know all about this trial that has come to me; but I must go on talking to you about it, because I think of it as a great grace, and it is one of the blessings which have come to me during your term of office.

Last year, God granted me the happiness of observing the Lenten fast in all its rigour. I had never felt so strong, and this strength lasted me out till Easter. But on Good Friday Jesus had a present for me; nothing less than the hope of seeing him, quite soon, in heaven. What a wonderful day to look back on! I went up to bed after watching till midnight at the altar of repose, and I had scarcely laid my head on the pillow when I became conscious of what seemed like a warm tide that rose up, up, till it reached my lips. I wasn't sure what it was, but my soul was flooded with joy at the thought that I was going to die; surely I must be spitting blood? Only the lamp was out, so I had to wait till morning to make certain that it was all right. It wasn't a long wait; my first thought on waking was of good news coming to me, and as soon as I got to the window I realised that there was no mistake. With an intense feeling of inward happiness, I cherished the conviction that Jesus, on the anniversary of his own death, was sending me his first summons. The cry, "The Bridegroom is

198

on his way,"[1] had reached me in the form of a soft murmur from a distance.

I attended Prime and the Chapter of Faults very devoutly; I was impatient for my turn to come, so that in asking for your pardon I might have the chance of confiding to you, dear Mother, my hopes and my happiness. I added (what was perfectly true) that I was in no pain, and begged you, Mother, not to treat me differently from anybody else. That was all right; much to my relief, I was allowed to spend Good Friday in my own way. Never had it appealed to me so much, the severe way of practising austerities we have in Carmel; I was buoyed up all the time by the thought of heaven being so near. At last the happy hours drew to an end, and bed-time came; but once more Jesus gave me the sign of dismissal; Eternity couldn't be far off now. I should explain that at this time I had a faith so living and so lucid that the thought of heaven was the sum of all my happiness. I couldn't believe that there really were godless people who had no faith at all; it was only by being false to his own inner convictions that a man could deny the existence of heaven. What, no beautiful heaven, where God himself would be our eternal reward?

But there are souls which haven't got any faith, which lose, through misuse of grace, this precious treasure, fountain of all pure and true happiness. And now, in those happy days of Easter-tide, Jesus taught me to realise that. He allowed my soul to be overrun by an impenetrable darkness, which made the thought of heaven, hitherto so welcome, a subject of nothing but conflict and torment. And this trial was not to be a matter of a few days or a few weeks; it was to last until the moment when God should see fit to remove it. And that moment hasn't come yet.

I wish I could put down what I feel about it, but unfortunately that isn't possible; to appreciate the darkness of this tunnel, you have to have been through it. Perhaps, though, I might try to explain it by a comparison. You must imagine that I've been born in a country entirely overspread with a thick mist; I have never seen nature in her smiling mood, all bathed and transfigured in the sunlight. But I've heard of these wonderful experiences, ever since I was a child; and I know that the country in which I live is not my native

[1] Matthew 25, 6.

country; *that* lies elsewhere, and it must always be the centre of my longings. Mightn't that, you suggest, be simply a fable, invented by some dweller in the mist? Oh no, the fact is certain; the King of that sunlit country has come and lived in the darkness, lived there for thirty-three years.

Poor darkness, that could not recognise him for what he was, the King of Light! But here am I, Lord, one of your own children, to whom your divine light has made itself known; and, by way of asking pardon for these brothers of mine, I am ready to live on starvation diet as long as you will have it so—not for me to rise from this unappetising meal I share with poor sinners until the appointed time comes. Meanwhile, I can only pray' in my own name, and in the name of these brothers of mine : " Lord, have mercy on us, we are sinners! Send us home restored to your favour. May all those who have no torch of faith to guide them catch sight, at least, of its rays. And, Jesus, if the table they have defiled must be cleansed by the sacrifice of a soul that still loves you, let me go on there alone, taking my fill of trials, until you are ready to receive me into your bright kingdom. All I ask is that no sin of mine may offend you."

Dear Mother, I seem to be writing just anyhow; here is my fairy-story about the country of darkness turning all of a sudden into a kind of prayer. I can't imagine how it can interest you, trying to master ideas so badly expressed and so confused as mine. But after all, Mother, I'm not writing for the sake of literary effect, I'm simply writing under obedience, and even if you find it tedious, you will at least realise that I've done my best. So I will make bold to take up my parable where I left off. What I was saying was that the sure prospect of escaping from this dark world of exile has been granted me from childhood upwards; and it wasn't simply that I accepted it on the authority of people who knew more of the matter than I did—I felt, in the very depths of my heart, aspirations which could only be satisfied by a world more beautiful than this. Just as Christopher Columbus divined, by instinct, the existence of a New World which nobody had hitherto dreamt of, so I had this feeling that a better country was to be, one day, my abiding home. And now, all of a sudden, the mists around me have become denser than ever; they sink deep into my soul and wrap it round so that I can't recover

the dear image of my native country any more—everything
has disappeared.

I get tired of the darkness all around me, and try to refresh
my jaded spirits with the thoughts of that bright country
where my hopes lie; and what happens? It is worse torment
than ever; the darkness itself seems to borrow, from the
sinners who live in it, the gift of speech. I hear its mocking
accents; "It's all a dream, this talk of a heavenly country,
bathed in light, scented with delicious perfumes, and of a God
who made it all, who is to be your possession in eternity!
You really believe, do you, that the mist which hangs about
you will clear away later on? All right, all right, go on
longing for death! But death will make nonsense of your
hopes; it will only mean a night darker than ever, the night of
mere non-existence."

Dear Mother, I've tried to give you some picture of the
darkness in which my soul is blindfolded; only of course it
does no more justice to the truth than an artist's first sketch
does to his model. But how can I go on writing about it
without running the risk of talking blasphemously? As it
is, I'm terrified of having said too much. If I've done Jesus an
injury, may he forgive me for it; he knows well enough that
I do try to live the faith, even when I get no satisfaction out of
it. I don't suppose I've made as many acts of faith in all the
rest of my life as I have during this past year. Every time the
conflict is renewed, at each challenge from the enemy, I give
a good account of myself—by meeting him face to face? Oh
no; only a coward accepts the challenge to a duel. No, I turn
my back in contempt, and take refuge in Jesus, telling him
that I'm ready to defend the doctrine of heaven with the last
drop of my blood. What does it matter, that I should catch
no glimpse of its beauties, here on earth, if that will help
poor sinners to see them in eternity? And so, though it robs
me of all enjoyment in life, this ordeal God has sent me, I
can still tell him that everything he does is delightful to me;[1]
because after all there's no greater joy than to accept suffering
for the love of him. And if it's interior suffering, hidden away
from one's fellow-creatures, he is all the better pleased.
Although, for that matter, if he took no notice at all (supposing that were possible), it wouldn't worry me; I should still be

[1] Psalm 91, 5.

glad to suffer if there were any chance of making reparation, in that way, for a single sin of unbelief.

Dear Mother, does it sound as if I were exaggerating my symptoms? Of course, to judge by the sentiments I express in all the little poems I've made up during the last year, you might imagine that my soul was as full of consolations as it could hold; that, for me, the veil which hides the unseen scarcely existed. And all the time it isn't just a veil, it's a great wall which reaches up to the sky and blots out the stars! No, when I write poems about the happiness of heaven and the eternal possession of God, it strikes no chord of happiness in my own heart—I'm simply talking about what I'm determined to believe. Sometimes, it's true, a tiny ray of light pierces through the darkness, and then, just for a moment, the ordeal is over; but immediately afterwards the memory of it brings me no happiness, it seems to make the darkness thicker than ever. Mother, I don't think I'd ever quite realised before how gracious and merciful God is to us; he's sent me this ordeal just when I was strong enough to bear it—earlier on, I might well have given way to discouragement, whereas now it only serves to purge away all that natural satisfaction which my longing for heaven might have brought me. Dear Mother, what's left now to hinder my soul from taking its flight? The only thing I want badly now is to go on loving till I die of love.

Chapter XXXIII

THERESE AND THE FOREIGN MISSIONS

MOTHER, I can hardly believe my eyes when I look at the scrawl I produced for you yesterday. My hand shook so that I had to stop, and I'm sorry now that I tried to write at all. Let's hope my writing will be more legible to-day, because I'm no longer tucked up in bed; I shall do better in this dear little white arm-chair. Mother, I quite see that I'm always wandering off the point; but I did want, before going on to recall the past, to say something about my feelings at the moment, for fear I should forget about them later on. And the first thing I want to say is that I really am touched by all these motherly attentions of yours; my heart really is overflowing with gratitude, and I shall never forget what I owe you, never. The most touching thing of all is this novena which you're making to our Lady of Victories, all the Masses you're having said for my recovery. What a wealth of spiritual resources! No wonder I feel, already, that it's done a lot of good to my soul. At the beginning of the novena, I told you that the Blessed Virgin really must either cure me or carry me off to heaven; I couldn't bear the thought of you and the community being burdened with the care of a young religious who had fallen ill. But now I'm ready to be an invalid all my life if God wants to have it like that, and I don't care how long my life is; the only grace I ask for is that it shall be a wounded life, wounded by love.

No, it's not that I'm afraid of having a long life. I'm not going to shirk the field of battle; the Lord is my rockfastness, he makes these hands strong for battle, these fingers skilled in fight; he protects me and gives me confidence.[1] So I've never asked God for an early death, but I've always hoped that this may be his will for me. You see, when it's a question of undertaking work for his divine glory, he often allows the

[1] Psalm 143, 1.

will to count for the deed; and you know what my ambitions have been like—enormous.

You know, too, Mother, that Jesus has more than once put a cup of bitterness to my lips, and then taken it away before I could drink it, but not before I had tasted how bitter it was.[1] Dear Mother, King David was quite right when he said: " Gracious the sight, and full of comfort, when brethren dwell united ";[2] it's true, and I've felt it often enough, but always, here on earth, unity like that has to be cradled in sacrifice. I didn't enter Carmel for the joy of living with my sisters; I did it entirely in answer to the call of Jesus. And I knew well enough that it was going to be a mortification all the time, living with one's sisters when one was determined to restrain one's natural affection for them. I don't mean it's a virtue to keep your distance from your own relations in the convent; how can people think that? Nobody has ever blamed a set of brothers for fighting on the same field of battle, or sallying out in company to win the crown of martyr-dom; obviously they will encourage one another, and, what is more, the martyrdom of each will be a kind of martyrdom for the rest. And there is the same kind of solidarity about the religious life—which, indeed, has been described by theolo-gians as a martyrdom. One's heart, in giving itself to God, does not lose its natural sensitivity; on the contrary, it grows more tender as its love becomes purer and more divine. I have my full share of this sensitiveness, in the love which I bear towards you and my sisters; nothing would please me better than to go on living among my own family, to fight God's battles side by side with the rest. But at the same time I'm quite ready to hurry off at a moment's notice to some other battle-field, if my Divine Commander wanted me to. I shouldn't wait for express orders from him; a mere look, a mere gesture, would be enough.

Ever since I took shelter in the Ark of holy religion, I've had the idea that if Jesus didn't take me away to heaven quite soon, he might make the same use of me as Noé made of that poor little dove. One day, God would let me out of the window and tell me to fly far away, far away, to some heathen

---

[1] Perhaps referring especially to the possibility of being sent out to the missions; cf. the next paragraph.
[2] Psalm 132, 1.

shore, carrying a tiny olive-branch with me. The very thought, Mother, lent wings to my soul; I felt as if I were flying through the air with all creation at my feet! And I realised that there could be such a thing as separation, even in Carmel; there could be no complete or lasting union except in heaven. I determined that my soul would make its dwelling-place there, and see everything that happens on earth as if it were happening a long distance away. I used to resign myself to the idea of exile in an unknown country, and—what hurt much more—to the idea of my own sisters having to undergo that exile. I shall never forget the second of August, 1896, the date when the missionaries did actually sail, and it was an open question whether Mother Agnes of Jesus wouldn't be one of them. Oh, I wouldn't have lifted a finger to prevent it; but there was a terrible load on my heart. Surely a soul like hers, with all that sensitiveness, that delicacy of feeling, was never made to live among people who couldn't possibly appreciate her! A thousand anxieties of this sort came surging up into my mind, and Jesus wouldn't interfere, wouldn't calm the waves. So I said: " Dear God, I'm ready to put up with anything for the love of you; I'm quite ready to die of sorrow, if that is your will for me." And with that act of resignation, Jesus was satisfied.

A few months later, there was talk of two other sisters going out; Sister Geneviève and Sister Mary of the Trinity. This, too, was a searching test; it went very deep. I used to picture to myself all the trials and disappointments they would have to undergo, till I could see no rift in the clouds; it was only at the very depths of my heart that there was any peace and calm left. Dear Mother, you were wise enough to know what God wanted done about it, and in his name you told your novices not to think of leaving the nursery yet. It wasn't that you didn't understand their ambitions; you yourself, in earlier days, had asked to be sent out to Saigon. How often it happens that a mother's wish finds an echo in the hearts of her children!

In my own soul, dear Mother, this apostolic ambition of yours, as you know, has found a faithful echo. Just let me tell you why it is that it has always been my wish, and still is my wish, if our Lady should restore me to health, to go out into the wilderness, and leave this delightful oasis, where I live so happily under your motherly care. You told me once that being a Carmelite in a missionary country needs a special vocation, and many people think they've got it when they haven't; you also told me that I have got it, and my health is the only obstacle which makes the idea impossible for me. Clearly, if God wanted me to serve him in distant parts, this obstacle would disappear, so I can make my mind easy about it. But supposing I had to leave you, leave this dear Carmel of mine? Don't imagine that such a parting could be painless; Jesus didn't mean me to have a heart of stone! And it's just because my heart suffers so easily that I mean it to offer Jesus all the suffering it's capable of.

Mother, look at the life I live here! Untouched by the anxieties which make the world such a miserable place—all I've got to do is to carry out the work you've given me to do, such pleasant, such easy work! And then, all this motherly care you shower on me! I never feel the pinch of poverty; I've always got everything I want. But above all, here at Carmel I have your love and the love of all the sisters, and it means so much to me! So my dream, you see, is of a convent where I should be quite unknown, where I should really have to face poverty, and the want of affection; exile of the heart. If I'm ready to give up so much that's dear to me, it's not because I imagine I could be of any use to the foreign Carmel which would take me in. Of course I'd do whatever was expected of me, but I know how incompetent I am; I should do my best, but I should do everything badly, because as I was saying just now I've no head for anything practical. No, my only aim would be to do God's will, and sacrifice myself to him in whatever way pleases him best.

A disappointing experience? Clearly it couldn't be that; when you are looking forward to pure, unadulterated suffering, the least ray of happiness comes to you as a surprise packet! And besides, Mother, as you know very well, the greatest happiness of all is the suffering itself, once you've come to regard it as the only treasure worth looking for. But if I'm anxious to go off to the missions, it's not with the idea of having anything to shew for my pains. If that were in my mind, I shouldn't be enjoying this delicious sense of peace; I should be suffering from the mere fact of not being able to follow up my vocation. As it is, I've ceased to be my own mistress, this long while back; I've given myself up entirely to Jesus instead, so he is at liberty to do exactly what he likes with me. He gave me this longing for complete exile, and at the same time he made it clear to me what sufferings such a life would involve; was I ready to drink the chalice of its dregs? Immediately, I put out my hand to take it, this cup Jesus was offering me; but he, thereupon, held it back, and let me see that all he wanted was my willingness to accept it.

Isn't it extraordinary, Mother, what a lot of anxiety you can avoid by taking the vow of obedience? How enviable it is, the simple creed of the religious, who has only one compass to steer by, the will of her superiors! She knows for certain, all the time, that she is on the right path; there's no fear that she can go wrong, even when she feels fairly certain that her superiors are wrong. When people lose sight of this unfailing guide, refusing to follow it and claiming to follow the will of God, which has been misunderstood by his representatives, they find themselves, all at once, wandering about on desert paths where the supply of grace is bound to dry up before long. As far as I'm concerned, dear Mother, you are the compass; Jesus means you to guide me safe to the shore of eternity; and I can't tell you what a comfort it is to look at you, look hard at you,* and keep on doing God's will like that. Ever since he began to let me have temptations against the virtue of faith, he has established the spirit of faith more firmly than ever in my heart; so that I see in you not merely a mother, greatly loving and greatly loved, but beyond all that Jesus himself, alive in your soul and communicating his will to me through you. Of course, you treat me like a special case, like a spoilt child, so that obedience costs me nothing. But something deep down in my heart tells me that I should act just as I do, love you as much as I do, if you saw fit to treat me harshly. I should still know that it was the will of Jesus; you would only be doing it for the greater good of my soul.

Chapter XXXIV

LITTLE SACRIFICES OF THE CLOISTER

DURING THIS last year, dear Mother, God has been very gracious to me in making me understand what is meant by charity. Well, of course, I did understand it before, but only in a very imperfect way; I hadn't got to the bottom of what Jesus meant when he said that the second commandment is like the first, "Thou shalt love thy neighbour as thyself."[1] I was making a special effort to love God better; and in doing that, it was borne in upon me that it was no use as long as my love simply expressed itself in words: "The kingdom of heaven will not give entrance to every man who calls me Master, Master; only to the man who does the will of God, my Father."[2] What was this will of God? Jesus kept on telling us about that; you might almost say on every page of his gospel. But at the Last Supper he makes it clearer still. He knows that the hearts of his disciples are aglow, more than ever, with love for him, because they have just received him in that wonderful mystery of his, the Holy Eucharist. So he gives them, this dear Redeemer of ours, a new commandment. He says to them—oh, so tenderly!—" I have a new commandment to give you, that you are to love one another; that your love for one another is to be like the love I have borne you. The mark by which all men will know you for my disciples will be the love you bear one another."[3]

Well, how did Jesus love his disciples? And why did he love his disciples? You may be quite sure that their natural qualities did nothing to attract him. After all, he stood at an infinite distance from them; he was eternal Knowledge, eternal Wisdom—they were only poor sinners, so ignorant, their thoughts so earth-bound; and yet Jesus calls them his friends, his brothers. He wants them to reign with him in his Father's kingdom; he is determined to win them admission, even if it means dying on a cross for it; " this is the greatest

[1] Matthew 22, 39.   [2] Matthew 7, 21.   [3] John 15, 12.

208

love a man can shew," as he put it himself, "that he should lay down his life for his friends."[1]

Meditating on these words of Jesus, Mother, I began to see how imperfect my own love was; it was so obvious that I didn't love my sisters as God loves them. I realise, now, that perfect love means putting up with other people's short-comings, feeling no surprise at their weaknesses, finding encouragement even in the slightest evidence of good qualities in them. But the point which came home to me most of all was that it was no good leaving charity locked up in the depths of your heart. "A lamp," Jesus says, "is not lighted to be put away under a bushel measure; it is put on the lamp-stand, to give light to all the people of the house."[2] The lamp, I suppose, stands for charity; and the cheerful light it gives isn't meant simply for the people we are fond of; it is meant for everybody in the house, without exception.

To love your neighbour as yourself—that was the rule God laid down before the Incarnation; he knew what a powerful motive self-love was, and he could find no higher standard by which to measure the love of one's neighbour. But this wasn't the "new commandment" Jesus gave to his apostles, his own commandment, as he calls it a bit lower down.[3] I am not just to love my neighbour as myself; I am to love them as Jesus loves them, and will love them till the end of time. Dear Lord, you never tell us to do what is impossible, and yet you can see more clearly than I do how weak and imperfect I am; if, then, you tell me to love my sisters as you love them, that must mean that you yourself go on loving them in and through me—you know it wouldn't be possible in any other way. There would have been no new commandment, if you hadn't meant to give me the grace to keep it; how I welcome it, then, as proof that your will is to love, in and through me, all the people you tell me to love!

Always, when I act as charity bids, I have this feeling that it is Jesus who is acting in me; the closer my union with him, the greater my love for all the sisters without distinction. What do I do when I want this love to grow stronger in me? How do I react, when the devil tries to fix my minds' eye on the defects of some sister who hasn't much attraction for me? I remind myself, in a great hurry, of all that sister's good qualities, all her good intentions. True enough, she's made a slip this time; but who's going to tell us how often she's fought temptation and conquered it, only she was too humble to let us notice it?

It's even possible that what I think of as a fault was in reality a praiseworthy act—it depends on the intention. I don't need to be assured on that point, because I once had experience of it myself in a small way; the moral being that you shouldn't pass judgement on other people. It was during recreation; the portress had rung twice, and that meant the enclosure door had got to be opened, to let the workmen bring in some trees for the Crib. You weren't there, dear Mother, so the recreation wasn't much fun, and I thought it would suit me quite well if I were sent out to lend an extra hand.* Sure enough, Mother sub-Prioress called on me and the sister who was next to me; one of us was to go. So I started at once to undo the strings of my apron, but rather slowly, so as to let the other sister finish first; I thought she might like the chance of lending a hand outside. The sister who was in charge of things* stood there, smiling as she looked at us, and when she saw me get up last she said: " I thought as much, slowcoach! No extra jewel for your crown that time." And of course all the community must have thought I was just being selfish.

I can't tell you what a lot of good this tiny little incident did me, in making me kinder about other people's faults! Another thing—it's good for my vanity; when people speak well of me, I say to myself: " They mark it down as a fault in me, when I try to do a bit of good; what about these good qualities they find in me? Mayn't they really be faults?" And then I add, quoting from St. Paul: " I make little account of any human audit-day; I am not even at pains to scrutinise my own conduct; it is the Lord's scrutiny I must undergo."[1] And what is the best way to ensure that God will judge you favourably—or rather, won't judge you at all? Why, I do my best to have none but charitable thoughts in my own mind; hasn't our Lord said: " Do not judge others, or you yourselves will be judged "?[2]

Dear Mother, to read what I've just written, you might imagine that keeping the commandment of charity has no

[1] I Corinthians 4, 3, 4.   [2] Matthew 7, 1.

difficulties for me! Well, it is true that for some months past the practice of this lovely virtue hasn't been the pitched battle it used to be; but I don't mean there haven't been any lapses; dear me, I am much too full of imperfections for that! I only mean that I don't find much difficulty, now, about picking myself up after a fall. The fact is that I had the best of it in one particular fight against temptation; and now the holy Angels rally to my side, because they can't bear to see me beaten, after the epoch-making victory which I'm going to describe to you!

There's one sister in the community who has the knack of rubbing me up the wrong way at every turn; her tricks of manner, her tricks of speech, her character, just strike me as unlovable. But then, she's a holy religious; God must love her dearly; so I wasn't going to let this natural antipathy get the better of me. I reminded myself that charity isn't a matter of fine sentiments; it means doing things. So I determined to treat this sister as if she were the person I loved best in the world. Every time I met her, I used to pray for her, offering to God all her virtues and her merits. I felt certain that Jesus would like me to do that, because all artists like to hear their work praised, and Jesus, who fashions men's souls so skilfully, doesn't want us to stand about admiring the façade— he wants us to make our way in, till we reach the inmost sanctuary which is his chosen dwelling, and admire the beauty of that. But I didn't confine myself to saying a lot of prayers for her, this sister who made life such a tug-of-war for me; I tried to do her every good turn I possibly could. When I felt tempted to take her down with an unkind retort, I would put on my best smile instead, and try to change the subject; doesn't the *Imitation* tell us that it's better to let other people have their way in an argument, than to go on wrangling over it?[1] We used often to meet, outside recreation-time, over our work; and when the struggle was too much for me, I used to turn tail and run.

She was quite unconscious of what I really felt about her, and never realised why I behaved as I did; to this day, she is persuaded that her personality somehow attracts me. Once at recreation she actually said, beaming all over, something like this: " I wish you would tell me, Sister Thérèse of the

[1] *Imitation of Christ*, III, xliv, 1.

Child Jesus, what it is about me that gets the right side of you? You've always got a smile for me whenever I see you." Well, of course, what really attracted me about her was Jesus hidden in the depths of her soul; Jesus makes the bitterest mouthful taste sweet. I could only say that the sight of her always made me smile with pleasure—naturally I didn't explain that the pleasure was entirely spiritual.

In the last resort, dear Mother, as I've told you, my recipe for victory is to run away; I used to try this even in my noviciate, and I always found it worked. I must tell you about one instance of that kind, Mother, because it will amuse you. One morning, when you were having one of your attacks of bronchitis, I stole along very quietly to put some keys in your room—it was the keys of the communion grille, because I was sacristan at the time. In my heart of hearts I rather welcomed this chance of getting a sight of you, but of course I took great care not to shew it. And one of the sisters saw me; actually she was very fond of me, but in the goodness of her heart she was afraid I would wake you up, so she offered to relieve me of the keys.* I'm afraid I was too cantankerous to give up my rights like that, so I told her, very politely, that I was just as anxious not to wake you as she was, but giving back the keys was my job. Of course I realise now that it would have shewn a much better spirit if I had let her have her way; she was only a young nun, but she was my senior. At the time I thought otherwise; so there was I doing my best to follow her into your room, while she held the door fast to prevent me getting in,* till the dreadful thing happened we were both afraid of—the noise we made woke you up.

Naturally after that I was the villain of the piece, and the poor sister I'd fallen foul of began to indulge in a long diatribe, of which the burden was: "That was Sister Thérèse of the Child Jesus making that noise! Oh dear, how difficult she is!" My story was quite different, and I wanted badly to stick up for myself, but fortunately a bright idea came to me— if I started to defend myself, could I hope to preserve my peace of mind? At the same time, I didn't think I'd enough patience to stand by and hold my tongue while I was being attacked like this; I'd only one chance left, and that was to run away. No sooner said than done; I quitted the field without beat of drum, leaving the sister to go on with her speech, which was reminiscent of Camilla's curse against Rome.[1] My heart was beating so fast that I couldn't go any distance, I just sat down on the stairs to be alone with the spoils of my victory. It wasn't very heroic, was it, Mother? But I have a strong feeling that it's best not to engage in a battle when defeat is quite certain.

Oh dear, when I look back at my noviciate, I see how unfledged I was; it makes me laugh, now, to think what heavy weather I made over nothing at all. How can I thank God enough for having made my soul grow up since then, given it the use of its wings? The arts of the fowler have no terrors for me now; " the snare is laid to no purpose, if the bird is watching."[2] Later on, no doubt, the present state of my soul will appear to me, in its turn, as full of imperfections! But at least I've learnt not to be surprised at anything—it doesn't worry me to discover that I am frailty itself; on the contrary I go about boasting of it. Every day, I expect to find out a fresh lot of imperfections in my character; charity, we are told, " draws the veil over a multitude of sins," and here is a rich mine Jesus has shewn me.[3]

---

[1] Corneille's *Horace*, iv, 5.   [2] Proverbs 1, 17.

[3] I Peter 4, 8, quoting Proverbs 10, 12. The Saint seems to imply that she has a rich supply of faults, which encourage her to counterbalance them by the exercise of charity.

Chapter XXXV

TOWARDS THE HEART OF CHARITY

WHAT IS the novelty of our Lord's New Commandment? He has told us himself, in the Gospel: "You have heard that it was said, Thou shalt love thy neighbour and hate thy enemy. But I tell you, Love your enemies, pray for those who persecute you."[1] Of course, you don't meet enemies in Carmel; but when all is said and done you have your sympathies. One sister attracts you; another sister—well, you'd go a good long way round to avoid meeting her; without knowing it, she is your persecutress. Good; then Jesus tells me this is the sister I've got to love, the sister I've got to pray for. Her behaviour, to be sure, suggests that she isn't any too fond of me; yes, but, "What credit is it to you, if you love those who love you? Even sinners love those who love them."[2] And just loving her isn't enough; you've got to prove it. We find a natural satisfaction in making presents, especially if they're surprise presents, to people we are fond of, but that's not charity—sinners find the same. Another point in our Lord's teaching; he says: "Give to every man who asks, and if a man takes what is thine, do not ask him to restore it."[3] Giving what one's asked for—how much less enjoyable than offering something of one's own accord, out of the goodness of one's heart! Moreover, people have different ways of asking for a thing; if they do it nicely, the gift doesn't cost you much, but if they don't succeed in wording the request so tactfully, your pride is up in arms at once—unless your soul is well grounded in charity. You hit upon a thousand reasons for refusing it altogether; first of all, you have to impress on the wretched woman a sense of her great tactlessness, and only after that do you do what she asks, as a special favour—probably some tiny service which wouldn't have taken a twentieth of the time you spent in airing your imaginary grievance!

And when it comes to letting people take away what

[1] Matthew 5, 43. [2] Luke 6, 32. [3] Luke 6, 30.

214

belongs to you, without asking to have it back—that's much harder than giving things to people who ask for them. Of course, Mother, when I say it's more difficult I really mean it *seems* more difficult. The Lord's yoke, after all, is a light and easy yoke, and once you have taken it on your shoulders you feel the charm of it—those words of the Psalmist come to your lips: " Do but open my heart wide, and easy lies the path thou has decreed."[1] What is going to open my heart wide? Nothing but love. Once the heart has been melted down in this gentle flame, what a pleasure it is, dear Jesus, to run along this new path you've traced for us, your *new* commandment! I mean to go on running like that, till the blessed day comes when you let me join the retinue of virgins that escorts you to the marriage-feast; then, with no narrow path, but infinite space at my feet, I shall be able to follow you with a *new* song; what song will it be? It can only be the song of love.

What was I saying? Oh yes, Jesus tells me not to claim the restoration of my own property; surely I ought to find that easy and natural enough—it isn't as if there were anything I could call *mine*. I've taken a vow of poverty, renouncing all worldly goods; so I've no right if somebody takes away a thing which doesn't belong to me; how nice to feel really poor! Arguing like that, I used to imagine that I was completely free from all attachments; it's only since I've begun to understand what Jesus meant, that I've realised how bad I am at rising to the occasion. When I'm painting, for instance, I know perfectly well that none of the things belong to me. Then I sit down to work, and find the brushes and the colours all jumbled up anyhow; or there's something missing, a ruler or a pen-knife; and there I am, all at once, at the end of my patience! I have to hold myself in with both hands, or I'm sure to make myself unpleasant when I ask if I can have the missing things back. Naturally, one has to ask for them sometimes, if one can't get on without them; but that's all right—it's not disobeying Jesus if you do it humbly. The thing is to behave like a beggar, holding your hand out (because you've got to make a living), but not being in the least surprised if people refuse—after all, you've no rights.

Oh, how peace comes flooding into the soul, when once it

learns to rise above its natural sensitiveness! To be really poor in spirit—there's no joy like it. You ask, with complete unconcern, for something you really need, and the other person not only refuses, but wants you to hand over something you've got already; what do you do? Why, what our Lord advises us to do: " If a man is ready to go to law with thee over thy coat, let him have it and thy cloak with it."[1] I suppose the idea of giving up one's cloak is renouncing the last shred of dignity, treating oneself as everybody's drudge, everybody's slave. Well, now that you've taken off your coat, you're in a good position for walking—running, if you want to; so our Lord goes on: " If he compels thee to attend him on a mile's journey, go two miles with him of thy own accord."[2] You see, it's not enough to give people what they ask for; we've got to go one better. When I do a service to other people, they ought to get the impression that I'm grateful and honoured to have the opportunity; when they take away something I'm wanting to use, there must be no show of reluctance; I must look as if I was glad to be rid of it. Of course, dear Mother, when I tell you that I've got these ideas, I don't mean for a moment that I carry them out. But somehow I get peace merely from wanting to carry them out.

To-day, more than ever, I seem to have expressed myself very badly; I've written a sort of sermon about charity, and it must have been uphill work for you reading it. Please forgive me, dear Mother; you've got to consider that the infirmarian sisters, at the moment, are treating me just in the way I've been describing—they don't hesitate to walk a mile where twenty yards would do; so I'm in a good position for watching charity in action! This devotion of theirs, which ought of course to be balm to my soul, has a rather paralysing effect on my brain; so that my pen has lost something of its briskness. I can't put down my thoughts properly unless I'm as lonely as a sparrow on the house-top, and this isn't a common experience. The moment I take up my pen to write, one of the dear sisters comes along with a pitch-fork on her shoulder, passing close by me—a little chat, she thinks, would do me good. First it's the hay-making, then it's the ducks, then it's the chickens, then it's a visit from the doctor, one thing after another. It doesn't really last long, but there are quite a lot

[1] Matthew 5, 40.   [2] Matthew 5, 41.

of the sisters who are kind to me like this. . . . Sudden appearance of another haymaker, who puts down some flowers in my lap, presumably by way of giving me some ideas for writing poetry! But I'm not wanting to write poetry just now, and I'd rather the flowers were left to wave on their stalks. So it goes on; at last I get tired of opening and shutting the famous autobiography, and open a book instead (not that it will stay open), with the intimation that now I'm going to copy out some texts from the Psalms and the Gospels, for our Reverend Mother's feast—that's quite true, because I'm always free with my quotations.

It would make you laugh, Mother, if I told you about all my adventures in the tangled undergrowth of Carmel; I don't think I've ever managed to write ten lines without being interrupted. No laughing matter, you'd think, for me; but I'm so grateful to God, and to the dear sisters themselves for all their charity to me, that I do try to look pleased and above all to *be* pleased about it. . . . What's this? A hay-making nun has just taken leave of me with the words: " Poor little sister, it must be very tiring for you to be writing like that all day." " Don't worry about that," I said, " I look as if I were writing a great deal, but there's hardly anything to shew for it." She seemed rather relieved at that. " A good thing too," she said, " but all the same it's just as well we're getting the hay in; a bit of a distraction for you." I should think it did distract me, quite apart from the infirmarians' visits; it was no exaggeration to say that I hardly got anything written.

Fortunately, it takes a lot to discourage me. In proof of that, Mother, I'm going to go on telling you about the light Jesus has given me on the subject of charity. So far, I've only spoken of its outward manifestation; now I want to let you know my ideas about a charity which is wholly spiritual. I'm certain to get the two kinds mixed up before I know where I am; but it's you I'm talking to, and I'm perfectly certain you'll be able to see what I mean—it won't be the first time you've taken my skein out of tangle.

In Carmel, one can't always carry out the gospel precepts to the letter; sometimes you've got work to do, and an act of kindness has to be refused. But if charity is deep rooted in the soul, it shews up for all that. If you've got to say No, there are more ways of doing it than one; a refusal can be so

gracious as to afford almost more pleasure than the gift. . . .
If you are an obliging sort of person, the other sisters will
have less compunction about asking you to do things for
them; but don't forget that our Lord has told us we mustn't
turn away from the borrower; it wouldn't do to edge away
from the sister who's always wanting something, merely on
the excuse that you would have to refuse this time in any case.

Another thing; you mustn't shew obligingness merely so as
to create an impression, perhaps in the hope that your good
offices will be repaid in kind. Our Lord has said: "What
credit is it to you, if you lend to those from whom you
expect repayment? Even sinners lend to sinners, to receive as
much in exchange. No, you must lend without any hope of
return; then your reward will be a rich one."[1] A rich one,
even here on earth . . . on this path of generosity, it's only
the first step that takes it out of you. To lend without expecting to see your money back—that does go against the grain;
you would rather give the things outright, and see it pass out
of your possession. Someone comes up to you and says, with
an air of complete assurance: "Dear sister, could you
give me some help for an hour or two? It's all right, I've got
Reverend Mother's leave to give you some of my own time in
return; I know how busy you are." Knowing, as you do, that
she won't really repay the loan of your time, you're tempted to
say: "Not at all; I'll make you a gift of it." That would
gratify one's self-esteem; a gift is more generous than a loan
—and besides, it would shew the sister exactly how much
confidence you have in her offer.

Ah yes, our Lord's teaching does run counter to the
instincts of nature; without his grace, we shouldn't merely be
unable to carry them out—we shouldn't even understand
them. Charity, Mother, has mysterious depths; and if our
Lord has given a daughter of yours the grace to get to the
bottom of them, it ought to sound like heavenly music in your
ears when she tells you about them. But from me, unfortunately, you only get childish prattling; if his own words
didn't lend me support, I would be tempted to ask if you
would excuse me, and throw away my pen. Never mind; I
started under obedience, and under obedience I'll go on.

[1] Luke 6, 34, 35.

Dear Mother, I was saying yesterday that if somebody robs me of any worldly possession, I mustn't ask to have it back again. I ought to be able to do without it, because it doesn't really belong to me. That's true about the good things of earth; what about the good things of heaven? They don't belong to me either; they're only loans from God, and I've no right to complain if he takes them back. But . . . there are certain movements of the mind and the heart, certain deep-reaching thoughts, that go to form a treasury of your very own; nobody else, you feel, has a right to tamper with it. For instance, I tell one of the sisters, when we have leave to talk, about some light that has been given to me in prayer; and she, quite soon afterwards, mentions it to a third party in conversation as if it were an idea of her own; isn't that pilfering? Or again, in recreation, I whisper some remark to the person next me, a good remark, absolutely to the point; and she repeats it aloud without mentioning where it came from; isn't that a theft of my property? I can't say so at the time, but I'd like to; and if opportunity arises, I determine to let it be known, with all the delicacy in the world, that somebody's been misappropriating my thoughts.

If I can describe them so exactly, Mother, these deplorable instincts of our nature, it is because I have felt them in my own heart. How gladly I would have nourished the illusion that I was the only person affected by them! But it was no good, because you put me in charge of these dear novices, and I had to hear all about their temptations too. I can't tell you how much I've learnt from doing this work for you; and, best of all, I've had to practise what I preach! I really think I can say, now, that our Lord's given me the grace to care as little about gifts of the mind and the heart as about worldly posses-sions. An idea occurs to me, and I say something which is well received by the other sisters—why shouldn't they adopt it as their own? I find it quite natural. You see, this idea doesn't belong to me, it belongs to the Holy Spirit. Doesn't St. Paul tell us that we can't even say "Father" to our Father in heaven without the aid of his loving Spirit?[1] Surely, then, he can make use of me if he wants to convey to any soul some profitable thought? To suppose that this "thought" belongs

[1] Romans 8, 15.

to me would be to make the same mistake as the donkey carrying the relics, which imagined that all the reverence shewn to the Saints was meant for its own benefit!

Don't think that I undervalue them, these deep-reaching thoughts which help to feed the soul and unite it to God. But it has been borne in upon me, long since, that you must never make them the ground of your confidence; perfection has nothing to do with receiving a whole lot of lights in prayer! They don't amount to anything without action. To other people, of course, they may be very useful; people who are humble enough to thank God for letting them share in such a treat, and for enriching a soul with such dainties. But the person so enriched mustn't take credit to herself for these profitable thoughts, plume herself on them like the Pharisee in the temple. That would be like a man dying of hunger in full sight of his own well-stocked table, while his guests, helping themselves generously, looked round with envy at a man who was so well off!

How true it is that only God can see into the depths of our hearts, and all our human views are short-sighted! The moment we see a soul more highly gifted than others, we say to ourselves: "Jesus doesn't love me as he loves that soul; I can't be called to the same level of perfection as that!" Really? And since when has our Lord lost the right to use one of his creatures for his own purposes, to provide the souls he loves with their appropriate nourishment? He hadn't in Pharaoh's time; this is what he says to Pharaoh: "This is the very reason why I have made thee what thou art, so as to give proof, in thee, of my power, and to let my name be known all over the earth."[1] Since those words were spoken, century after century has gone by, and still he has not altered his way of dealing with us; he is always using this or that creature of his to produce an effect in the lives of others.

[1] Romans 9, 17.

Chapter XXXVI

THERESE AS NOVICE-MISTRESS

IF THE CANVAS on which an artist is working could think and speak, it obviously wouldn't be annoyed with the brush that kept on touching and retouching it; and it wouldn't be envious either, because it would know perfectly well that all its beauty came from the artist who held the brush, not from the brush itself. And on the other side, the brush couldn't claim any credit for the masterpiece on which it was at work, because it would know quite well that artists are never at a loss; they are the sort of people who enjoy coming up against difficulties, and find it amusing, sometimes, to make use of shoddy and imperfect instruments.

Well, dear Mother, I'm the poor little brush our Lord has picked out to be the means of imprinting his image on the souls which you have entrusted to me. An artist isn't content to work with one brush, he'll need at least two; there's the really valuable one with which he sketches in the general colour-scheme, covering the whole canvas in no time, and then there's the little tiny one which fills in the details. I see you, Mother, as the favourite brush which Jesus takes up, oh so lovingly, when he wants to produce some important effect in the lives of your children; I'm the little tiny brush which he uses afterwards, to put in the extra flourishes.

When did he first make use of it? About the eighth of December, in the year 1892; a time I shall always remember as one when special graces were granted me. I had the privilege of being admitted to Carmel when I was only fifteen; and I found there a fellow-novice, who had entered a few months before me, eight years my senior, but so child-like in character that the difference of age didn't seem to make any difference. It wasn't long, Mother, before you had the satisfaction of seeing that these two young novices of yours hit it off perfectly, and had become inseparable friends. This growing affection, you felt, might have useful results; so you allowed us to meet, now and again, and have a talk about spiritual things. She was so innocent, so confiding, this fellow-novice of mine, that you couldn't help loving her; but at the same time she puzzled me. Her affection for you was so different from mine; and I thought her behaviour towards the other sisters left room for improvement.

By that time, God had already taught me one important lesson—that with some souls he shews great patience, waits for them, and lets his illumination come to them by degrees. So I wasn't going to forestall the hour of grace; I would wait quietly until Jesus shewed me that it had come. Then, one day, I was thinking about the permission you had given us to have these talks, by way of "fanning" (as our constitution says) "the flame of our love for the heavenly Bridegroom"; and I had to admit, ruefully enough, that they weren't getting us anywhere. Then God let me see that the moment had come; either I must speak out bravely, or I must give up these conversations which might just as well have been conversations between two worldly friends. That was on a Saturday; and the next day, in my thanksgiving, I asked God to put the words into my mouth, words that would be quite gentle and yet bring conviction; or rather, I asked him to speak through me. Our Lord answered my prayer; indeed, he allowed the results to surpass all my expectations. How true it is that those who look to him will be enlightened; that light dawns in the darkness for those who are true at heart![1] The first of those quotations applied to me, the second to my friend; what a true heart she had! When the time came for us to meet she, poor thing, saw at a glance that there was something different about me. She blushed as she sat down by me; and I, making her rest her head close to my heart, told her just what I thought. There were tears in my voice, and I spoke with such tender expressions, made my affection for her so clear, that her tears were soon mingling with mine. Very humbly, she admitted the truth of all I said, promised to begin a new way of life, and asked me as a favour always to warn her of her faults. In the end, when we parted, our affection for one another had reached an entirely spiritual level, it wasn't a human thing any longer. It was true of us, what

[1] See Psalm 33, 6 and Psalm 111, 4.

Scripture says: "When brother helps brothers, theirs is the strength of a fortress."[1]

Of course, it was only the little brush at work—the effect of all this would have been obliterated in no time if our Lord hadn't made use of you, Mother, as well; it was for you to realise his design fully in this soul which was to be all his own. This meant a trying time for my poor friend, who found it a bitter experience; but your firm methods triumphed in the end. It was my task to console her, this sister whom you had made my sister in a very special sense; and in doing so I managed to explain to her about what love really means. I pointed out that it was herself, not you, she was loving all the time; my own love for you was something quite different. From the very beginning of my religious life I had had to sacrifice my own inclinations, for fear of getting attached to you in the wrong way—the merely natural attachment which a dog has for its master. The food of real love is sacrifice; just in proportion as you deny yourself any kind of self-indulgence, your affection for the other person becomes something stronger, and less self-regarding.

How well I remember the violent temptations I had, when I was a postulant, to make my way into your room, just for the pleasure it gave me; a crumb of comfort now and again! I had to pass the office at full speed, and cling tight to the banisters. Couldn't I go and ask leave to do this and that? Such thoughts crowded into my mind; I can't tell you, Mother, what a lot of excuses occurred to me for getting my own way. And how grateful I am now that I kept myself in hand during those early days! There's a reward promised to people who fight bravely, and I'm glad to say I've got it already. I don't find it necessary any longer to turn away from any consolation my heart craves, because I made up my mind to love our Lord above anything else, and my soul is now fixed in that resolve. I find, to my great delight, that when you love him the capacities of your heart are enlarged, so that your feelings towards those who are dear to you are infinitely more tender than they would have been, if you had devoted yourself to a selfish kind of love which remains barren.

Well, dear Mother, that was the first piece of work on

1 Proverbs 18, 19.

which you, or rather our Lord, made use of me. It was only a beginning; plenty more were to be entrusted to me. I was to work in the hallowed ground of human souls. I saw at once that this was beyond my powers, so I went to God in the spirit of a child that throws itself into its father's arms, and nestles its head against his shoulder. "Lord," I said, "I'm such a poor thing—I haven't got it in me to give these children of yours their food. If you want each of them to get what she needs, you'll have to put it here, in my hand. I'm not going to leave your arms, I'm not going to turn my head and look at them: I'll simply pass on what you give me to each soul that comes to me for its food. Some will find it to their taste; so much the better—I shall know that it's thanks to you, not to me. Some will complain, and make sour faces over it; that won't worry me—I shall do my best to make them understand that it comes from you, and I shan't dream of offering them any other food instead."

It hasn't seemed difficult any longer, Mother, this work you gave me to do, since I realised that I couldn't do anything in my own strength. I came to see that only one thing matters: uniting myself more closely to our Lord all the time; whatever else I want will be given me "without the asking." That's my experience—that my hopes haven't once been disappointed; whenever my sisters were in need of spiritual food, God has seen fit to put it into my unworthy hands. I assure you, dear Mother, that if I had had to depend in the slightest degree on my own strength, I should have handed in my papers long since. When you look at it from a distance, it all seems plain sailing; what's the difficulty about doing good to souls, making them love God better—in a word, turning them out on your own pattern, according to your own ideas? But when you look at it from close to, it's not plain sailing at all, nothing of the kind. You discover that trying to do good to people without God's help is no easier than making the sun shine at midnight. You discover that you've got to abandon all your own preferences, your own bright ideas, and guide souls along the road our Lord has marked out for them; you mustn't dragoon them into some path of your own choosing.

But that's not the real difficulty; what takes it out of me most is having to mark down every fault in them, even the slightest imperfection, and declare war on it, war to the death. Unfortunately for me—no, that's a cowardly way of looking at it; fortunately for these sisters of mine, ever since I put myself in the arms of Jesus I've been like a sentry on the watch-tower of a fortress, keeping a look-out for hostile attack. Nothing escapes me; I've been astonished, again and again, at the clear view I get. I begin to sympathise with the prophet Jonas in his desire to run away,[1] sooner than warn Ninive of its downfall! I would so much rather be blamed myself than have to find fault with other people! But I realise it's a good thing that it *should* go against the grain with me. If it comes natural to you, telling other people about their faults, you're no use as a Novice-mistress. Instead of seeing what's wrong with her, the offender has only one thought: "Here's the Novice-mistress in a bad temper, so she's taking it out of *me*, a thoroughly well-meaning person like me!"

Of course, they think I'm terribly strict with them, these lambs of your flock. If they read what I'm writing now, they would say: "That's all very well, but she doesn't *seem* to mind it much, running about after us and lecturing us." Oh dear, the spots I have to point out on those white fleeces, the wool that gets caught in wayside hedges for me to retrieve! Never mind; let them say what they will, at the bottom of their hearts, they know that I really do love them; I'm not like the hireling, who runs away and deserts the flock when he sees the wolf coming. I'm quite ready to lay down my life for them;[2] but my love for them is on such a rarefied level that they're not allowed to feel it. Never, by God's grace, have I made any attempt to engage their affection for myself; I know well enough that my business is to bring them to God, and to tell them that if our Lord is to have a visible representative on earth, all their love and respect must be kept for you.

---

[1] Jonas 1, 3.   [2] John 10, 11 and 12.

Chapter XXXVII

ON PRAYER

I said just now, dear Mother, that in teaching others I've learnt a lot myself. One thing I've noticed is this: all souls, more or less, have to put up the same sort of fight, but on the other hand no two souls are alike. One sees what Père Pichon meant when he said: "Souls differ more than faces do." You can't therefore, treat them all in the same way. With some, I can see that I've got to fold myself up small; I mustn't scruple to humiliate myself by telling them about my own conflicts, my own defeats. Once they've realised that I've got the same weaknesses myself, these younger sisters of mine are ready to admit the faults that lie on their consciences, glad to think that I know what it's like by experience. Others, I saw from the first, needed the opposite treatment; you've got to be quite firm with them, and never go back on what you've said. In dealing with people like that, you mustn't come down to their level; it would be weakness, not humility. God has given me one grace—I'm not afraid of a fight; I have to do my duty, come what may. More than once these people have protested: "If you want to get anything out of me, you'll have to go gently; blustering won't get you anywhere." Unfortunately, I haven't to be told that nobody is a good judge in his own cause! When some doctor decides that a child has got to have a painful operation, there will be plenty of screaming, and he will be told that it's hurting worse than the pain did; but how glad the child is, a day or two later, to be well again, able to play and run about! And so it is with souls; they soon come to realise that a dose of medicine does more good than sugar, sugar all the time; and they aren't afraid to admit it.

Sometimes I can't help having a quiet smile to myself over the magical change that comes over these people between one day and the next. They come to me and say: "You were quite right to be strict with me. It put my back up at the time, but, thinking it over, I've come to see that you were quite justified. Do you know what? When I left you yesterday, I thought I'd had enough of it; I told myself I'd go to Reverend Mother and say I wasn't going to have anything more to do with Sister Thérèse of the Child Jesus. But I realised, afterwards, that it was the devil who was putting that into my head; and then I got the idea that you were praying for me, and I quieted down. A sort of light has begun to dawn on me, but I want you to get the whole thing cleared up properly; that's what I've come about." That sort of thing is a good opening for conversation; and I'm glad, this time, to follow my natural instincts, and leave out the scolding.

Yes, I know; but I soon see that we mustn't go ahead too fast; one unguarded word, and the whole structure it cost so many tears to build will come down in ruins. If I'm unlucky enough to use a single phrase which seems to take the edge off what I said yesterday, I can see my novice finding a loophole there. When that happens, I breathe a short, silent prayer, and always the truth comes out uppermost. What should I do without prayer and sacrifice? They are all the strength I've got; the irresistible weapons our Lord has granted me. I've proved it again and again—they touch souls much more surely than any words could. Here's one instance out of many, which comforted me a lot and made a deep impression on me.

It was during Lent; we had only one novice* then to claim my attention—I was a sort of guardian angel to her. One morning she came to see me, beaming all over: "You'd never guess," she said, "what a wonderful dream I had last night! I was with my sister, and I was trying to turn her mind away from the worldly vanities she is so fond of. By way of doing that, I gave her an interpretation of those lines of yours in *All my Life Love*:

> " Jesus, thou dost repay a hundredfold
>   All that we lose in loving thee;
>   Take, then, the perfume of my life,
>   Nor give it back to me!"

I could tell that everything I said was sinking into the depths of her soul, and I was in transports of joy. When I woke up this morning, I was wondering if God does really mean me to make him a present of this soul? Couldn't I write to her, when Lent is over, and describe the dream, and tell her that our Lord wants her all to himself?"

I didn't give the matter much thought; I just told her that she could try, but first she'd have to get our Mother's leave. Lent had still a long way to go; and I imagine, dear Mother, that you were a bit surprised at the request, which must have seemed premature. You said—and it was obviously God who inspired you to say it—that Carmelites are meant to save souls by prayer, not by writing letters. When I heard about your decision I saw at once that it came from our Lord, and I suggested to Sister Mary of the Trinity: "We'll have to put our noses to the grindstone; let's pray hard about it. How wonderful it would be if at the end of Lent our prayers were granted!" There's no limit, is there, to the Lord's mercies, listening as he does to the prayers of his children—sure enough, at the end of Lent one more soul gave itself to God. A real miracle of grace, secured by the devotion of one humble novice!

What an extraordinary thing it is, the efficiency of prayer! Like a queen, it has access at all times to the Royal presence, and can get whatever it asks for. And it's a mistake to imagine that your prayer won't be answered unless you've something out of a book, some splendid formula of words, specially devised to meet this emergency. If that were true, I'm afraid I should be in a terribly bad position. You see, I recite the Divine Office, with a great sense of unworthiness, but apart from that I can't face the strain of hunting about in books for these splendid prayers—it makes my head spin. There are such a lot of them, each more splendid than the last; how am I to recite them all, or to choose between them? I just do what children have to do before they've learnt to read; I tell God what I want quite simply, without any splendid turns of phrase, and somehow he always manages to understand me. For me, prayer means launching out of the heart towards God; it means lifting up one's eyes, quite simply, to heaven, a cry of grateful love, from the crest of joy or the trough of despair; it's a vast, supernatural force which opens out my heart, and binds me close to Jesus. I don't want you to think, dear Mother, that when we are saying prayers together in choir, or at one of our shrines, I say those without any devotion. No, I love prayers said in common; hasn't our Lord told us that he'll be in our midst when we gather in his name?[1] On those occasions, I'm conscious that the warmth of my sisters' piety is making up for the coldness of my own. But when I'm by myself . . . it's a terrible thing to admit, but saying the rosary takes it out of me more than any hair-shirt would; I do say it so badly! Try as I will to put force on myself, I can't meditate on the mysteries of the rosary; I just can't fix my mind on them.

For a long time I was in despair about it, this want of devotion. I couldn't understand it, because I've such a love for the Blessed Virgin that there ought to be no difficulty about saying prayers in her honour; her own favourite prayers, too! Now I don't distress myself so much; it seems to me that the Queen of heaven, being my Mother, must be aware of my good intentions, and that's enough for her. Sometimes, when I'm in such a state of spiritual dryness that I can't find a single thought in my mind which will bring me close to God, I say an Our Father and a Hail Mary very slowly indeed. How they take me out of myself then; what solid satisfaction they give me then! Much more than if I'd hurried through them a hundred times over. Meanwhile, the Blessed Virgin isn't angry with me; she shews that by always coming to my rescue the moment I ask her to. Any anxiety, any difficulty, makes me turn to her at once, and you couldn't have a more loving Mother to see you through. Again and again I've appealed to her, and found out the advantage of having a mother like that, when I've been trying to talk to the novices.

The novices themselves can't understand it; they often ask me: "How do you manage to have an answer for everything? I did think I'd got you guessing that time. Where do you go for these inspirations of yours?" Some of them have such nice natures that they really believe I can read their hearts, just because I sometimes know what they're going to say before they've said it. One night, one of them had gone to bed in real anguish of mind, but she was determined to keep it dark from me; so she met me next morning with a smile

[1] Matthew 18, 20.

on her face as she talked to me. And I, taking no notice of her remark, just said to her, as if I knew all about it: "Something is worrying you." She couldn't have been more surprised if I'd made the moon drop down at her feet. Indeed, her amazement was so complete that it communicated itself to me; just for a moment I felt an uncanny sense of alarm. I knew perfectly well that I hadn't the gift of reading people's hearts, and yet it had all fallen out so pat! Then of course I realised that God was there, at my elbow, and I'd simply used, like a child repeating its lesson, words that came from him, not from me.

The novices, Mother, as you're aware, are quite free to tell me exactly what they think, pleasant or unpleasant, without the least restraint. That comes easy to them, because they don't feel bound to treat me with respect, as if I were a real Novice-mistress. Does our Lord, then, give me a path of public humiliation to tread? No, I can't say that; the humiliation all takes place in the depths of my soul—outwardly, to all human appearance, everything goes well with me. It's a kind of triumphant progress, as far as that's possible in religion! A dangerous path, you would think; but then, I quite see why I've got to tread it—for other people's sake, not for my own. After all, if the community here saw in me a religious full of defects, incompetent, without either a clear brain or a good judgement, you'd find it difficult, Mother, to find any use for me. So God has thrown a veil over my defects, inward and outward alike; and this disguise of mine does sometimes bring me compliments from the novices. I'm sure there's no intentional flattery; it's just the way their innocent minds see the thing. And quite honestly it doesn't make me vain, because my mind is continually haunted by the thought of what I really am.

All the same, I sometimes get a terrible longing to hear something said about me which isn't praise! As you know, Mother, I prefer savouries to sweets; and my soul is like my palate—it gets tired of food which has too much sugar in it! When that happens, our Lord arranges for somebody to give me what I call a nice little salad. Plenty of vinegar, plenty of spice about it; nothing left out except the oil, and that makes it all the more tasty. These nice little salads are served up to me by the novices at the moment when I least expect it. God lifts the veil that hides my imperfections, and these dear young sisters of mine see me just as I am; they don't care for that very much. They tell me, with delightful frankness, all about the rough time I give them, and my unpleasant habits, with so little embarrassment that you would imagine they were talking about somebody else. You see, they know they're giving me an enormous amount of pleasure by doing it; indeed, pleasure isn't a strong enough word; it's a delicious treat that simply fills my heart with joy. How a thing which runs counter to all one's natural instincts proves a source of such happiness, is more than I can explain; it's a thing I couldn't believe if I hadn't experienced it. One day, when I was particularly anxious to be humiliated like that, one of the novices carried out my wishes so conscientiously that it reminded me, all at once, of Semei cursing King David. "Yes," I said to myself, " sure enough, she must have had her orders from Heaven, to talk to me like that."[1] No stint, there, of well-seasoned food, in which my soul took an epicure's delight! That's the sort of way in which God, mercifully, keeps me going. He can't be always supplying me with the food that really gives me strength—I mean, public humiliation of this kind—but every now and then there are crumbs falling from the nursery table[2] to sustain me. His mercy is so wonderful that I shall have to be in heaven before I can tell the full story of it.

[1] II Kings 16, 11.   [2] Mark 7, 28.

Chapter XXXVIII

MORE ABOUT SACRIFICES

ALL THE SAME, Mother, since I am trying with your help to tell the story of that boundless mercy while I'm still on earth, I mustn't omit to mention one great advantage I've derived from this work you entrusted to me. Earlier on, if I saw one of the sisters behaving in a way I didn't like, or in a way that seemed to me unsuitable, I used to say to myself: "How I wish I could tell her what I think of her, point out to her where she's wrong! It would do me all the good in the world." Now that I've been in the trade myself for a bit, I can assure you, Mother, that I feel quite differently about it. Now, if I happen to notice some behaviour of theirs which falls, as I think, below the right standard, I heave a sigh of relief and say to myself: "Thank goodness *she's* not a novice, so it isn't my job to put her right about it." And it's not long before I begin to make excuses for the sister concerned, and credit her with the good intentions which, beyond question, she had. . . . And then, Mother, since I've been ill, I've learnt a lot about charity from the care you yourself have lavished on me. Letting me have the most expensive kinds of treatment, and never tired of trying fresh ones! And all the trouble you took, when I still went to recreation, to keep me out of a draught! If I started trying to write it all down, I should never stop. All this loving care of yours, Mother, has shewn me how sympathetic I ought to be towards my sisters over their spiritual ailments.

Here's a thing I've noticed—not that there's anything surprising about it. The holiest people in the community are the people one loves best; everybody is ready to talk to them, does them a good turn without being asked; in fact, it's exactly the people who could do without these attentions, without all this politeness, that are surrounded by marks of affection on every side. It's like what our father St. John of the Cross said: "Since I gave up trying to secure the good

232

things of life, out of self-love, every kind of good thing has come my way." On the other hand, people who suffer from imperfections get left out of things. Of course, one has to shew them all the politeness that is expected to religious, but, if only for fear of saying something unpleasant to them, one avoids their company.

When I describe such people as less than perfect, I'm not thinking only of spiritual imperfections; after all, the holiest of us won't actually be perfect till we get to heaven. I'm thinking of things like want of judgement, want of education, the touchiness you find in certain people's characters, which spoil the amenities of life. It's true, moral disabilities of this kind are chronic, there's no real hope of curing them. But then, what about Reverend Mother? If I went on being ill all my life, she would still look after me, still do her best to make me comfortable. What follows? Why, this: that at recreation, and at all time when freedom is granted us, I ought to single out the sisters who are least attractive to me, roadside casualties who need a good Samaritan. Often just a word or a friendly smile are enough to make these difficult natures open out; but the charity I'm speaking of isn't practised merely with that end in view. Because it won't be long before I meet with discouragement; some remark of mine, quite innocently meant, will be taken up all wrong. So in order not to waste my time, my object in being kind to everybody, and especially to the less attractive ones, is to rejoice the heart of our Lord.

What's the advice he gives us in the gospel? Why, something like this: " When you make a feast, don't invite your relations and friends; they might ask you back again, and then you've had your reward already. Send out your invitation to the poor, to lame people and cripples, and congratulate yourself that they can't make any return, because it means that your Father, who sees what is done in secret, will reward you."[1] The only feast a Carmelite nun can give to her sisters is a spiritual feast, made up of kindness and gaiety; at least, that's the only kind I know of, and I try to live up to St. Paul's principle of rejoicing with those who rejoice.[2] It's true he also mourned with the mourner, and in my feasts tears have got to be included in the bill of fare sometimes, but always

[1] Luke 14, 12.   [2] Romans 12, 15.

with the hope of cheering up the mourner in the end; "it is the cheerful giver God loves."[1]

I can remember one act of charity God inspired me to do while I was still a novice; it was a very trifling thing, but our Father who sees what is done in secret doesn't care about the importance of what you do, as long as you do it in the right spirit, and he has rewarded me already, without waiting to do it in the next life! It was when Sister St. Peter still went into choir and refectory. I used to kneel just behind her at evening prayers, and I knew that at ten minutes to six trouble was coming to somebody, because she had got to be piloted into the refectory, and the infirmarian sisters had their hands too full to deal with her. A trifling service, but it cost me something to make the offer, because I knew poor Sister St. Peter wasn't easy to please; she was very ill, and didn't like having a change of guides. But it seemed too good an opportunity to be missed; what did our Lord say about charity? He told us that if we did anything for the most insignificant of his brethren, we should be doing it for him.[2] So I swallowed my pride and offered my services; I had quite a lot of trouble in getting her to accept them. Well, as it turned out, when I got down to the job it was a complete success. Every evening, the moment I saw Sister St. Peter shaking her hour-glass at me, I knew that meant: "Let's go."

You wouldn't believe how much I minded being disturbed in this way, at first anyhow. But I lost no time in making a start, and we had to make a real ceremony of it. I had to move the bench and carry it away just so, without any sign of hurry—that was important—and then the procession began. The thing was to walk behind the poor invalid holding her up by her girdle; I did this as gently as I could manage, but if by some piece of bad luck she stumbled, she was down on me at once—I wasn't holding her properly, and she might easily fall; "Heavens, girl, you're going too fast; I shall do myself an injury." Then, if I tried to walk still slower, it was: "Here, why aren't you keeping up with me? Where's your hand? I can't feel it, you must have let go. I shall fall, I know I shall. How right I was when I told them you were too young to look after me!"

We would get to the refectory at last, without accidents.

[1] II Corinthians 9, 7.   [2] Matthew 25, 40.

There were more obstacles to be got over; Sister St. Peter had to be steered into a sitting position, with the greatest possible care, so as not to hurt her. Then her sleeves had to be turned up, again in a particular way; then I could take myself off. But I noticed before long the difficulty she had, with her poor crippled hands, about arranging the bread in her bowl; so that was another little thing to do before I left her. She hadn't asked me to do it, so she was greatly touched by having this attention paid to her; and it was this action (on which I'd bestowed no thought at all) that established me firmly in her favour. There was something even more important, though I only heard about it later; when I'd finished cutting her bread I gave her, before I left, my best smile.

Dear Mother, it must seem very strange to you that I should be writing about this tiny act of charity, long since over and done with. Well, I have a reason for it—I feel it's my duty to record, in his own honour, the mercies the Lord has shewn me, and this is one of them; he's allowed this incident to remain in my mind like a scent in the nostrils—a scent which lures me on to perform fresh acts of charity. There are details in connexion with it which still have, for me, the freshness of a spring breeze. Here is one that comes back to my memory; a winter evening when I was doing my bit as usual—the cold—the darkness. . . . All of a sudden I heard, far away, lovely music being played. And I constructed a picture in my imagination of a drawing-room splendidly lit up, with gilded furniture; of young fashionably dressed girls exchanging compliments and the polite small-talk of society. Then I looked back at the poor invalid I was helping along; there was no music here, only a piteous groan every now and then; there was no gilding, only the plain brick of our bare convent walls, faintly visible in the flickering light.

Of the inner experience I had, I can tell you nothing; I only know that God enlightened my soul with rays of truth, which so outshone the tawdry brilliance of our earthly festivities as to fill me with unbelievable happiness. I tell you that I wouldn't have exchanged those ten minutes of charitable drudgery for a thousand years of worldly enjoyment. . . . Here we are struggling on painfully, in the thick of the fight, and even so the thought that God has taken us out of the world can give us, for the moment, this feeling of happiness above all earthly happiness, so what will heaven be like? All will be lightness of heart there, all repose; and we shall see what an estimable grace the Lord has bestowed on us in choosing us out to live in this earthly home of his—the anteroom, did we but know it, of heaven itself. I don't mean that acts of charity were always accompanied by this uplifting of the heart; but from the very beginnings of my life in religion our Lord did make it clear to me what a comfort it is to see him as present on earth in the souls of his elect. When I was helping Sister St. Peter along, it was like that; I couldn't have done it with a better will if I'd been helping our Lord himself.

Still, as I said just now, dear Mother, acts of charity aren't always such easy going. In proof of that, I'll tell you about some of my skirmishes with the enemy, which ought to amuse you. For a long time, at evening prayers, my place was just in front of a sister who had an odd nervous affection;* I expect she had a lot of lights, too, in her prayer, because she hardly ever used a book. What made me notice she was rather odd was that the moment she came in she began to make a curious little noise, rather like what one would make by rubbing two shells together. Nobody noticed it except me; but then I've got a very sensitive ear—perhaps too sensitive on some occasions. I simply can't describe to you, Mother, how that tiny noise got me down. I longed to turn round and give the offender one look; obviously she was quite unconscious of fidgeting, and it didn't seem as if there was any other way to let her know about it. But something told me—something deep down inside me—that the right thing to do was to put up with it for the love of God, and spare the sister any embarrassment. So I stayed still, and tried to get closer to God; perhaps I could forget it altogether, this tiny noise. . . . Absolutely useless; there was I with the sweat pouring down me, in the attempt to make my prayer into a prayer of mere suffering! Suffering—but somehow I must get rid of the nervous irritation, and suffer peaceably, joyously; that is, with peace and joy deep down in my soul. So I hit on the idea of trying to *like* this exasperating noise, instead of trying vainly not to hear it. I devoted myself to listening hard, as if the sound were that of some delightful music, and all my prayer—it certainly wasn't the prayer of quiet!—consisted in offering this music to our Lord.

Another time I was helping to do the washing, and there was a sister opposite me who managed to splash my face with dirty water every time she lifted up the handkerchiefs from the ledge.* My first instinct was to step back and wipe my face, by way of suggesting to this over-effusive sister that I should be obliged if she kept herself to herself. But all at once the thought occurred to me: "You're a fool not to take what's going free"; so I took good care to hide my annoyance. I devoted myself, instead, to cultivating a taste for dirty water; and really in the end I was so fond of this new kind of Asperges that I determined to come back another time to this lucky dip where one was so well treated!

Dear Mother, you can see for yourself that I am a very insignificant person, who can't offer to God anything but very insignificant sacrifices. Sometimes I miss the chance of making them, sacrifices that give me such peace of soul; but I don't lose heart, I just resign myself to the loss of one peaceful hour, and try to be more on my guard another time. God is so good to me that it's out of the question to be afraid of him—he always gives me exactly what I want; or rather, he always makes me want exactly what he's going to give me. That's what happened about these temptations I have against the faith. Just before they started, I'd been saying to myself: "I don't seem to have any great trials outwardly, and I don't see how I'm going to have any interior trials, unless he calls on me to follow some other path—and I don't think he's likely to do that. But I can't go on and on living in undisturbed peace like this. What means can our Lord possibly devise for putting me to the proof?" Well, the answer wasn't long in coming. He is never at a loss, this Lord who commands my love. He left me to follow exactly the same path, and yet he sent me a trial all the same—a bitter medicine that mingles its taste with all my happiness.

Chapter XII

THERESE AND HER BROTHERS ON
THE MISSION

WHEN OUR Lord means to send me trials, he gives me warning of them and a desire for them beforehand. That applies to other things as well as trials. To have a brother a priest—that was a longing of mine for years, and one, it seemed, that could never be fulfilled. If only, I thought, those two little brothers of mine hadn't been carried off to heaven, I might have seen them going up to the altar! As it was, God had decided to make little angels of them, so my dream could never be more than a dream. And now, not content with granting me the grace I'd longed for, our Lord has linked me by a spiritual bond to *two* apostolic missionaries of his, who have become my brothers. I'd like to give you the details, dear Mother, of the way in which our Lord satisfied my longing, and went further than that. I wanted a priest who would remember me every day at the altar—what, only one?

The first of these younger brothers was a present from our holy Mother St. Teresa for my feast day, in the year 1895. I was helping with the washing and hard at work when Mother Agnes of Jesus took me aside and read me a letter she'd just had by the post. It was from a young seminarist acting (so he claimed) under inspiration from St. Teresa, who wanted to have a sister devoting herself to the cause of his salvation, and helping him later on, when he went out to the missions, by her prayers and sacrifices, so that he could be the means of saving many other souls as well. He promised, on his side, that he would remember this sister of his continually when it became possible for him to offer the holy sacrifice of the Mass.

Well, Mother Agnes told me I was the person she wanted to be a sister to this missionary in the making. I simply can't explain, Mother, the happiness I felt over that. It was such a strange fulfilment of my wish! I can only describe it as a childish joy; I had to go back to my childhood to recover the memory of joys like that, so keen that the soul isn't big enough to contain them. Not for years had I experienced happiness of this kind; I felt as if my soul had taken fresh roots, as if chords of music, long forgotten, had stirred within me.

Meanwhile, I realised the responsibility I was taking on, and set to work with redoubled fervour. I must confess that I didn't get much encouragement at first, to keep me up to the mark. My young brother wrote a charming letter of thanks to Mother Agnes, full of cordiality and fine sentiments, but he didn't give any other sign of life till the next July, apart from a card in November to say that he was off to the barracks! *

So it was left for you, dear Mother, in God's Providence, to put the finishing touch to this undertaking. Prayers and sacrifices, no doubt, are the best help one can give to missionaries; but when our Lord sees fit to bring about a union between two souls, for his greater glory, he does *sometimes* allow them to exchange ideas and to kindle the love of God in one another's hearts; and this can only be done at the express direction of those in authority. (Otherwise, I fancy, such correspondence would do more harm than good. Whatever may be said of the missionary, a Carmelite nun leads a life which tends to throw her back on herself; and if she invited a correspondence of this kind, even at rare intervals, it would divert her mind instead of helping her to achieve union with God. She would imagine that she was making history, when she was only mistaking a love of useless distractions for a love of souls. Here, as everywhere, I'm afraid of self-indulgence; if my letters are to do any good, they must be written under obedience, and there must be more reluctance than pleasure in writing them. It's the same when I'm talking to one of the novices; my own mortification has to be kept in view. I never ask questions to satisfy my own curiosity; and if she starts talking about something interesting and then, without finishing up, passes on to some subject which bores me, I don't try to steer her back to the original topic. Nothing's done well when it's done out of self-interest.)

Oh dear, Mother, I'm quite incorrigible; who's going off at a tangent now? Myself, as usual, with all these long dissertations. Please forgive me, and allow me to do the same next time, for I have to tell my story this way. You know, Mother, talking to you is rather like talking to God; he never gets tired of listening to the tale of my joys and griefs as if he didn't know about them already. It's the same with you, Mother; you've had plenty of opportunity to know all about my way of looking at things, and about the leading events in my life; I've got nothing new to tell you. I can't help laughing at myself for writing down so carefully a whole lot of things you know just as well as I do. But there it is, dear Mother; I'm under your orders. Perhaps if you don't find this very interesting at the moment, later on it'll cheer up your old age, and then you can put it on the fire; I shan't have written in vain. I write as children do, for amusement; so you mustn't imagine that I'm concerned to know how such poor stuff can possibly be of any use. I'm under orders, and that's all that matters; if you burn it under my eyes without reading it, I shan't mind.

Well, it's really time I got back to my story, and talked about these brothers of mine who are now such an important feature in my life. It was, as I remember, at the end of May last year that you sent for me just before we went into refectory. I can tell you, Mother, my heart was beating pretty fast when I came into your room; what could you possibly have to say to me? It was the first time I had ever been summoned like this. Well, you told me to sit down, and asked whether I would make myself responsible for forwarding the spiritual aims of a missionary, who was to be ordained and sent abroad almost at once? And you shewed me the young priest's letter, so as to let me know just what it was he wanted.

I was overjoyed at first; then I felt frightened. I explained to you that I'd already offered such poor merits as I have on behalf of one apostle-to-be; surely it wouldn't be possible to do it all over again for the intentions of a second? And any-how there were plenty of the sisters who were much better nuns than I was; couldn't one of them do what he wanted? But you overruled all my objections, telling me that it wasn't impossible, after all, to have more than one brother. And when I suggested that perhaps my obedience to your orders would give my actions a double value, you said Yes, it would, and added several other considerations which suggested that I ought to have no scruple about adopting a new brother.[1] In my heart I already agreed with you; indeed, since (as we are told) a Carmelite's zeal ought to encircle the earth, I don't see why I shouldn't manage, with God's grace, to be of use to more than two missionaries at the same time. How can I cease to pray for all missionaries everywhere? Not to mention those ordinary parish priests whose work is sometimes quite as uphill work as preaching to the heathen. No, I mean to be a true daughter of the Church, like our Mother St. Teresa, and pray for the intentions of the Pope, which after all include the whole universe. Such is my aim in general; but if my brothers had lived to become priests instead of becoming angels, that wouldn't have prevented me from praying specially for them, associating myself especially with their apostolic work.

Well, that's the story of how I came to be linked up spiritually with these two missionaries our Lord had given to me as brothers. All that I have belongs equally to them, and to each of them; God is so good, it wouldn't be good enough for him to start working out fractions; God is so rich, he can give me what I ask for in any quantity he chooses. Not that I waste my time in drawing up long lists of the things I want! Here am I with two brothers, and these novices for my younger sisters; if I started praying for all their needs in detail, the day wouldn't be long enough for it, and I should always be worrying about having left out something important. Complicated methods of prayer are all very well, but they're not meant for simple souls like me. So, one morning, during my thanksgiving, our Lord gave me a quite simple recipe for satisfying my obligations. He let me into the meaning of that phrase in the Canticles, "Draw me after thee where thou wilt; see, we hasten after thee, by the very fragrance of those perfumes allured."[2] Dear Jesus, you don't even expect us to say: "Please attract all those I love, not just me"; the expression "Draw me" is all that's wanted. As I understand you, Lord, there is a fragrance about the thought of you, and when I allow that fragrance to cast its spell over me, I don't hasten after you in the first person singular—all those whom I love come running at my heels. This happens without effort

[1]This last clause cannot be deciphered with certainty in the manuscript.

[2] Canticles I, 3.

or constraint; it is the automatic consequence of that attraction which you exercise over me. Just so, the swirling river rushing down to the sea bears along with it everything it has met in its course. Your love, Jesus, is an ocean with no shore to bound it; and if I plunge into it, I carry with me all the possessions I have. You know, Lord, what those possessions are—the souls you have seen fit to link with mine; nothing else

Chapter XL

HER APOSTOLATE OF PRAYER

THEY ARE possessions with which you yourself have entrusted me; and when I think of them, I am emboldened to make your words my own—those words which you addressed to your heavenly Father, on the last evening that saw you on earth, a pilgrim, a mortal still. Dear Jesus, I don't know how long it will be before my banishment comes to an end; there may be many evenings yet that will find me telling the tale of your mercies, still in exile. But for me, too, there will be a last evening; and then, my God, I would like to be able to offer to you the same prayer. "I have exalted thy glory on earth, by achieving the task which thou gavest me to do. I have made thy name known to those whom thou hast entrusted to me; they belonged to thee, and now they are mine by thy gift. Now they have learned to recognise all the gifts thou gavest me as coming from thee; I have given them the message which thou gavest me, and they, receiving it, recognised it for truth that it was thou who didst send me. I am praying for those whom thou hast entrusted to me; they belong to thee. I am remaining in the world no longer, but they remain, while I am on my way to thee. Holy Father, keep them true to thy name, thy gift to me. Now I am coming to thee, and while I am still in the world I am telling them this, so that the joy which comes from thee may reach its full measure in them. I am not asking that thou shouldst take them out of the world, but that thou shouldst keep them clear of what is evil. They do not belong to the world, as I, too, do not belong to the world. It is not only for them that I pray; I pray for those who are to find faith in thee through their word. This, Father, is my desire, that all those whom thou has entrusted to me may be with me where I am, and that the world may know that thou hast bestowed thy love upon them, as thou hast bestowed it upon me."[1]

[1] John 17, 4-24, with many omissions and some adaptation.

Those are the words I would like to repeat after you, dear Lord, before I take refuge in your arms. Am I being rash? I don't think so; you've allowed me to take liberties with you this long time past. You've said to me what the father said to the elder brother of the Prodigal Son in the parable: " Everything that I have already is thine ";[1] and as these are your words, dear Jesus, they belong to me. So I'm at liberty to use them, in the hope of bringing down on the souls that are linked with mine whatever blessings our Heavenly Father has to give. But of course when I ask that the people you've entrusted to my care may be " where I am," I'm not suggesting that they may not reach a much higher degree of glory than you see fit to give me. I'm merely asking that we may all meet, one day, to share with you the splendours of heaven.

My God, you know that the only thing I've ever wanted is to love you; I have no ambition for any other glory except that. In my childhood, your love was there waiting for me; as I grew up, it grew with me; and now it is like a great chasm whose depths are past sounding. Love breeds love; and mine, Jesus, for you, keeps on thrusting out towards you, as if to fill up that chasm which your love has made—but it's no good; mine is something less than a drop of dew lost in the ocean. Love you as you love me? The only way to do that is to come to you for the loan of your own love; I couldn't content myself with less. Dear Jesus, I can have no certainty about this, but I don't see how you could squander more love on a human soul than you have on mine! That's why I venture to ask that these souls you've entrusted to me may experience your love as I have. One day, maybe, in heaven, I shall find out that you love them better than me, and I shall be glad of that, glad to think that these people earned your love better than I ever did. But, here on earth, I just don't find it possible to imagine a greater wealth of love than the love you've squandered on me without my doing anything to earn it.

Dear Mother, it's time I came back to you. I can't think how I came to write what I've written above; I never meant to, but there it is, so it had better stay there. Only, before I go back to the story of my brothers, I do just want to explain two things. When I talk about handing on the message God

[1] Luke 15, 31.

has given to me, I'm not thinking of them, only of the
novices. I don't after all, set up to teach missionaries; it's a
good thing I'm not conceited enough for that. And indeed, if
I've managed to give some advice to these sisters of mine, it's
to you, Mother, as God's representative, that I owe the grace
for it. On the other hand, when I say that I don't want them
taken out of the world, or pray for those who will come to
believe through their words, I'm only thinking of those others,
spiritual sons of yours, spiritual brothers of mine. I can't
help praying for the souls that will be saved, in those distant
mission-fields, by their preaching.

And now, Mother, about that passage in the Song of
Songs: "Draw me after thee; we hasten"—I think some
further explanation is called for, because what I've tried to
write about it is a bit difficult to follow. Our Lord says:
"Nobody can come to me without being attracted towards
me by the Father who sent me."[1] Then, by those splendid
parables of his, and often by less popular ways of talking, he
teaches us about the door that will be opened if we only
knock, about finding what we want if we only look for it,
getting what we ask for if we only stretch out our hands in
humble supplication.[2] Again, he tells us that if we ask the
Father for anything in his name, it will be granted to us.[3]
All that, surely, explains why the Holy Spirit, long before our
Lord came into the world, looked on ahead and prescribed for
us this formula of prayer: "Draw me after thee; we hasten."

When we ask to be "drawn" we mean, surely, that we want
to be united as closely as possible with the object which has
cast its spell over our hearts. Suppose that fire and iron were
capable of reason; suppose that a piece of iron says to the fire:
"Draw me to yourself"; doesn't that mean that it wants to be
identified with the fire, to be penetrated with it, steeped in it,
this burning force, till the two seem to be merged into one?
My prayer, Mother, is like that; I want our Lord to draw me
into the furnace of his love, to unite me ever more closely
with himself, till it is he who lives and acts in me. Still, as
that flame kindles, I shall cry out to be drawn closer, closer;
and its effect on those around me will be the same, although I
am only a poor piece of iron filing, that outside the furnace
would be inert. They will be as active as I am—like those

[1] John 6, 44.   [2] Matthew 7, 7.   [3] John 16, 23.

women of the Canticles who ran, allured by his perfumes, where the royal lover went. The soul that is enfolded by Divine love can't remain inactive; though it may, like Magdalen, sit at the feet of Jesus and listen to those words of his, so full of fire, so full of comfort; not appearing to contribute anything, but really contributing so much! More than Martha, as she hurries distractedly to and fro, and wishes her sister would do the same. (Not that our Lord has any fault to find with Martha's exertions; his own Mother, Mother of God though she was, put up with humble work of that kind all her life; didn't she get the meals ready for the Holy Family? Martha is a devoted hostess, but she won't keep calm, that's the trouble.) All the Saints have seen the importance of Mary's attitude, and perhaps particularly the ones who have done most to fill the world with the light of Gospel teaching. Surely those great friends of God, people like St. Paul and St. Augustine and St. John of the Cross and St. Thomas and St. Francis and St. Dominic, all went to prayer to find the secret of their wisdom; a Divine wisdom which has left the greatest minds lost in admiration.

" Give me a lever and a fulcrum," said the man of science, " and I'll shift the world." Archimedes wasn't talking to God, so his request wasn't granted; and in any case he was only thinking of the material world. But the Saints really have enjoyed the privilege he asked for; the fulcrum God told them to use was himself, nothing less than himself, and the lever was prayer. Only it must be the kind of prayer that sets the heart all on fire with love; that's how the Saints shift the world in our own day, and that's how they'll do it to the end of time.

And now, dear Mother, I must just tell you what I understand by these " perfumes " which tempt the soul to set out on its loving search. Our Lord has ascended into heaven, so I can only follow him by means of the traces he has left behind him. But they're so full of light, so full of fragrance! One glance at the holy Gospel, and the life of Jesus becomes a perfume that fills the very air I breathe; I know at once which way to run. Oh, I don't try to jostle into the front rank, the last is good enough for me; I won't put myself forward, like the Pharisee, I'll take courage from the humble prayer of the publican. But the Magdalen, she, most of all, is the model I like to follow; that boldness of hers, which would be so amazing if it weren't the boldness of a lover, won the heart of Jesus, and how it fascinates mine! I'm certain of this—that if my conscience were burdened with all the sins it's possible to commit, I would still go and throw myself into our Lord's arms, my heart all broken up with contrition; I know what tenderness he has for any prodigal child of his that comes back to him. No, it's not just because God, in his undeserved mercy, has kept my soul clear of mortal sin, that I fly to him on the wings of confidence and of love . . . .

NOTES ON THE MARTIN FAMILY

The Parents

FATHER : Louis Martin. Born Bordeaux 1823. Son of Captain Pierre-François Martin. Set up as watchmaker and jeweller at Alençon. He had considered becoming a monk but was prevented from doing so by his delicate health. d. 29th July, 1894.

MOTHER : Zélie-Marie. Born at Saint-Denys-sur-Sarthon (near Alençon) in 1831. Daughter of M. Guérin, a retired officer. She too considered entering religion but found her vocation lay in marriage. She became a lace-maker. M. 13th July, 1858. d. 28th August, 1877.

The Children

MARIE-LOUISE, b. 22nd February, 1860. In religion Sister Marie of the Sacred Heart. Entered Carmel of Lisieux 1886. D. 29th January, 1940.

MARIE-PAULINE, b. 7th September, 1861. In religion Sister Agnes of Jesus. Entered Carmel of Lisieux 1882. Prioress 1893–6; made Prioress for life in 1923. D. 28th July, 1951.

MARIE-LEONIE, b. 3rd June, 1863. Sister Françoise-Thérèse, a nun of the Order of the Visitation, at Caen, which she entered in 1899. D. 16th June, 1941.

MARIE-HELENE, b. 13th October, 1864, d. 22nd February, 1870.

MARIE-JOSEPH-LOUIS, b. 20th September, 1866, d. 14th February, 1867.

MARIE-JOSEPH-JEAN-BAPTISTE, b. 19th December, 1867, d. 24th August, 1868.

MARIE-CELINE, b. 28th April, 1869. Sister Geneviève of the Holy Face and of St. Teresa. Entered Carmel of Lisieux, 1894.

MARIE-MELANIE-THERESE, b. 16th August, 1870, d. 8th October, 1870.

MARIE-FRANCOISE-THERESE (St. Thérèse of the Child Jesus). Born 2nd January, 1873, at 36 (now 42) Rue Saint-Blaise, Alençon. She lived there until her mother's death of cancer on 28th August, 1877. On the 16th November of the same year the family moved to a house called *Les Buissonnets* at Lisieux. Went to school as a weekly boarder to the Benedictines of Lisieux on 3rd October, 1881. Made her First Communion 8th May, 1884, and was confirmed on the 14th June that year. On 29th May, 1887, told her father of her wish to be a Carmelite; appealed to the Bishop of Lisieux on 31st October and to the Pope on 20th November of that year. Entered the Carmel of Lisieux 9th April, 1888, was Clothed 10th January, 1889, made her Profession 8th September, 1890, and took the veil on 24th September that year. Was appointed assistant to the Mistress of Novices in 1893. d. 30th September, 1897.

First publication of *The Story of a Soul*, 1898. Cause of Thérèse's Beatification introduced 1914. Decree of Beatification 29th April, 1923. Decree of Canonisation 17th May, 1925.

Relations

UNCLE: Isidore Guérin, brother of Mme. Martin, b. Saint-Denys-sur-Sarthon on 2nd January, 1841. Established himself at Lisieux 22nd April, 1866, as a chemist. M. Céline Fournet, 1866. He died 28th September, 1909.

AUNT-BY-MARRIAGE: Céline Elisa Fournet, b. 1847, d. 13th February, 1900.

COUSINS: Jeanne Guérin, eldest daughter of the above. M. 1st October, 1890. D. 25th April, 1938.

Marie Guérin, younger sister of Jeanne, b. Lisieux 22nd August, 1870. Entered the Lisieux Carmel 15th August, 1895, under the name of Sister Marie de l'Eucharistie. Was a novice under her cousin Thérèse. d. 14th April, 1905.

Religious

REVEREND MOTHER MARIE DE GONZAGUE: Marie-Adèle-Rosalie Davy de Vircille. Entered the Carmel of Lisieux 29th September, 1860. Held the office of Prioress of the Carmel six times: 1874-1883, 1886-1893, 1896-1902. The prioresses are elected for a period of three years and can be elected twice in succession but special permission has to be obtained for periods over six years. She died on December 17th, 1904.

REVEREND MOTHER GENEVIEVE DE ST. TERESA: Claire Marie Radegonde Bertrand. Born Poitiers 1805. Entered the Poitiers Carmel 1830. Took part in the foundation of the Lisieux Carmel as sub-Prioress, 16th March, 1838. Was three times elected Prioress. Died 1891.

SISTER MARIE DES ANGES ET DU SACRE COEUR: Jeanne de Chaumontel. b. Montpinçon, 1845. Novice-mistress of St. Thérèse. Died 1924.

SISTER MARIE DE LA TRINITE: St. Thérèse's favourite novice Marie-Louise-Josephine Castel. Born 1874 at Saint-Pierre-sur-Dives. Entered the Carmel of the Avenue de Messine, Paris, in 1891, but became ill. Entered the Lisieux Carmel as a postulant in 1894.

PUBLISHER'S NOTE

Monsignor Knox did not live to correct the proofs of his translation; therefore it is natural that some mistakes remained uncorrected. In addition, after the publication of *Autobiography of a Saint*, which was based on the photostatic edition of Saint Thérèse's work, the Carmel of Lisieux published a printed edition of the original text in which certain additional passages were recovered.

A number of critics, as well as the Carmel of Lisieux, have drawn attention to the need, in the circumstances, to make some revisions in this new edition.

It is never an easy task to achieve a perfect balance between the spirit and the letter in a translation, nor will everyone agree where this balance lies. The task becomes still more difficult when the original has been written in a period style.

The alteration of single words presented no difficulty, but where a correction involved the rewording of a sentence, the text has been left unchanged and the passage marked by an asterisk, as it would be impossible to recreate Monsignor Knox's style. The asterisk refers the reader to an appendix in which the passage is given in French and in a transliteration. A number of factual notes are also included in this section.

The Reverend Étienne Robo has given us valuable help in revising the translation and our thanks are due to him. (This is in no way to be taken as suggesting that the Carmel of Lisieux are in agreement with his view of St. Thérèse as set out in his study of the Saint.)

APPENDIX AND NOTES TO THE TEXT

p. 25: " You, who are my mother twice over "
After Madame Martin's death, Thérèse had chosen Pauline as her " little mother." In January *1895* when she began to write her autobiography, Pauline was Prioress and had again over her sister the authority of a mother.

p. 33, l. 7: " Nurse has just brought in little Thérèse "
More correctly, foster mother. This refers to Rose Taillé with whom Thérèse was then living on a little farm at Semaillé about six miles away. On market days (Thursdays) she took the child to Alençon and left her with the family until she was ready to go home. When Thérèse was fifteen months old, on April 2nd, *1874*, she went back to live at Les Buissonets.

p. 33, l. 13: " Une bonne figure de prédestinée "
Literally : " The innocent face of a future saint "

p. 34: " When you came back from school "
This was a boarding school at Le Mans, kept by the Sisters of the
Visitation. The terms lasted about three months, which explains why
Pauline had to keep the slab of chocolate so long for her little sister.

p. 35: Monsignor Knox translated this passage as it appeared to read
in the photostat of the manuscript. The text had been considerably
corrected and the original version is now given in the printed French
text as follows :
" Je suis obligée de corriger ce pauvre bébé qui se met dans des furies
épouvantables quand les choses ne vont pas à son idée, elle se roule par
terre comme une désespérée croyant que tout est perdu, il y a des moments
où c'est plus fort qu'elle, elle en est suffoquée. C'est une enfant bien
nerveuse."
Literally : " I have to punish the poor baby who gets into frightful rages
when things do not go the way she likes. She rolls on the ground in
desperation as if she thought that all was lost. There are times when
she loses all control of herself and nearly chokes. She is a very nervous
child."

p. 36, l. 9: Louise was the Martins' maid.

p. 36, l. 23: " Take part in their pious practices "
This refers to a custom which existed in many French convents of the
period. The pupils were taught to count their acts of self-denial either
on a knotted cord or in a special booklet—each page had a number of
small flaps which were folded back, one for each act of mortification.

p. 36, l. 23: " Fine comme l'ombre "
A deformation of the well-known French expression : " Fine comme
l'ambre "

p. 37, l. 4: " Cercle catholique "
These clubs existed in many parishes ; they were open every evening
and occasionally put on plays or choral evenings. They were intended
for working men but many people of the standing of the Martins dropped
in without being members.

p. 37, l. 31: " The Préfet's daughter "
The girl referred to was Jeanne Béchard, the daughter of the Préfet of
the Département de l'Orne, an office which has no equivalent in England.

p. 38: " Pain bénit "
The custom of having a loaf cut into small pieces and distributed during
the Sunday Mass existed in England in the pre-Reformation times, and
the name of the donor was given out in the bidding prayers on Sunday
morning. In the nineteenth century the same custom still survived in

France and the pieces of bread, blessed at the beginning of the Mass, were taken round the congregation in large baskets during the High Mass ; and on certain feasts cake was given instead of bread. To partake of the same food is a symbol of unity, and the partaking of unconsecrated bread was a symbolic substitute for sacramental Communion.

p. 40, l. 16: " She foresaw that her exile on earth wasn't going to last much longer "
This letter is dated March 22nd, *1877.* Madame Martin was suffering from cancer and died in August of the same year.

p. 40, l. 26: " Rule of life "
The word of the French text is " pratique ". This, in the context, means acts of mortification and should be read as such throughout the text.

p. 41: " In the park "
These words are not found in the French text. The pavilion was not in a park, it stood in one corner of a garden bought by Monsieur Martin at Alençon before his marriage. It consisted of a little rustic tower with one room downstairs and one above it and it was a great treat for the children to spend the afternoon there.

p. 45: " I got five marks "
These were not marks such as are customary in English schools, they were little tokens of thick, coloured paper which the children were given for good conduct. When they had collected enough of them they could exchange them for pretty devotional or historical pictures.

p. 46: " Soldiers on the march "
The manuscript does not mention soldiers on the march. These " faint echoes " were probably those of a regimental band giving an afternoon concert on the market place for the benefit of the townspeople.

p. 48: " Me donna un grand sujet de m'humilier "
Literally : " It gave me great cause for humiliation"

p. 49: Monsieur Ducellier was one of the curates of the Cathedral.

p. 60: " Une pièce de quatre sous "
Literally : " A twopenny piece "

p. 62: This was a ten sous piece, a silver coin, the value of which was about fivepence.

p. 78: The practices were " acts of mortification ". See note for p. 36, l. 23.

p. 84: " Ah, ma joie fut sans amertume, j'espérais la rejoindre bientôt et attendre avec elle le Ciel "

Literally: "My joy was unclouded, soon I hoped I would join her and that together we would look forward to Heaven." This sentence has been left out of the translation.

p. 87: "Et là je contemplais le coup d'œil"
Literally: "And from there I watched the scene." This sentence has been left out of the translation.

p. 95, l. 17: "Des péchés que Marie m'avait permis de confesser, pas un de plus"
Literally: "The sins Marie had allowed me to confess, not one more."

p. 95, l. 31: "Pêche a l'équille"
Literally: "Digging for sand-eels"

p. 95, l. 37: "Ma cousine . . . qui était toujours souffrante et pleurnichait souvent"
Literally: "My cousin . . . who was always ailing and whimpered a good deal"

p. 96: "Je me mis donc en devoir de larmoyer"
Literally: "I got all set for a good snivel"

p. 99: "Comme nous, il trouvait, cela bien drôle"
Literally: "He thought it very odd, as we all did." One day Léonie went with her father to the Convent of Poor Clares and expressed a wish to become a member of their Community. The Abbess, taking her at her word, gave her the postulant's habit there and then and Léonie did not come home that night. Two months later she returned to Lisieux.

p. 100: "Or fetch Céline's flower-pots in from the garden *in the evening* when she was out"
The words "*le soir*" have been left out of the translation.

p. 101: "Mes souliers dans la cheminée"
Lace or button boots which were set out in a row in front of the empty grate and filled by the parents with sweets made in a variety of shapes —pipes, mice, pigs, etc., or even small sugar cribs.

p. 103: "Un grand criminel qui venait d'être condamné a mort"
Pranzini was condemned to death for the murder of two women and a child; the murders were committed in the course of theft. Just before he was to be executed, having previously refused religious help, he suddenly cried out, "Quick, the crucifix", and kissed it.

p. 108: "Ce n'est pas pour rester dans le ciboire d'or qu'il descend chaque jour"
It is to be noted how far in advance of the views of her time was Thérèse's wish for frequent Communion. In those days nuns needed the permission of their superiors in order to go daily to Holy Communion.

p. 109, ll. 24-30: " Oh si des savants ayant passé leur vie dans l'étude
étaient venus m'interroger, sans doute auraient-ils été étonnés de voir
une enfant de quatorze ans comprendre les secrets de la perfection,
secrets que toute leur science ne leur peut découvrir puisque pour les
posséder il faut être pauvre d'esprit "
Literally : " If learned men having spent a lifetime studying had come
and questioned me, no doubt they would have been amazed to find a
fourteen-year-old girl who understood the secrets of perfection, secrets
which all their science could not discover for them since to possess
them it is necessary to be poor in spirit "

p. 111: " J'avais résolu "
Literally : " I was determined". It was Thérèse who had first had the
idea of approaching the Pope. It had come to her after reading the
letter which she had received from Sister Agnes at Loreto. She wrote
to her about the project on November 4th, *1887*. " The last hope is to
speak to the Holy Father . . . but it would have to be possible ".

p. 119: This " Palace " is now a museum where the celebrated Bayeux
tapestry is exhibited. The present Bishop's house is situated on the
same side of the Place de la Cathédrale, but nearer to the chancel end of
the Cathédral.

p. 121: " Mon âme était plongée dans l'amertume, mais aussi dans la
paix car je ne cherchais que la volonté du Bon Dieu "
Literally : " My soul was steeped in bitterness and yet at the same time
filled with peace as I only sought the will of God "

p. 130: " de gratter furtivement "
Literally : " Stealthily to scrape "

p. 136: " Il me suivit longtemps des yeux "
These words which Monsignor Knox translated are not in the handwriting of the Saint.

p. 139: This Agnes must not be confused with the Roman matyr of the
same name. She was the sister of St. Clare and was born at Assisi
towards the end of the thirteenth century.

p. 144: " I was told "
The French printed edition of the photostat reads : " A letter from
Mother Marie de Gonzague told me "

p. 149, ll. 29-36: From " I know she was very fond of me . . ." to
". . . his earthly representative ". A look at the MS. shows that this
passage has been extensively corrected.

155, ll. 13-16: " Les trois années du martyre de Papa me paraissaient
les plus aimables, les plus fructueuses de toute notre vie "
Literally : " The three years of Papa's cruel suffering seemed to me
the most gracious and the most rewarding of our whole life "

p. 155, l. 23: " Mon cœur déborde de reconnaissance "
Literally : " My heart overflows with gratitude "

p. 158: " Le réfectoire qui fut mon emploi aussitôt après ma prise d'habit "
The work in the refectory was divided between several nuns ; it consisted in sweeping the refectory and placing the bread and drink at the nuns' places at table.

p. 159: " Je devrais me désoler de dormir (depuis 7 ans) pendant mes oraisons et mes actions de grâce, et bien je ne me désole pas "
Literally : " I ought to be distressed that I fall asleep during my meditations and my thanksgiving as I have done for the last seven years. But it doesn't distress me "

p. 160: " En faisant mon chemin de la croix après matines "
It was the custom in the Carmel to remain in choir till midnight on the eve of a profession.

p. 165, l. 31: " The time of our greatest distress "
This is an allusion to their father's mental breakdown.

p. 165, l. 35: " Vraiment ce spectacle était ravissant "
Literally : " It was a beatific spectacle "

p. 167: " L'influenza se déclara dans la communauté "
All the sisters except two or three were in bed. The offices were suspended. There was a silence of death in the community. Three nuns died. Sister Thérèse gave herself up to the care of the sick and dying sisters and to the work of the sacristy. She gave proof of a calmness, a presence of mind and a degree of intelligence which were quite unusual. The Superior, Monsieur Delatroëtte, who had been against her entry into the Carmel, was impressed and began to see the great hope which the Community might have of this child. (Abridged from the evidence of Sister Marie des Anges, taken at the Process.)

p. 168: " Les petites langes "
Literally : " Swaddling clothes "

p. 175: " Ce n'est pas le plus souvent pendant mes oraisons qu'elles sont le plus abondantes, c'est plutôt au milieu des occupations de ma journée "
Literally : " It is not generally in the course of my prayers that this light comes more abundantly, but more often in the middle of my daily tasks "

p. 177: " Transplantée sur d'autres rivages "
Thérèse alludes to the possibility of going to one of the missions. At the time at which she wrote the first MS. the Saigon Carmel, which had been founded from Lisieux, was asking for nuns to found another

Carmel at Hanoi. In a letter to Father Roulland Thérèse says: " I shall leave one day for Hanoi, for there is a Carmel in that town ".

p. 188: " Elle recueillera mes fleurs effeuillées par amour "
An allusion to the shower of roses related to the reading aloud of the life of St. Louis de Gonzague.
Deposition by Sister Marie of the Sacred Heart. *Bayeux,* Vol. I:—" In the refectory I was reading aloud an episode from the life of Saint Louis de Gonzague where it is said that a sick person who was praying to be cured saw a shower of roses falling on his bed, as a symbol of the grace which was about to be granted to him. Afterwards, during the re-creation, she said to me: ' After my death I too shall make roses rain ' ".

p. 192: The Saint refers here to the day on which she took her vows.

p. 207: " Qu'il m'est doux de fixer sur vous mon regard "
Literally : " How it comforts me to fix my eyes on you "

p. 210, l. 14: " To lend an extra hand "
Servir de tierce. On many occasions, notably in the Parlour, a Carmelite must have the company (tierce) of another sister.

p. 210, l. 20: " La Sœur qui remplaçait la dépositaire "
Literally : " The Sister who was acting for the Bursar "

p. 212, l. 20: " Elle voulut me prendre les clefs "
Literally : " She tried to take the keys away from me "

p. 212, l. 28: " Voulant absolument entrer à sa suite, malgré elle qui poussait la porte pour m' empêcher d'entrer "
Literally : " Being determined to follow her in, in spite of the fact that she was pushing the door to prevent me "

p. 227: " We had only one novice "
This was Sister Marie de la Trinité.

p. 236: It was an odd habit: she was grinding one of her finger-nails against her teeth.

p. 237: " Les mouchoirs sur son banc "
The washing was put out on a wide ledge and beaten with a wooden bat.

p. 239: " Off to the barracks "
A recent law had decreed that seminary students should join the army at twenty-one and do one year's military service, like everyone else.